A HISTORY OF FRONTIERS

A HISTORY OF FRONTIERS

The Strategic Crossroads of Gilgit-Baltistan, 1839 to 2019

ASHUTOSH SINGH

MANOHAR
2026

Cover photograph: A view of Nanga Parbat, the ninth highest mountain in the world at 8,126 metres above sea level. It is the western anchor of the Himalayas, around which the Indus River skirts into the plains of Pakistan. By Tahsin Anwar Ali - Own work, CC BY-SA 3.0, https://commons.wikimedia.org/w/index.php?curid=40616492

First published 2026
First eBook edition 2026

ISBN 978-93-6080-164-9 (hardbound)
ISBN 978-93-6080-364-3 (eBook)

Published by

Ajay Kumar Jain *for*
Manohar Publishers & Distributors
4753/23 Ansari Road, Daryaganj
New Delhi 110 002

Typeset by Kohli Print, Delhi 110 051

Cover design by Manoj Kumar

Printed and bound in India

Contents

Preface

The region of Gilgit and the Khyber Pass has long been a contested frontier, situated at the crossroads of Central Asia, South Asia, and the Middle East. Throughout history, various powers have sought to control this strategically important area, leading to conflicts and political manoeuvring. The history of this region is a testament to the enduring importance of natural frontiers and the strategic value of controlling them. In this research report sponsored by the Indian Council of Historical Research (ICHR), it has been the author's endeavour to explore the complex interplay of local power struggles and geopolitical tensions between the British and Russian empires in Central Asia, which shaped British policy towards the northern Indian frontier region of Gilgit-Baltistan. The Great Game, a strategic rivalry between the British and Russian empires for dominance over Central Asia and control over the passage to India, played a crucial role in shaping British policies towards the region.

This work delves into the historical narrative of the Gilgit Agency and its strategic role within the political framework of British India's northern frontier region. It traces the establishment of the agency and the appointment of Major Biddulph as its first political officer in Gilgit, with the aim of maintaining amicable relations with the local tribes and safeguarding India's northern borders. It highlights the challenges faced by the British in establishing control and pacifying the frontier, with the Dogras acting as their agents and the resistance from local tribes such as Chitral and Hunza.

Through this work a comprehensive account is provided of the region's history and its enduring impact on international relations. The events surrounding the Gilgit Agency and its strategic importance to British India shed light on the significance of natural frontiers in shaping political and military strategies. The report also underscores the complexities of colonialism and its impact on local populations, highlighting the resistance of the tribes in the region and offers a nuanced perspective on the history of the Gilgit-Baltistan region and its relevance to contemporary geopolitics.

Chapter 1 explores the concept of natural frontiers and their impact on the development of societies, with a focus on the northern region of the Indian subcontinent. While natural frontiers have shaped political boundaries historically, they do so ultimately because they act as natural barriers to more prosperous but vulnerable lands. The chapter examines the region of Gilgit-Baltistan, its ethnic and linguistic makeup, and its historical significance as a centre of local confederacies. The chapter also delves into the collapse of the Sikh Empire and the British policies towards the mountainous kingdoms in India's northern frontier during the nineteenth century, driven by their need to control the frontiers of India and their wariness of Russian expansionism. The chapter highlights the geo-strategic significance of the Gilgit-Baltistan region and the establishment of formal contact between the British and the frontier region. On the whole, the chapter provides insight into the complex political and strategic dynamics at play in the region during the nineteenth century.

Chapter 2 discusses the Great Game, which was a geopolitical struggle between the British and Russian empires in Central Asia throughout the nineteenth century. The British were concerned about Russian expansion in Central Asia and its potential impact on their northern Indian frontier region of Gilgit-Baltistan. The chapter explores the ways in which the British policies towards the region were shaped by their concerns over Russian inroads and the desire to pre-empt any possible Russian moves. The events surrounding the Witkiewicz Mission and subsequent Russian expeditions to Afghanistan also had significant implications for British policies towards the North-West Frontier. The chapter also discusses the establishment of the Gilgit Agency, which was established by the British to establish control and maintain friendly relations with the local tribes of the remote frontier of the Indian subcontinent and highlights the challenges faced by the British in pacifying the frontier and establishing friendly relations with the local tribes. The establishment of the Gilgit Agency under the leadership of Captain Algernon Marion Durand marked a significant turning point in the British presence in the region. The chapter concludes by discussing the Chitral crisis of 1895, which changed the British attitude towards the frontier and the region.

Chapter 3 discusses the end of the Great Game between Britain and Russia in the nineteenth century after the Chitral crisis and the signing of the Pamir Boundary Commission in 1895. The report of this commission emphasized the importance of the mountain passes to the west of the Indus River as the primary invasion routes into India. The British government then carried out regional military reforms to reduce the cost of maintaining a military force in the Gilgit Agency. This included concentrating troops in fewer locations and reorganizing the Kashmir Imperial Service troops. In 1913, the Government of India constituted the Gilgit Scouts to replace the local levies in the Agency. The chapter also discusses the changing geopolitical situation at the start of the twentieth century, including the defeat of Russia in the Russo-Japanese War and the realization in Britain that Germany posed a greater threat than Russia. Lord Kitchener initiated a series of military reforms to make the British Indian Army capable of missions, including developing and maintaining transportation infrastructure and promises of military reinforcements.

Chapter 4 provides an overview of the historical events that led to the current dispute over the Gilgit-Baltistan region, which is now a part of the Indian state of Jammu & Kashmir. The chapter begins by discussing the Partition of India in 1947, which resulted in the formation of East and West Pakistan as autonomous states for Muslims. The Maharaja of Jammu & Kashmir attempted to maintain the independence of the princely state, but after a series of events, the state ultimately acceded to India, leaving Pakistan in control of the strategic region of Gilgit-Baltistan. The chapter also delves into the United Nations Commission for India and Pakistan (UNCIP) resolutions, which were introduced to address the dispute over the state of Jammu & Kashmir. The 1971 Indo-Pak War resulted in Indian troops securing 804 sq. km of territory in Baltistan, which is now a part of the Indian state of Jammu & Kashmir. The chapter also covers the post-war administrative reforms implemented in the northern areas by Zulfiqar Ali Bhutto's administration to consolidate Pakistan's control over the region, as well as the cultural and ethnic connections of the region to India.The chapter further examines the dissolution of the last princely state of Hunza in September 1974, which marked the end of the old order in the region. It also analyses the complex political and legal issues surrounding Pakistan's control over the Gilgit-Baltistan region, a strategically important frontier with close ties to China. The construction of the Karakoram Highway and the abolition of the State Subject Rule allowed for a significant influx of outsiders, resulting in a change in the demographic profile of the region and upsetting the delicate balance of the local population. Furthermore, it traces the history of conflict between India and Pakistan over the Siachen Glacier, which has significant implications for the control of the region. Pakistan's efforts to exert direct control through various orders and policies have had a detrimental impact on the local populace, resulting in frustration and a desire for greater autonomy. The chapter also examines the implications of the Pakistan Supreme Court's intervention in the region and its increasing association with China.

To conclude, this study provides a comprehensive and detailed examination of the historical, political, and strategic factors that have shaped the Gilgit-Baltistan region and its ongoing dispute. Through an analysis of the Great Game, the establishment of the Gilgit Agency and the challenges faced by the British in pacifying the frontier, this study highlights the intricate history of a region, pot marked by local power struggles and geopolitical tensions. The post-independence conflict over the state of Jammu & Kashmir, which began with raiders attacking the princely state on 22 October 1947, had far-reaching consequences on the relations between India and Pakistan. The UNCIP resolutions passed in 1948 failed to resolve the dispute, and subsequent wars and administrative reforms by India and Pakistan left the region with a complex and unresolved status. The construction of the Karakoram Highway and the conflict over the Siachen glacier have further complicated the situation. The people of the region have suffered from neglect, inadequate development and cultural changes brought about by external factors. Ginger attempts by the Pakistani state to extend its control over the frontier territory continue, absent an increase of local representation. This has had significant implications for this frontier, leading to frustration among the populace. The China-Pakistan Economic Corridor (CPEC), meanwhile, is expected to exacerbate Pakistan's persistent trade deficit with China. Moreover, the local populace may not benefit from the financial proceeds obtained from the exploitation of their resources. The risk of land loss and population displacement looming in the background, make for a gloomy future. With the twenty-first century rise of China and Pakistan's increasing dependence on its northern ally, the direction of geopolitical power projection has moved in the opposite direction across this strategic region. The stakes were never higher for the Indian subcontinent with the risk that a power outside the subcontinent may achieve de facto control over this strategic northern frontier.

Acknowledgements

I would first like to express my gratitude to the Indian Council of Historical Research (ICHR) without whose assistance and support this research project would not have been possible. The Research Division of ICHR was always ready to lend a supporting hand in case of any difficulties and queries regarding the disbursement of funds of the project grant.

The acknowledgement would be incomplete without mentioning the continuous encouragement and support of Professor S.L. Kothari, Vice-President ASTIF (Amity Science Technology and Innovation Foundation) and his office staff in ensuring the smooth processing of my project grant at the university level. I would like to take this opportunity to thank Professor Amit Jain, Vice-Chancellor and Dr Nitin Bhardwaj, Registrar Amity University Rajasthan in ensuring all necessary institutional support in bringing this project work to a successful conclusion.

For most of the nineteenth and the mid-twentieth centuries, the territory in question was either frequented by British explorers or was under direct or indirect British control. Consequently, most of the relevant primary documents were to be found in the National Archives at New Delhi. The National Archives played a critical role in providing necessary documents in this research work. A special thanks, therefore, is in order for the National Archives, New Delhi for providing access to all requested documents and facilitating copies of the same. The Srinagar State Archives, also provided and facilitated access to all the documents at their disposal despite being in the midst of a relocation and reorganization at the time of my visit there.

A special thanks is due to the microfilm section of the Nehru Memorial Museum and Library (NMML), where I could access old newspaper articles of historical relevance to the topic. I also express my gratitude to Dr Dinesh Kumar who was instrumental in obtaining the photocopies from the National Archives, once they were made available and dispatching them to me by post.

A necessary mention must be made of the names of Alok Bansal whose work *Baltistan and Its Saga of Unending Human Rights Violations* and Dinkar Srivastava's *Forgotten Kashmir* provide important insights into the post-1947 history of Gilgit-Baltistan for which no archival sources are available in India. As such they comprise essential readings for any scholar on the topic. I would finally express my gratitude to my dear wife for standing by me these last two years when my time has been completely absorbed by this project.

ASHUTOSH SINGH

Abbreviations

AJK	Azad Jammu & Kashmir
AKHC	Azad Kashmir High Court
AMC	Azad Muslim Conference
API	Associated Press of India
BRI	Belt and Road Initiative
Brig. Gen.	Brigadier General
Brig.	Brigadier
Capt.	Captain
CFTA	China-Pakistan Free Trade Agreement
CGS	Chief of General Staff
CO	Commissioned Officer
Col.	Colonel
CPEC	China-Pakistan Economic Corridor
DMO	Director of Military Operations
EAD	External Affairs Department
FCR	Frontier Crimes Regulation
FCRA	Frontier Crimes Regulation Act
FM	Field Marshal
GB	Gilgit-Baltistan
Gen.	General
GHQ	General Headquarters
GOI	Government of India
HDI	Human Development Index
HuM	Harkat-ul-Mujahideen (Islamic jihadist organization)
ICS	Indian Civil Service
IGP	Inspector General of Police
J&K	Jammu & Kashmir
JCO	Junior Commissioned Officer
JeM	Jaish-e-Muhammad (Army of Muhammad)
KANA	Ministry of Kashmir Affairs and Northern Areas
KKH	Karakoram Highway

LeJ	Lashkar-e-Jhangvi (Army of Jhangvi)
LeT	Lashkar-e-Taiba (Army of the Pure)
LoC	Line of Control
LSE	London School of Economics
Lt.	Lieutenant
Maj. Gen.	Major General
Maj.	Major
MC	All Jammu & Kashmir Muslim Conference
MKA	Ministry of Kashmir Affairs
MMG	Medium Machine Gun
MRD	Movement for the Restoration of Democracy
NAAC	Northern Areas Advisory Council
NACC	Northern Areas Consultative Council
NALC	Northern Areas' Legislative Council
NAP	National Assembly of Pakistan
NC	National Conference
NHP	Net Hydel Profit
NWF	North-West Frontier
NWFP	North-Western Frontier Province
OSD	Officer on Special Duty
PM	Prime Minister
PoK	Pakistan Occupied Kashmir
PPP	Pakistan People's Party
RFM	Russian Foreign Ministry
RGS	Royal Geographic Society
SMP	Sipah-e-Mohammedi (Soldiers of Muhammad) Pakistan
SSP	Sipah-e-Sahaba (Prophet's Companions) Pakistan
USSR	Union of Soviet Socialist Republics
UN	United Nations
UNCIP	United Nations Commission for India and Pakistan
UNDP	United Nations Development Programme
UNSC	United Nations Security Council
VCO	Viceroy's Commissioned Officer

CHAPTER 1

Introduction

THE IDEA OF A FRONTIER

Natural geography and the environment have defined and shaped the progression and evolution of human cultures and civilizations throughout history. Geographical barriers can result in isolating a culture from neighbouring influences or protect it from hostile invaders. The question as to why the Myceneans were a sea-faring cultural tradition, or the Mongols a nomadic equestrian one, cannot be answered convincingly without understanding the role that geography played in their development. More specific to the topic at hand, throughout recorded history, geographical features have acted as markers of boundaries within which communities with a common language and culture dwelled. In ancient Greece, the Pindus mountains marked the border between Greater Epirus or Thessalonica from Macedonia and later the Rhine River came to mark the frontier between the Roman Empire and the Germanic lands to the east. The phrase 'a Limes on the Rhine' came to refer to this territorial delimitation. Over a period of time, as national consciousness emerged, these natural features have come to mark the boundaries of states created along national lines called nation states. These nation states replaced the monarchies and empires of old. The Alps still form the frontier between Italy and France, the Pyrenees the Franco-Spanish frontier and the Rhine largely demarcating the Belgian, Swiss, Austrian and Bulgarian frontiers. More recently, in the nineteenth century, the Rio Grande River came to demarcate the frontier between the United States and Mexico.

Whether natural geographical features should form the political boundaries of states has been a contentious issue. Arnold Toynbee in his book, *The New Europe: Some Essays in Reconstruction* (1916) observes in chapter IV titled, 'Natural Frontiers and Economic Rights of Way', 'Natural Frontiers are, in fact, the most artificial that can be drawn, and are simply a euphemism for the momentary conquests of brute force'.[1] While it may be true, that politicians may whimsically interpret where such natural frontiers of a nation may lie, it is an equally undeniable reality that natural frontiers have had a significant political and cultural impact on the development of societies. The term 'Indian subcontinent' itself, refers to the geographical landmass, which while being located in Asia, is physically isolated from the rest of the continental landmass by a series of natural barriers. Professor Dudley Stamp would go on to remark, 'Perhaps there is no other part of a landmass anywhere else in the world that was so well demarcated by physical features than the Indian subcontinent'. These natural frontiers of the subcontinent include the great Himalayan Mountain range running from Brahmaputra in the east to the Indus in the west and Pamir and the Hindukush and Karakoram Mountain ranges to the west and north. On its west and east, great deserts and forests respectively formed natural redoubts. These natural barriers while daunting and formidable, are by no means impermeable. In certain locations narrow passes have allowed many adventurers, soldiers and traders to traverse their vales, both in and out of the Indian subcontinent over the millennia. However, despite these limited exchanges of people, the physical separation so achieved was adequate for the subcontinent to develop a distinct cultural identity despite several instances of cultural similarities and exchanges over a period of time with the rest of Asia. The most formidable of these barriers were doubtlessly the northern mountain ranges of South Asia. Home to some of the highest mountain ranges in the world, the Pamir Knot is an intersection of the three mountain ranges namely Himalayas, Hindukush and the Karakoram. It is on this region of the natural frontier presented by the northern mountains that this study is concerned with.

The term 'frontier' itself has got specific connotations in political geography. J.R.V. Prescott in his book *The Geography of Frontiers and Boundaries*, defines it either as the political division between two states, or the division between the settled and unsettled parts of a state.

> The term 'frontier' in political geography has two different meanings: it can refer to either the political division between two states or the division between the settled and uninhabited parts of one state. In either case the frontier may be considered as a line or a zone. While the context normally prevents confusion between the two meanings, problems of interpreting the sense can easily arise. It is for this reason that some geographers have attempted to restrict the use of the term to features possessing width, referring to simple linear divides as boundaries.[2]

As such, this particular region historically fell somewhere between the two definitions. It was very sparsely populated, though never absent of population, but was always a bulwark of the more densely populated regions as the terrain gently descended into valleys of Kashmir to the south-east and Swat to the south-west. Moreover, in the ages preceding the clearly defined political boundaries of modern nation states, it would form the frontier, of whichever state was strong enough to exert control over it.

GILGIT AND BALTISTAN: A TOPOGRAPHICAL SKETCH

The region of Gilgit-Baltistan is geographically contiguous with Ladakh, to its east and Afghanistan to its west. To the north-west of Gilgit lies the Wakhan Corridor, which runs west to east, connecting Afghanistan to Chinese Xinjiang while a narrower pass, running to the south connects the corridor to Gilgit-Baltistan. Historically, this region has been the point of congruency of three cultures, namely Central Asian, Chinese and Indian. The Khyber Pass lying to the south-west of Chitral, a western part of this natural frontier of the Indian subcontinent has been the most prolific invasion route into India. Persians, Greeks, Parthians and Kushanas invaded the subcontinent through this route, while later, the Turks, Timurids, Mughals and the Afghans would use this doorway into the Indian subcontinent. All major political powers including the Delhi Sultanates and the Mughals were very particular about securing the Khyber Pass to defend themselves from any threats emanating from Central Asia. Indeed, a strong argument can be made here that the ability of the Indian states to exert control over this western doorway into the country would decide their political futures. The attack on Delhi by Nadir Shah in 1739 was preceded by his victory at the Battle of the Khyber Pass in 1738. This would soon be followed by Ahmad Shah Abdali's incursion into India and his victory in the Third Battle of Panipat in 1761. On both occasions, the Mughals and later the Marathas could not ensure control of the Khyber Pass. With the British victory over the Sikhs in the Second Anglo-Sikh War, the British would arrive and seek to control these natural frontiers of the subcontinent.

The British, astute students of history that they were, understood the significance of protecting these natural access ways into India. However, the nature of the geostrategic challenge from Central Asia had changed by the nineteenth century. The threat was no longer from a Central Asian power, but from a European power expanding over-land from Europe to Central Asia, namely Russia. The British were primarily interested in maintaining Afghanistan as a buffer zone, between the British Indian Empire in India and the Russian Empire to the north. This geopolitical struggle, known as the Great Game, was the determining factor behind the British political policies that gave this region its present political shape.

A BRIEF ETHNOGRAPHICAL SKETCH

One of the most important first hand accounts from the nineteenth-century British explorers to the northern region about the ethnic and linguistic make up of the regional population of Gilgit-Baltistan is *Tribes of the Hindukush* by Col. John Biddulph. Biddulph visited the region between the years 1873 and 1878. It was only the outbreak of the second Anglo-Afghan war in 1878, that would cut short his survey of the region. Biddulph mentions some peculiarities regarding the geography of the region which had affected the mannerism of the local population. He observes that topographically, the region of Gilgit and Baltistan had unusually low and deep valleys which were quite narrow especially at their entrance. This makes these passages difficult to approach and are easily cut-off during the long winter months leading to a sense of isolation and separate identity from the adjoining regions.

The population density of Gilgit and that of the adjoining region of Baltistan to a lesser extent, is far higher than that of the much larger region of Ladakh. Biddulph points out that the valleys in the Gilgit region widen as they widen at higher altitudes and that despite the close proximity of the region to Punjab, it has been historically isolated. He observes that the region of Gilgit and that which lies to its west, is inhabited by warlike tribes who have always had blood feuds and lawlessness as part of their way of life.

The word 'Dard' was first brought into focus in the nineteenth century by the British traveller William Moorcroft, who was unable to reach Gilgit-Baltistan. He talked about the 'Dardic people'. It was Dr William Leitner who went to the region and lived among the people whom he considered to be an 'Aryan' race of people who had survived unadulterated without mixing with non-Aryan populations in their inaccessible and remote mountainous abodes for hundreds and possibly thousands of years. According to Leitner, these people spoke a family of languages known as the 'Dardic' languages, which he considered to be proto-Indo-Aryan languages and these people were referred to as the 'Dards'. He was heavily influcenced by Alexander Cunningham's contemporary ideas of the Aryans as a civilizing force, coming to India from their Eurasian Urheimat,[3] a small group of whom survived high in the remote and inaccessible frontier of India, and would go on to attract many an ethnologist to the region.

The idea that all of these people in the regions formed a single ethno-linguistic group was later proven to be a fallacy. In fact, the entire region referred to as Dardistan comprised several distinct ethnic groups who, while having contact with one another in varying degrees, chose mostly not to intermarry and maintain their distinctiveness. Many of the western territories of the region described as Dardistan, fall in Afghanistan today. Dardistan, as one heads north from Kashmir Valley would include the regions of Darel first and Chilas, Gilgit, with Nagar and Hunza further north in that order. To the west of Gilgit, lay Yasin followed by Chitral further west. To the south-west of Yasin, as the Indus descends into the valley, is the region of Kohistan inhabited by the Hazara people before it enters the Swat Valley further south. Both Chitral which is contiguous with Afghanistan to its west and Kohistan to its south-east, were considered to be a part of the Dardic lands by Leitner. To the west of Chitral in Afghanistan, is the region known traditionally as Kafiristan or the land of the non-believers. This is indicative of the population following pre-Islamic practices having great similarity with Hinduism. It is this vast region from eastern Afghanistan to Gilgit in the east and Yasin in the north to Kohistan in the south, that comprised Dardistan. Being a great cultural meeting point as well as remotely located, it was certainly not likely that this vast region would consist of people from the same cultural group but rather small groups of people as a consequence of contact between different cultural units.

The region of Gilgit is strategically extremely important for the greater region of Gilgit-Baltistan. Biddulph observes in his memoirs that roads converge onto Gilgit from all the nearby valleys.[4] As such Gilgit has historically been the centre of many local confederacies and logically also a strategic location for any major power from an external area to the region. Being relatively easy to access, Gilgit has also provided an extension on occasions, protruding into Kashmir from the north-west. It is therefore, natural that rulers of Yasin and Chitral on different occasions in the nineteenth century, would attempt to exert their control over Gilgit. The people of Hunza are referred to as being 'warlike' whereas those of Nagar are mentioned as being 'timid' (Biddulph 1880: 25) with the implication being that this has something to do with their being followers of the Shiite sect of Islam, with a history of traditional rivalry between the two peoples. The idea that the Sunnis were warlike, while the Shia lacked martial prowess was commonplace in the nineteenth century and these views are reflective of the same. Biddulph goes on to add that there has been a popular perception that the people of Hunza have traditionally had the reputation of being robbers (ibid.: 28). This cultural notion of the Hunza being warlike is attributed to their raids on the adjoining regions, while being secure in their inaccessible mountainous strongholds. This entire region has a long-standing tradition of tribal conflicts over grazing lands and livestock which are highly prized.The Hunza do have extensive cultivation in their territory, to the north of which lies the Wakhan corridor (Biddulph 1880: 28).

The language spoken by the people of Hunza, especially in its upper reaches is known locally as the Burushaski or 'Boorishki' as mentioned by Leitner.[5]

> Having been on a special mission by the Panjab Government, in 1866, when I discovered the races and languages of 'Dardistan', and gave the country that name, and again having been on special duty with the Foreign Department of the Government of India in 1886 in connection with the Boorishki language and race of Hunza, Nagyr, and a part of Yasin, regarding which I have recently completed Part I of a large work, I may claim to speak with some authority as regards these districts, even if I had no other claim. (Leitner 1996: 16)

Leitner points out that despite the people speaking Boorishki, the songs are all in the 'Shina' language. Shina is one of the Dardic languages and does not have any script, although it is now written using the Arabic script. Biddulph elaborates that even the non-Shina-speaking populations in the region sing in Shina without actually understanding the language. The Shina language features more prominently in the region of Gilgit, where most of its prominent speakers are located along the western most reaches of Ladakh.

As late as the 1880s, the risk of frequent tribal raids was significant enough in the regions of Hunza and its adjoining regions so much so that people would retreat every night into small fortresses, at least one of which was present in each village. Such forts are described by Biddulph in his accounts, as being built of sun-dried bricks, with walls 15 ft tall. He observes that while such forts were also present in Gilgit, they had fallen out of use under Dogra rule. This is indicative of relative peace and security and a reduction in tribal conflict as a result of Dogra rule. The aspect of religiosity of the tribes of Hunza attracts Biddulph's attention, in that it seems to diverge significantly from more puritanical versions of Islam compared to its neighbourhood tribes.It is claimed that the people of Hunza are given more to wine drinking and consume food which is unorthodox:

> Mahommedanism sits but loosely on the Hunza people, who make no secret of their preference for easy-going tenets. Though professing to be Maulais, they are disowned by their own Pirs, who refuse to visit the country, and no contributions are sent by them to their spiritual chief. They are great wine drinkers, and are reproached by their neighbours for their readiness to eat unorthodox food, and for the immorality of their women. (Biddulph 1880: 30)

It therefore becomes clear, that the people of this remote region, home to a multitude of tribes and peoples, each with their own distinct languages and cultures, briefly interacting yet not assimilating with each other reflected a sort of a melting pot of various communities. Located near ancient trading routes, it would always receive a trickle of new languages and religions, yet this could never become a deluge owing to the remoteness of the region. Great empires have at various times controlled the region, ever since at least the Mauryan Empire. The Mongols followed by the Mughals and even the Chinese to whom the Hunza briefly pledged allegiance as suzerains, did leave behind their genetic footprints among the populace, however, the primordial cultural elements still visible, remind one of their Indic cultural roots. The rulers of Hunza and Nagar, the regions north of Hunza are known as Thum and were addressed in reverence as Soori; Biddulph observes in his account, that Soori is very close to the word 'Shri' which is one of the names of Goddess Laxmi.

> Both Thums are still addressed as Soori, as a title of respect. This appears to be the same as Sri, an appellation of Lakshmi, the Hindoo goddess of wealth, commonly prefixed to the names of Hindoo princes in India to denote their honour and prosperity. The Thum's wives are styled 'ganish', which is almost identical with the original Sanskrit word for mother, and their sons are called 'gushpoor'. (Biddulph 1880: 30)

The region of Chilas to the south of Gilgit has some similarities with the Pashtun culture. The Chilasi have a system of council of elders known as the Jushteros, and like the Pashtun Jirga, the Chilasi have the Sigas. The Sigas decide on issues such as war as well as issues regarding their local communities. However, it is here that the similarities end. Criminal cases are not decided by the Sigas, as they are by the Pashtun Jirga. Criminal cases, especially murder is decided by the *ulema* as per the *sharia*. Biddulph also points out that unlike the Pashtun, blood feuds are not allowed to continue indefinitely (Biddulph 1880: 17).

THE EARLY NINETEENTH CENTURY AND THE SIKH EMPIRE

The scope of the study starts in 1839, the year of the death of Maharaja Ranjit Singh, which would effectively begin the process of collapse of the Sikh Empire. A series of intrigues would follow at the Lahore court, the seat of Sikh power and Maharaja Gulab Singh would emerge as the de facto ruler of Jammu. Dr A.H. Dani writes favourably about the leadership role provided by Gulab Singh after the death of Maharaja Ranjit Singh. Gulab Singh had joined the Sikh Army in 1809, one year after the capture of Jammu by the Sikhs. Jammu, which had till then been a Dogra ruled state, now became a part of the Sikh Empire and provided the latter with a gateway to Kashmir. Gulab Singh's father Kishore Singh, was appointed as the Hakim, or Governor of Jammu in 1820 in recognition of the sterling service provided by his family, especially Gulab Singh, to the Sikh Empire. After Kishore Singh's death in 1822, Gulab Singh became Governor of Jammu.

The ascendancy of Gulab Singh to the throne of Jammu would mark the early beginnings of the modern state of Jammu & Kashmir. Gulab Singh was instrumental in expanding the boundaries of the Sikh Empire towards the west from the Kashmir Valley, beyond Rajouri towards Khyber Pakhtunkhwa where the Sikh general defeated Afghans at Shaidu in 1827. This battle was a culmination of the struggle between the Afghan Durrani Empire and the Sikh Empire and cemented Sikh control over the region.

Dr A.H. Dani observes that the Sikh Empire under Maharaja Ranjit Singh considered itself as the successor of the Mughal Empire in the Punjab and the western regions.[6] As such, it was to be expected, that it would attempt to impose its writ over the northern and western passages into the subcontinent. The Sikhs as such, would go on to demand tribute from both Ladakh and Baltistan which at that time, were still ruled by local rulers, both of whom were opposed to any Sikh expansion. Starting from 1834, the Sikh general Zorawar Singh began military campaigns in Ladakh (Dani 1991: 245). However, the British historian Alexander Cunningham points out, that here were underlying differences between the Sikh and Dogra objectives, even though the latter were Sikh feudatories. Mihan Singh, the Sikh governor of Kashmir was trying to instigate the Ladakhi people to revolt against their Dogra rulers, because Dogra control over Ladakh would open up alternate trade channels to India through Jammu, bypassing Kashmir, which would have been adversarial to the interests of the Lahore court. Ladakh and Baltistan meanwhile were eager for British support against the Sikh threat. These underlying tensions within the Sikh nobility would manifest themselves after the demise of Ranjit Singh, when the Lahore court would be beset by a series of conspiracies and political instability. After the death of Ranjit Singh, Gulab Singh would be increasingly alienated from the Lahore Court, his younger brother and nephew murdered. In 1844 Lahore would order the invasion of Jammu to compel Gulab Singh into paying tribute. After the defeat of the Sikh Empire in the first Anglo-Sikh War in 1846, as a reward for his good behaviour, Gulab Singh was sold the right to continue ruling his territory of Jammu & Kashmir for the price of 75,00,000 Nanakshahi Rupees.[7]

The region of Gilgit historically had subsidiary relations with the state at the center of political power in India. As an example, it became a part of the Mughal Empire in 1634.[8] This control was maintained by a series of marital ties and relationships of kinship. The region of Gilgit was ruled by an old local Trakhan Dynasty at the beginning of the nineteenth century, but by 1839, witnessed several years of conflict and had been significantly weakened. Mughal authority long having faded away, this frontier region was now about to be subjugated by the new political power in the vicinity, namely the new princely state of Jammu & Kashmir, with blessings from the British paramount power.

To the north-west of Gilgit, lay the kingdom of Hunza; further towards the west of Hunza, was the kingdom of Chitral which bordered Afghanistan on its west. These former frontier regions of the Mughal empire, had by the late eighteenth century chosen new masters. Hunza had pledged allegiance to the Qing court in China as its suzerain by 1760. The weakening of the Mughal power, the arrival of the Europeans into India and the ensuing political instability had resulted in these small kingdoms, ruled by small local dynasties, either becoming independent or pledging their loyalty to powers who were externally relative to the subcontinent. Yasin, the western most edge of the Gilgit region, itself emerged as a local power by the early nineteenth century and would go on to try to extend its influence and control over Gilgit. The ruler in Yasin, was opposed to the expansion of Sikh power, which was pushing northwards against the former remnants of the Durrani Empire and beyond. According to A.H. Dani, by 1842, the Sikh governor in Kashmir dispatched an expedition of about 1,000 troops under Nathu Shah, authorized by the Lahore Darbar. This force would continue to administer Gilgit with the cooperation of Karim Khan (Dani 1991: 247). Karim Khan was the son of Tahir Shah, the ruler of Nagar, who was apparently opposed to any efforts by Yasin to take over Gilgit and as such accepted Sikh suzerainty for all practical purpose. Despite the opposition of Gohar Aman, the ruler of Yasin, by the mid-1840s, Sikh power was firmly entrenched in the region with its base in Kashmir.

The process of integration of Baltistan, the region to the east of Gilgit adjoining Ladakh, has to be understood in the context of the Dogra general Zorawar Singh's campaigns into Ladakh. Although, Zorawar Singh himself would be killed in 1841,[9] by 1845 Baltistan would firmly be a part of the princely state of Jammu & Kashmir. A.H. Dani notes that while the Sikhs had failed to exact a tribute from the local rulers of Baltistan, the Dogras would succeed (ibid.: 249). It is important to note that A.H. Dani, while extremely thorough and articulate in his presentation of fact, takes great pains to do so, so that it seems that the region referred to as Gilgit-Baltistan always resisted foreign rule if it was non-Muslim in character. The petty politics of local rulers in the region is presented as 'Jihad' (ibid.: 249) when conducted against an outsider and their distinctiveness from the rest of Kashmir is emphasized. Despite this, he agrees that it was for the first time after the Mughals, that anyone, in this case the Dogras, would succeed in exacting tribute from this 'frontier region' (Dani 1991: 249).

While the Dogras under Gulab Singh had succeeded in extending their control over this region, the initial years till 1846 were marked by a series of local revolts and uprisings. Raja Ahmad Shah who was the erstwhile ruler of Skardu, was imprisoned after the capture of Gilgit by the Dogras. Following, the demise of Zorawar Singh in 1841, he was released from captivity and he used this opportunity to plot his return to power in collaboration with the other nobility of Gilgit and Baltistan. These nobles included chiefly local rulers such as Ali Khan of Skardu, Daulat Ali Khan of Khaplu and Khurram Khan of Kirisamong as well as other nobles from Baltistan. This disaffected band of nobles would raise the flag of rebellion and imprison Bhagwan Singh who was the seniormost Dogra official in Skardu and then proceed to loot the treasury and weapons stored in Skardu fort. Many of the nobles who did not align with the rebels such as Suleiman Khan of Shigar and Muhammad Shah of Skardu would also be imprisoned. To meet this threat, Gulab Singh sent a force of 3,000 men under Wazir Lakhpat from Kishtwar. This force made its way to Kargil via Suru. At Kargil, he was be joined by Ali Sher Khan of Kartaksho or Kharmang in Baltistan. Ali Sher Khan who was aligned to Gulab Singh advised Wazir Lakhpat to first march towards Baltistan. Upon arriving in the region, Wazir Lakhpat lead siege to the fort of Kharpocha, where Haider Khan, the leader of the uprising had taken refuge. The Dogras were successful in assaulting and burning the Kharpocha Fort to the ground. Haider Khan, the leader of this rebellion managed to escape, but was captured, by one of his own accomplices Daulat Ali Khan and handed over to Lakhpat and was taken to Jammu. Wazir Lakhpat then proceeded suppress the countryside and anyone suspected of having sympathies with the rebels. Bhagwan Singh was restored to his pre-rebellion position as the commander of the Kharpocha Fort after repairs. The year 1846, was the last in which a series of major uprisings took place against the Dogras in the region. This was in Zanskar in Ladakh which was suppressed by Basti Ram, a commander of Gulab Singh.

The year 1846, was a watershed in the history of the region. The British having crushed the Sikh power in the First Anglo-Sikh War, imposed the Treaty of Lahore on 9 March 1846 upon the Sikhs. A week later, on 16 March 1846, Gulab Singh was made the ruler of Gilgit under the Treaty of Amritsar. Fredrick Drew, a British officer at the court of Gulab Singh, mentions in his memoirs titled, *The Northern Barrier of India: A Popular Account of the Jummoo and Kashmir Territories*, that Kashmir and Gilgit were transferred to Gulab Singh under the Treaty of Amritsar, following which the ruler of Hunza broke his agreement with the Dogras.

> On Kashmir, and with it Gilgit, being ceded to Gulab Singh, Nathu Shah left the Sikhs and transferred his services to the new ruler, and went to take possession of Gilgit for him. In this there was no difficulty. The Dogra troops relieved the Sikh posts at Astor and Gilgit. Most of the Sikh soldiers took service under the new rulers; they were few in number, those at Gilgit being perhaps not more than one hundred. The state of peace did not long continue. It was broken by the Hunza Raja making an attack on the Gilgit territory and plundering five villages. Nathu Shah led a force up the valley of the Hunza River to avenge this attack; but his force was destroyed, and he himself was killed, as also was Karim Khan, the titular Raja of Gilgit, who had accompanied him.[10]

He goes on to add that, Nathu Shah, the former Sikh commander switched his loyalty to the Dogras, just as the fortunes of his former sovereign the Sikh empire had turned.

THE REGION UNDER GULAB SINGH FROM 1848 TO 1857

This narrative presented by Fredrick Drew is challenged aggressively by A.H. Dani. Dani, argues that Fredrick misrepresents facts and implies that his position as an English emissary to the Dogra court gave him a bias to represent things in favour of the Dogras (Dani 1991: 253). In line with his historical narrative of a *jihad* against Dogra and Sikh rule, he quotes an account by Dr Gottlieb William Leitner, a British orientalist and a member of the Indian Civil Services (ICS), who mentions a rebellion led by Gohar Aman, the ruler of Yasin, supported by rulers of Hunza and Nagar and the 'people of Gilgit'.

Gohar Aman accordingly sends troops under his brother Akbar Aman and captures the Bargu and Shukayot Forts in Gilgit territory. The Rajas of Hunza and Nagyr combine with Gohar Aman and assisted by the Gilgit people, with whom Karim Khan was unpopular because of his friendship for Kashmir, defeat and kill Nathe Shah and Karim Khan. Gohar Aman captures the Gilgit and Chaprot Forts—Dr Leitner in his note of 1848 (Dani 1991: 252)

Karim Khan who was allied with the Dogras, was naturally presented as unpopular because of this alliance. Of course, this fails to mention that Dr Leitner, an avid traveller, had adopted the name of Abdur Rasheed Sayyah during his sojourns to Turkey and frontier regions in India. Moreover, Dr Leitner was a well-known apologist for Islam and *jihad* in nineteenth-century Victorian England and his works were instrumental in formalizing the modern western perspective of *jihad*.

Germain claims that the notion of jihad was key in forming the image of Islam in the West in the last decades of the nineteenth century and that Leitner played an important role as an apologist for Islam and the 'true meaning' of jihad.[11]

This seems like a case of selecting facts which suit a particular narrative rather than an objective presentation of facts. With the success of the rebellion, Gauhar Rahman, the ruler of Punial and Yasin too joined in the fight against the Dogras. In response, Gulab Singh, sent two groups of forces, one from Baltistan and the other from Hasora against the rebels and succeeded in bringing peace to the region after meeting some resistance. For the following few years there was a marked absence of violence and rebellion until 1852. In 1852, there was an uprising which essentially resulted in the loss of Gilgit and Dardic lands to the south of Gilgit known as Dardistan for the remainder of Gulab Singh's reign.

It was Gauhar Rahman in 1852, who decided to renew his efforts to overthrow Dogra power in the region. Fredrick Drew mentions that he is not clear about why Gauhar Rahman decided to do it then (Drew 1877: 185). There seemed to have been two prominent Dogra strongholds in Gilgit in 1852; one under Sant

Singh who was the commander of the Gilgit Fort while the other at Naupura nearby. According to the account provided by Fredrick Drew, the following details of the Dogra debacle are available. The fort at Naupura was located just a couple of miles away from the fort at Gilgit. The Naupura Fort was under the command of Ram Din at the head of a Gurkha regiment, with the main Dogra reserve forces located at Bawanji in Astor. The approximate distance between Gilgit and Astor is approximately 100 km. Gauhar Rahman raised a force suddenly which surrounded the two forts and cut-off their lines of communication. Hearing of these developments, Bhup Singh rushed to their rescue, at a place, Drew refers to as 'Nila Dhar' which was on the banks of the Gilgit River (Drew 1877: 441). This was a tactically vulnerable position, surrounded on all sides by elevations, and Bhup Singh was surrounded. His route ahead had been barricaded, while the Dards had come to his rear, thereby cutting off any possible retreat. The Hunza forces collected on the other side of the river to prevent any escape. The Dogras, short on food supplies, were promised replenishment by the Dards, without any intention of delivering on the same. When the situation became extremely critical after seven days without food, the forces under Bhup Singh were assaulted on all sides by the rebels and annihilated (ibid.: 186). Drew, notices the remarkable similarity of the tactics used here with those used by the Afghans under Akbar Khan during the first Anglo-Afghan War when the latter ambushed and destroyed the British Indian army under Maj. Gen. Elphinstone.

> The Dards then began to play the game of double dealing, in which they are adepts. They promised Bhup Singh provisions, for of these he was quite short, and a safe passage back if he would agree to retire. This he consented to do, and he waited for days in hopes of the food coming. The Dards kept him in expectation, and fed his hopes; one might almost fancy that they had learnt a lesson from Akbar Khan of Kabul. (ibid.: 186)

Drew goes on to mention that almost a thousand men were killed at this spot and while this disaster was unfolding with Gulab Singh's reserve troops, a similar fate was befalling his garrisons in Gilgit and Naupura (ibid.: 442). Any forays by soldiers out of the forts were ambushed and destroyed. Without going into any further details, it can be said that Dogra power ceased to exist on the north or 'right' bank of the Indus River in Dardistan and Gauhar Rahman established himself in Gilgit. While Baltistan still continued to be under Gulab Singh's control, he did not attempt to exert his influence beyond Bawanji (modern-day Bunji) in Baltistan which marked the limit of his control in the region.

RANBIR SINGH AND CONSOLIDATION OVER GILGIT

Ranbir Singh ascended the throne after the death of his father Gulab Singh in 1857. It was during the reign of Ranbir Singh that Fredrick Drew was at the Kashmir court as an English geologist. Ranbir Singh was determined to extend his rule to the regions of Gilgit and beyond, where his father had before him, been largely unsuccessful. Ranbir Singh had provided troops to the English to help suppress the great Indian uprising of 1857. After some initial hesitation Ranbir Singh would finally commit troops in August 1857.[12] It would be 1860, by the time that effort and attention would be redirected towards the Gilgit region.

That year, a force was sent across the Indus under a formidable Dogra commander named Devi Singh. Just before Devi Singh's force reached Gilgit, Gauhar Rahman passed away leaving the local resistance leaderless (Drew 1877: 444). This led to the collapse of resistance in Gilgit and the capture of Gilgit Fort, a strong redoubt, which the Dogras had lost earlier. This force would continue its advance further to the north west of Gilgit towards Yasin, located in bordering Chitral further west. Once at Yasin, Devi Singh made Azmat Shah, a first cousin of Gauhar Rahman of Gilgit and son of Sulaiman Shah, the king. Sulaiman Shah, the old ruler of Yasin who had captured Gilgit in 1800 from Mohammad Khan, had great prestige among the local population of Yasin. However, as soon as the Dogra forces who had never intended to occupy Yasin physically, turned back, Azmat Shah was deposed by the local populace.

THE BRITISH AND THE GREAT GAME

The British had always had a special interest in the frontier region, as they called the entire region of Kashmir and westwards into Afghanistan. The entire British policy in the nineteenth century, known as splendid isolation, beginning after the end of the Napoleonic wars in 1815, was intended to remain isolated from continental European politics. The primary purpose of isolation was to focus all energy on expanding its overseas colonial possessions centred around its Indian empire. All possible threats to the British position in India were the focus of British foreign policy during this period.

There were however, few overseas threats to British India, with the Royal Navy ruling supreme at sea. The most significant great power that was gradually extending to India's doorstep was the Russian Empire, expanding towards the east from Europe, through Siberia and Central Asia, southwards towards India and further east through Manchuria towards China. Both India and China, with their huge populations, were seen as attractive markets for European factories, and Russian advances towards both were seen as a strategic threat to British interests, especially to India which was by the mid-nineteenth century a totally British colony. The possibility of Russian access to the Black Sea and subsequently cutting off British access to its Indian colony was the primary driving factor behind the British involvement in the Crimean War. The most significant and enduring form of this geopolitical struggle between the two European powers would be in the form of the Great Game that would take place in Central Asia and over the control and security of India's northern frontiers.

An important mention must be made at this juncture of the very influential English geographer, and the Director of the London School of Economics (LSE) at the time, Sir Halford Mackinder. His 'Heartland Theory' which was published in an article titled 'The Geographical Pivot of History' in 1904 by the Royal Geographic Society (RGS) has been the subject of geo-strategic thought with both its proponents and opponents. The proposition by Mackinder was that 'Afro-Eurasia', or the three continents of Asia, Europe and Africa, comprised the 'world continent'. The region including Eastern Europe, Siberia and Central Asia, comprised the 'pivot'; anyone who controlled the 'pivot' would control the 'world continent' and whoever controlled the world continent would control the world. Despite several criticism of this idea, it certainly was a distilled expression of British strategic thinking for most of the nineteenth century; of course, by the time the article came out, the entire territory in the 'pivot' was owned by the Russian Empire.

It is necessary to point out that at the time this article was published in April 1904, the Russo-Japanese War was already underway. One year later, after the final Russian defeat at the battle of Tsushima in 1905, British strategic thinking would shift from Russia to imperial Germany as the primary threat and culminate in the Anglo-Russian Entente of 1907. This would also relegate the 'Heartland Theory' to the periphery with a renewed emphasis on a maritime competition with Germany.

However, for most of the nineteenth century, both British and Russian explorers and geographers would continue to extend the limits of diplomacy and cartographical knowledge in the remotest regions of the Hindukush, Pamirs and Himalayas. According to British army Colonel John Biddulph, who was posted at Gilgit as the British Political Officer, the name of the region of Gilgit was earlier, Sargin. However, at a later date, this was changed to Gilit and later when the Sikh and Dogra ruled it, the name was further changed to Gilgit; however, this is rejected by A.H. Dani who claims that the name has always been Gilgit (Dani 1991: 162). It would be this great struggle for domination over Central Asia and the control over the passages to India that would determine British policy in Gilgit-Baltistan and be known as the 'Great Game'. As early as 1846, one of the reasons for having Gulab Singh in power in the region seems to have been, the intention of having a friendly state in power at the northern reaches of the geographical boundaries of India. Maharaja Gulab Singh's punitive expedition against Gauhar Rahman in 1851, happened after the British granted their permission for the expedition.

> Permission was granted by the British Government in 1851 for a successful raid, and two columns entered Chilas—one from Cashmere by the Lolab Valley, and one from Astor by the Mazenoo Pass. (Biddulph 1880: 31)

This is clearly indicative of the British desire to extend their influence over the northern mountains. However, some British explorers such as Wilhelm Leitner were of the opinion that the region of Gilgit-Baltistan must be left neutral, a sort of a 'no man's land' or a buffer zone between British and Russian zones of influence. In his accounts, Leitner observes:

> The neutralization of the Pamirs is the only solution of a difficulty created by the conjectural treaties of diplomatists and the ambition of military emissaries. Left as a huge happy hunting-ground for sportsmen, or as pasturage for nomads from whatever quarter, the Pamirs form the most perfect 'neutral zone' conceivable. That the wanderings of these nomads should be accompanied by territorial or political claims, whether by Russia, China, Afghanistan, Kashmir, or ourselves, is the height of absurdity.[13]

Nevertheless, by the time Leitner wrote this, Colonel Biddulph was already the British resident at Gilgit, indicating the British desire to extend their position as a paramount power to the region. The rule of Gulab Singh had served the British well, at a time when they desired to project power into the region without having yet consolidated their position in the Punjab and the north-western frontier. As such, the question of the nature of political relationship these minor mountain principalities had with the princely state of Jammu & Kashmir was mute. Indeed, all the British geo-strategic policy decisions since the 1830s can be explained by the British need to control the frontiers of India. All the major conflicts which led to the British coming into contact with India's northern and western frontiers such as the first Anglo-Afghan War and the Anglo-Sikh War can be explained by the British concerns of Russian plans in the region, as well as its own interests in Central Asia which was increasingly falling under increasing Russian domination.

Clearly, Kashmir under the Dogras, after the second Anglo-Sikh War was a major British asset in the region and the British support provided them with an opportunity to extend their own control over these minor states in the region. This was mutually beneficial to both the British and the Dogras; the Dogras could expand their influence to regions, hitherto out of their reach, while the British could through the Dogras, secure the frontiers of their Indian possessions. As John Keay, points out in his book, *The Gilgit Game: Explorers of the Western Himalayas 1865-95*, that this policy would eventually put the British into a situation where they would have to contend with these mountainous kingdoms, which had traditionally been independent in their geographical isolation.

Having committed itself to the idea of appropriating and defending such a remote frontier as the Hindu Kush, the Indian government was faced with the problem of how to control the tribes that lay within it. Their diversity proved as much a stumbling block as their ferocity. The study of the tribes, fascinating enough in itself, was expected to provide pointers as to how their loyalty could most readily be secured. It did up to a point; but such recommendations were usually ignored in favour of some supposed essential of imperial strategy. And as a result, just as the Great Game often seemed to have something to do with skirmishes with the Pathans on the northwest frontier, so the Gilgit Game had a way of deteriorating from the lofty ideals of Anglo-Russian rivalry into frantic and embarrassing fracas with the mountain peoples. On what became known as India's northern, as opposed to north-western frontier, actual hostilities lasted for only four years and were never as bloody as those round the Khyber.[14]

It is clear that the accounts of adventurers and explorers like Leitner and Drew, clearly served to prepare the British policy-makers to understand the levers which could be used to influence and eventually control these remote and difficult regions. It was at this time that the Russian expansion in Central Asia was gathering momentum. After being checked in the Crimean War in 1853, the Russians quickly took over Tashkent, Bukhara and eventually Samarkand in 1868. In 1873, the Russians would establish a protectorate over the Khanate of Khiva in modern-day Uzbekistan, bringing them to the doorstep of British India. This seemed to the British a validation of their long-standing fears of the expansion of Russian military power culminating into a threat to their Indian possessions.

This naturally rang alarm bells for British policymakers who now desired to establish Afghanistan as a 'neutral zone' between the 'Asiatic Empires of Russia and Britain'.[15] The direct consequence of the manifestation of the Russians at India's doorstep was that, in 1876, the British would send Colonel John Biddulph on a clandestine mission to Gilgit which would result in his establishment at Gilgit 1877, as an Officer on Special Duty (OSD). This was naturally to provide an official British political representation in the strategically important region to pre-empt any possible Russian moves no matter however unlikely.

Indeed, the British overtures to the native chiefdoms in the region of Gilgit-Baltistan, have to be understood in context of the second Anglo-Afghan War of 1878 and numerous British primary documents, reports and communications of the second half of the nineteenth century attest to this fact. In fact, all British reports from the Gilgit-Baltistan region and Chitral are categorized under 'Frontier' in the British indices of the time. The British would continue to maintain and gradually extend their grip on the larger frontier region which stretched from Ladakh in the east to the Durand Line along Afghanistan in the west.

The position of the British political officer in Gilgit would be upgraded to a full-fledged British resident in 1889, with Colonel Algernon Durand as its first resident and demonstrating the establishment of a more formal contact between the British and the frontier region. Colonel Durand highlighted British wariness of a Russian threat in the following manner:

> No man in his senses ever believed that a Russian army would cross the Pamirs and attack India by the passes of Hunza and Chitral, but we could not overlook the fact that in 1885, when war hung in the balance, some thousands of her troops were moved down towards the Pamirs. What was this for? hardly for change of air or to shoot big game, as the British public were asked to believe later, when similar moves were made. The object was to get a footing on the south side of the Hindu-Kush, and to paralyse numbers of our troops who would have to be kept in observation of possible Russian lines of advance.[16]

It is in this geostrategic significance of the Gilgit-Baltistan region, that one must now proceed, into the greater nuances of the course of historical developments that happened in the nineteenth century and later in Gilgit-Baltistan.

NOTES

1. Arnold Toynbee, *The New Europe: Some Essays in Reconstruction*, J.M. Dent & Sons Limited, New York, 1916, p. 39.
2. J.R.V. Prescott, *The Geography of Frontiers and Boundaries*, Routledge, New York, 2015, p. 33.
3. E. Bryant and L. Patton, *The Indo-Aryan Controversy Evidence and Inference in Indian History*, 2005, Routledge, 2005, p. 270.
4. J. Biddulph, *Tribes of the Hindoo Koosh*, Superintendent of Government Printing Press, Calcutta, 1880, p. 21.
5. G.W. Leitner, *Dardistan in 1866, 1886 and 1893*, Asian Educational Services, New Delhi, 1996, p. 16.
6. A.H. Dani, *History of the Northern Areas of Pakistan*, National Institute of Historical and Cultural Research, Islamabad, 1991, p. 244.
7. P. Gupte, *India the Challenge of Change*, Mandarin, United Kingdom, 1989, p. 170.
8. Irmtraud Stellrecht, *Perspectives on History and Change in the Karakorum, Hindukush, and Himalaya*, Rüdiger Köppe, University of Michigan, 1997, p. 219.
9. N. Sehgal, *A State in Turbulence Jammu & Kashmir*, Ocean Books, New Delhi, 2013, p. 57.
10. F. Drew, *The Northern Barrier of India: A Popular Account of the Jummoo and Kashmir Territories*, Edward Stanford, London, 1877, p. 184.
11. E. Kendall and E. Stein (eds.), *Twenty-First Century Jihad Law Society and Military Action*, I.B. Tauris, London, 2015, p. 20.
12. C. Snedden, *Understanding Kashmir and Kashmiris*, Hurst, London, 2015, p. 80.
13. Wilhelm G. Leitner, *Dardistan in 1866, 1886 and 1893*, Asian Educational Services, New Delhi, 1996, Appendix, p. 20.
14. John Keay, *The Gilgit Game: The Explorers of the Western Himalayas 1865-95*, Butler and Tanner Ltd., Frome and London, 1979, pp. 6-7.
15. Henry Dodwell, *The Cambridge History of the British Empire*, Volume 4, Macmillan, United Kingdom, 1929, p. 409.
16. A. Durand, *The Making of a Frontier*, John Murray, London, 1900, p. 42.

REFERENCES

Biddulph, John, *Tribes of the Hindoo Koosh*, Superintendent of Government Printing Press, Calcutta, 1880.

Dani, Ahmad H., *History of the Northern Areas of Pakistan*, National Institute of Historical and Cultural Research, Islamabad, 1991.

Drew, Fredrick, *The Northern Barrier of India: A Popular Account of the Jummoo and Kashmir territories*, Edward Stanford, London, 1877.

Leitner, Wilhelm G., *Dardistan in 1866, 1886 and 1893*, Asian Educational Services, New Delhi, 1996.

CHAPTER 2

Gilgit Agency and the Great Game

THE RUSSIANS AND THE INDIAN FRONTIER

All British Gilgit-Baltistan strategies were based on the nineteenth century Great Game between the British and Russian empires in Central Asia. The two big powers fought for control in China, Iran, and Afghanistan. British political connections and territory advances in Gilgit-Baltistan must be studied in the light of Russian Central Asian expansion.

Since the Third Anglo-Maratha War in 1819, British anxieties regarding the north-west Indian frontier had persisted. By the 1830s, the British wanted a neutral Afghanistan on their border to dominate India. The British buffer against Afghan and Persia to the west was the Sikh Empire and in 1836, the Viceroy of India Lord Auckland joined these three states under the 1838 Tripartite Treaty. The British, Maharaja Ranjit Singh, and Shah Shuja of Afghanistan signed a pact to topple Dost Mohammad Khan of Kabul and instate Shah Shuja, who was more responsive to British demands.

Under Peter the Great, Russia expanded into Central Asia rapidly in the eighteenth century. Peter supported Russian modernization and while being best known for founding the Russian Navy and supporting warm water port acquisition, he also stretched the Russian boundaries eastwards. This eastward approach targeted trade between Russia and India via Central Asia, however this progress into Central Asia stopped abruptly in 1717 following the failure of the Khivan Campaign.

Under Catherine the Great, the Russian strategic thought determined that war had to be waged on land without naval supremacy against Great Britain. This implied a military effort towards British India to force Britain to shift her military posture in Europe.[1] Napoleon's contemporary, Paul I of Russia, planned a Russo-French invasion of India via Herat and Kandahar.[2] These plans ended abruptly with the assassination of Paul I, but were briefly revived under Alexander I.

Napoleon's Continental System destroyed the friendship of Alexander I and Napoleon which had developed after the Treaties of Tilsit in 1807 and this would end any potential Russian moves towards India. However, the Russian Witkiewicz Mission to Kabul in the 1830s aiming to strengthen influence in Afghanistan, triggered British action. The Russian foreign minister Count Karl Nesselrode dispatched Russian orientalist and explorer Jan Prosper Witkiewicz to Kabul in 1837, triggering British involvement in Afghanistan before the first Anglo-Afghan War. It was in Afghanistan, that Witkiewicz would meet Alexander Burnes. Witkiewicz was recalled from Afghanistan upon British complaints to the Russian envoy in London. This set the foundation for failed Anglo-Afghan negotiations and the First Anglo-Afghan War in 1842. The British desire for friendly buffer states on the Indian border increased after the first Afghan War failed. Afghanistan under Dost Muhammad Khan was hostile to India and could potentially negotiate a pact with Russia.

Following Ranjit Singh's death in 1839, the Sikh Empire would lie in disarray and political instability, that increased British unease. The Sikh Empire under Ranjit Singh had balanced the court between Lahore, the Sikh capital, and Jammu, the Dogra feudatory capital skilfully. Infighting in Sikh courts after Ranjit Singh's death destroyed this delicate balance between the Sikhs and the Dogras. The British entered the fray now by encouraging the militarization of the Sikh Empire and supporting the dal Khalsa in 1845.

The Anglo-Sikh War and 1846 Treaty of Lahore expanded British borders westward with the acquisition of the Jalandhar Doab. British recognition of Gulab Singh as ruler of Jammu & Kashmir's was one of their first moves to safeguard the northern frontiers of British India. The British approached frontier security more carefully and methodically after the disaster of the First Anglo-

Afghan War. The British strategy towards Gulab Singh and his positive conduct in the 1848-9 Anglo-Sikh War are clearly referred to in documents from the National Archives of India. Gulab Singh went on to administer many semi-autonomous communities on the northern boundary for Britain.

Meanwhile, the Russians were consolidating their power in Central Asia while the British were engaged in Afghanistan and dealing with the aftermath of Ranjit Singh's death in Punjab. British protests forced the Witkiewicz Mission to retreat from Afghanistan. A later Russian expedition known as the Perovsky mission forced the Khanate of Khiva to negotiate with Russia, culminating in the 1842 Khiva-Russia Treaty, which had mostly symbolic significance.[3]

While the Great Game was gathering momentum, Central Asian tribes such as the Kirghiz were rallying to the Russians because they presented themselves as defenders and not colonial masters. The Crimean War in 1853 and Britain's alliance with the Ottomans against Russia affected the grand strategy of Central Asia. While, the Crimean War raged in Europe, the Russians desperately sought means to defeat the British. In 1854, the Russian General, Alexander Duhamel advocated invading British India again. All five of Duhamel's invasion routes into India passed through Afghanistan. These forces could enter India via the Khyber Pass. This plan was possible only with the help of a friendly Afghan government. The Russian defeat in the Crimean War stalled Russia's Indian ambitions again. In 1857 Khiva and Bokhara sent ambassadors to St. Petersburg, and in response, the Russian statesman Count Ignatieff sent missions to the two regions. Further, an expedition under Russian explorer Nikolai Khanikoff was accused of generating diplomatic issues for the English in Afghanistan during the 1857 Indian Revolt (Colquhoun 1900: 12).

As Russia expanded into Central Asia, there were worries about where the frontiers of the Russian Empire should lie. The Russian Foreign Ministry and military disputed a 'safe frontier' from 1861. The Foreign Minister Alexander Mikhailovich Gorchakov opposed expansion beyond southern Kazakhstan, while the War Minister Dmitry Alekseyevich Milyutin called for a more aggressive expansion. Russian General Tchermayyoff took advantage of a pro-Russian faction in Tashkent, resulting in an unconditional surrender of Tashkent to the Russians on 29 June 1865. On the Russians taking control of Uzbekistan, Sir John Lawrence, then Viceroy of India, declared 'Russia might prove a safer neighbour than the wild tribes of Central Asia' (Chohan 1997: 32).

Recent research indicates that there was no Russian Grand strategy in its expansion in Central Asia; rather separate factions within the Russian military acted independently and seized the initiative when it presented itself. Consequently, Tashkent and Khujand in Tajikistan were annexed to the Russian Empire on 8 and 26 September 1866 respectively on pretexts by regional Russian commanders. The Emir of Bokhara would panic at this aggressive Russian incursion and sought British support from India. However, his overture for assistance would be refused by the British saying that they were unlikely to interfere in a Russian 'civilizational mission' in uncivilized Central Asia.

St. Petersburg denied having any foreknowledge of the actions by Russian military commanders in the region and declared that if any Russian officers had acted independently, they would be brought before a court martial. This seems to have been done primarily to assuage British fears. Further, under 23 July 1867 Imperial Ukase or Declaration, these newly acquired territories were made independent of the Russian city of Orenburg which had served as the base of all Russian expeditions to Central Asia. The city of Khokand would emerge as a Russian trading hub in Central Asia and further expand their trade with Bukhara as explained by Col. Fred Burnaby in his travelogue *A Ride to Khiva.*[4]

The British authorities were confident that the Russians would not advance further to Khiva. Further, the Russians reinforced this belief when the Russian aristocrat, Count Pyotr Shuvalov told the British, that an imminent Russian expedition to the region was punitive in nature and did not intend to recover any territory. However, in 1873, a Russian invasion force of 14,000 men arrived resulting in a peace agreement between Russia and Khiva on 25 August 1873 making the latter a Russian vassal. Russia thus gained exclusive control of the Oxus River (Burnaby 1895: 250).

By 1876, Khiva and Khokand had been annexed as the Fergana Province of the Russian Empire.

Russia had expanded from the Caspian and Central Asia to the Oxus River north of Afghanistan. Multiple factors had pushed this expansion, with the Russian army playing an important role in shaping the expansion policy to the south of Kazakhstan. Only Afghanistan separated British India from Russian territories in Uzbekistan, which were adjacent to the Wakhan corridor in Yasin. Moreover, Chitral had close ties with Afghanistan—a country with which the British had fought the First Anglo-Afghan War. Consequently, the British could not ignore this strategic frontier.

BRITISH FRONTIER CONCERNS

The Russian expansion into Khiva in 1873 would renew the impetus for the British to seek some sort of a more formal control over the north-western passages into India. While Punjab and Afghanistan further to the north-west were the traditional axes of advance into India, the regions of Chitral and Yasin to the east were important flanks of these access routes. Chitral had been a constant threat to Gilgit, often supported by Afghans. Yasin under Malik Aman would attack Gilgit twice in 1867-8 to remove the Dogras who had captured Gilgit. The British were keenly observing the events happening in the frontier region and were clearly unhappy with the situation of political instability which they saw. Small local principalities were busy fighting each other and often attacked forces of the princely state of J&K. Chitral, as a minor state aligned with the Afghans, was a clear and present threat to British interests in the frontier region.

Sir Douglas Forsyth*, had in 1874, presented a secret report expressing his concerns about a possible Russian move against Kashgar and subsequently onto the Hindukush Mountains, with

* Sir Thomas Douglas Forsyth was a career diplomat in British India in the second half of the nineteenth century. He would visit Yarkand and Kashgar in the mid-1870s at the request of Yakub Beg who was the anti-Chinese leader of the region.

special reference to discussions with M. Berzenczey who was a Russian envoy of Hungarian descent:

> M. Berzenczey, now here says that the Russians at Almaty speak confidently of a speedy contact between Russian and British boundaries in Asia, and profess an indifference whether we advance our frontier to them or they push theirs on to India.[5]

The document further elaborates that while there was no immediate threat to India from Russian expansion, it expressed considerable wariness about any further Russian expansion southward:

> We have passed out of the region of speculation on the danger or advantage to British interests of an advance by Russia to the Hindoo Koosh. It has been publicly proclaimed to the world and is known to the people most interested, that Russia and England have accepted the Oxus as a line of boundary between them, and it is no matter of opinion now, but a certainty that a breach of this engagement by the occupation of Budakshan and Afghan Turkestan by the Russians, or by any one under their influence, would be fraught with danger to our prestige in India.[6]

Earlier in 1870 Sir Forsyth had been sent by the Government of India (GOI) on a mission of trade and exploration to Kashgar to explore the possibilities of such a Russian move to the south. This expedition entered Swat, Dir and Chitral through the Dorah Pass which connects Afghanistan with Chitral (Chohan 1997: 41). In a second mission by Forsyth in 1873, it was discovered that the two mountain passes, namely Baroghil and the Ishkoman Aghost Pass which separated Chitral and Yasin from the Oxus valley, were strategically critical because they provided military access to the Indian subcontinent. The Baroghil Pass connected the Wakhan region to Chitral and the Ishkoman Pass connected Wakhan to Gilgit and Yasin. Further, the expedition discovered that these passes had recently been used to transport artillery guns. The report also pointed out that whosoever controlled the Ishkoman Pass would also determine the movement of men and supplies through the Baroghil Pass.[7] This is also clearly pointed out in the Confidential Report of the Yarkand Mission by Sir Douglas Forsyth:

Both the Baroghil and Ishkaman have had guns taken over them within the last few years. By the former, the British frontier can be reached in 13 marches vid the Mastueh, Chitral, and Panjkora valleys. By the latter, Torbela on the Indus is reached in the same time vid Gilgit, Chelas, and the Indus Valley. Mir Futteh Ali Shah of Wakhan made special mention of the latter as the best and nearest road to India.[8]

He further explains the nature of the terrain which made it possible to use the passes for military movement:

So long as the mistaken idea was held that the Pamir was really the 'roof' of the world and quite impassable for troops, it mattered little how far Kashmir penetrated in that direction, or who held the petty principalities on the Hindoo-Kush. But as the mists of ignorance are gradually being dissipated, we are brought face to face with facts and are compelled to acknowledge danger from a quarter where we have a right to expect loyal assistance.[9] It further explains that: It is a fact, which is notorious, and of which we have had practical proof in the case of Abdul Subhan, that the Kashmir Government throws every obstacle in the way of our becoming acquainted with the country and people between Gilghit and the Hindoo-Kush, and her influence is exerted there against the interests of the British Government.[10] It continues: On the military question, whether Russia would ever think of sending a force down by Kokand, or Kashgar, and the Pamir, and direct to the Indus, I do not offer an opinion; but that the road is far easier than was supposed, and that it presents none of the obstacles which would render the Karakorum route next to impossible Col. Gordon's report shews.[11]

It is clear that the notion that the Pamirs presented an impassable barrier was now under question and it was now the assessment of British officials that the policies of the princely state of J&K were not necessarily in line with British interests. The report later goes on to elaborate, how the Russians, if they decided to press onwards in to India would have no logistical problems, facilitated by the fertile lands along the way:

Looking farther, we now know that from the Russian southern frontier to Surhud in Wakhan the difficulties of transporting troops are comparatively small. The most important strategical point on the Russian frontier is Osh in Khokund, the whole of which country may be considered for all practical purposes as Russian territory. Assuming that a force might be assembled at Osh for offensive purposes, the information we gained of the Pamir roads from the Kirghiz shows that there is nothing to prevent the rapid advance of an army fully equipped to within a few miles of Surhud. Not only is no road-making for the passage of field artillery necessary, but along the whole distance there is an unlimited quantity of the finest pasture in the world. The old saying recorded by Marco Polo that a lean horse gets into condition in ten days on the Pamir still holds good, and we were positively warned against giving grain to our horses while crossing, lest we should make them ill. Arrived within thirty miles of Surhud, road-making for guns becomes necessary, but a strong advanced guard, supported by mountain train batteries, would effectually secure the work from interruption, and the scanty poorly armed population of Wakhan can offer no opposition worth mentioning.[12]

Biddulph, in this part of the report explains the strategic significance of Osh in Khokand on the Russian frontier. The large pasture lands and natural access routes were natural threat axes into India. Finally, the report goes on to explain the strategic benefits of holding on to Gilgit to check any Russian expansion towards Kashmir into India:

In the event of Kashghar being in unfriendly hands, and so being liable to be used as a base of operations against India, the occupation of Gilgit and the Ishkaman Pass would appear sufficient to check an attack from the direction of the Pamirs. No hostile force could cross the Baroghil Pass in the face of one holding the Ishkaman. I assume that in such a case Kashmir would become practically British territory. The distance from Gaokuch, the Kashmir frontier village, to the Ishkaman Pass, along a valley, through a thinly populated country, is about 40 miles.[13]

It would be the recommendations of this report that would significantly influence future British policies towards this region and eventually result in a subsequent mission under Capt. John Biddulph in 1875. The purpose of this mission was to gather further information about the Ishkoman Pass. Capt. John Biddulph was the Aide-de-Camp to the then Viceroy of India, Lord Northbrook.* During his travel, Biddulph would visit the regions of Gilgit, Hunza and Yasin and present his findings upon his return. His findings about the nature of the terrain and the possible threat

* Lord Northbrook was the Viceroy of India from 1872 to 1876 during the Liberal Party government under Prime Minister William Ewart Gladstone.

of Russian inroads further increased concern about the strategic significance of the region:

> From Surhud to the top of either of the Passes, not above one mile and a half of road needs preparing for the passage of field guns, and the invader finds the choice of several routes open to him. By the Baroghil Pass he can follow the course of the Mastueh stream to Chitral, whence he can threaten both Jellalabad and Peshawur, or crossing by the Ishkaman Pass, he can reach Gilgit in three marches, and from there threaten the Punjab either by Cashmere or the Torbela route. This latter would in all probability offer the greatest physical obstacles, but the certain co-operation of the disaffected people of Swat offers counterbalancing advantages, while both the routes by the Ishkaman Pass have the advantage of turning the Indus line of defence.[14]

Biddulph emphasizes the direct threat that could be posed in this manner to the Punjab, if an invader were to gain access to Kashmir or the Tarbela, near the Swat region to the south-west. He goes on to explain, that such an attack did not require too much preparation, before they became suitable for military traffic:

> It is probable that the roads from the Passes to the plains of India need some preparation before bodies of troops can be brought by any of them, but this will tell as much against the defending forces as against the invader. None of them present any great natural obstacle, and once in possession of the Passes a powerful enemy will be able to take a strong initiative to which the defending army must conform. Under these circumstances, it would be well to consider what line of action remains open to us, before the course of events presses so hard on us as to cause the adoption of hasty and possibly ill-considered measures.[15]

These reports by Douglas Forsyth and Biddulph together with the Russian expansion in Central Asia, edging ever closer to British India, resulted in an appraisal of British policy towards the frontier. The primary debate that was ongoing in the British policymaking circles, was how to secure this frontier from any possible Russian inroads. There seemed to have been two possible alternatives; the first was to annex Chitral, Yasin, Hunza, and Nagar directly and the second was the use of the princely state of J&K to exert greater control over these frontier territories. However, any direct British annexation of these frontier territories risked a direct contact with the Russian frontier and was therefore not politically feasible. The second option was therefore considered more suitable. This meant that the J&K government would be encouraged to extend its control over the frontier and thereby control the Ishkoman Pass. In this endeavour, the J&K government would be ensured active support of the British, who would then be assured de facto control over these vital strategic passages. This policy had the advantage of achieving British strategic objectives without direct commitment of British men and material while also extending the British outposts closer to Afghanistan, which for all effects and purposes was considered to be a hostile country. However, this British Carte Blanche to the J&K government was conditional to the appointment of a British resident at Gilgit.[16]

It was with this backdrop that meetings were held between the then British viceroy Lord Lytton* and Maharaja Ranbir Singh at Madhopur near Pathankot on 17-18 November 1876. It was decided here that it was in British interests that the small principalities such as Yasin and Chitral, lying beyond the then northern borders of J&K State should come under the control of J&K rather than under the influence of some foreign power.

> Expressing his anxiety in regard to Kashmir frontier, he observed that the country beyond the Maharaja's borders was inhabited by a rude and barbarous people who owed allegiance to various chiefs in no respect more advanced than the populations over whom they exercised suzerainty and stated that it was essential that such states as Chitral and Yasin should come under the control of a friend and ally of the British Government, like His Highness, rather than be absorbed in the course of events by power enemical to Cashmere; this became the more necessary from their being certain passes through the mountain range bounding these territories on the north, which passes, it is believed, are more or less practicable or can be made practicable, for the passage of troops. (Dani 1991: 260)

As mentioned above, in the meeting on 17 November 1876, the Viceroy, Lord Lytton informed Maharaja Ranbir Singh, the incumbent ruler of J&K, that in the interests of the peace and security of the Indian borders, certain steps were necessary. The

* Lord Lytton was the Viceroy of India from 1876 to 1880 during the Conservative Party government under Prime Minister Benjamin Disraeli.

Viceroy expressed his specific concerns about the borders of J&K and how territories adjoining those borders were home to uncivilized tribes who owed loyalty to their respective tribal leaders and that it was of the utmost importance to the security of India that these regions be brought under the control of a British ally such as the state of J&K. This was preferable than these regions coming under the control of some hostile power at a subsequent date, especially since such regions were very easily accessible to hostile troops.

Maharaja Ranbir Singh suggested to the Viceroy that there were three possible approaches to achieve these aims. The first approach was to take advantage of a suitable opportunity to intervene in the internal politics of these frontier states arising out of their frequent dissensions. The second approach would be to engage in negotiations with these states to arrive at a political settlement which allowed political control and the third would be direct military action resulting in annexation. Ranbir Singh was open to pursuing any of these policies as long as British support was ensured.

The British, were also concerned with winning over the local population, in order to maintain their own political stability, preferred the second option which involved some sort of a negotiated settlement between J&K and the frontier states, specifically Chitral and Yasin with British support. Ranbir Singh agreed to pursue the second option as the Viceroy had consented but desired a written British assurance for any such actions that he may initiate. This was communicated to the Viceroy who agreed to provide any form of assurance that would be satisfactory to his highness the Maharaja. Moreover, the Viceroy assured to provide the Maharaja with 5,000 rifles for his army. It was then, that the Viceroy further added the British desire to have a British officer posted at Gilgit so that the British could have continuous information about the happenings on the frontier (Chohan 1997: 42).

The proposal of posting a British resident at the frontier caught the Maharaja off guard who did not expect any such British official to be based there. The Dogras had been very cautious about letting British explorers enter the frontier regions. Such a proposal naturally made Ranbir Singh wary. In response, Ranbir Singh proposed that a telegraph line could be established to Gilgit, permitting a constant transfer of information from the frontier. However, the Viceroy insisted on the idea of a British officer at Gilgit; in response to which Ranbir Singh requested some time to think about this British proposal, which ended the first day of their meeting.

The next day on 18 November, Ranbir Singh agreed to the British request for an officer posted at Gilgit but requested permission to address the GOI regarding certain assurances which he desired before proceeding on this endeavour, which Lord Lytton agreed to. A.H. Dani, refers to this as the 'Madhopur Declaration' and it was clear that this represented a clear shift to a far more direct British role in this part of the Indian Frontier. This greater British focus on frontier issues, however, is not a coincidence considering the several contemporary Russian territorial acquisitions in Central Asia occurring in quick successions. In essence, the revised British policy following the Madhopur Declaration towards the frontier states would be two pronged; on the one hand, the princely state of J&K, would enter into a series of direct arrangements with these frontier states and on the other hand, smaller states, would be directly annexed to J&K.

Six days later, on 26 November 1876, the Maharaja wrote a letter to the Viceroy requesting him a 'Sanad' or title deed giving him certain assurances.[17] The assurances included that the appointment of the political officer would be selected in consultation with him, his duties would be confined to the matters regarding the territories beyond the Kashmir borders and he would not in any way act to impair the powers and prestige of the Maharaja (Gadru 1973: xxi). These requests were accepted by the Viceroy in a reply dated 22 December 1876, in which he agreed that the demands of the Maharaja were reasonable and further added that:

> The function of the officer stationed at Gilgit would be confined to (1) collecting and furnishing information regarding the frontier and the progress of events beyond it, accompanied by such advice to the Maharaja and to the British government as his military experience might enable him to offer in regard thereto, (2) the organization of any military measures on the border which might have previously received the free assent and full approval of the Maharaja. (Chohan 1997: 48)

The Viceroy assured the Maharaja that the British officer at Gilgit would work with the complete confidence of the Maharaja and if he did not strictly adhere to the conditions of this appointment then that officer would be immediately recalled. It was also agreed to by the Viceroy, to consider the Maharaja's opinions regarding the selection of the officer for Gilgit. Finally, the Maharaja was reassured that the intention of appointing such an official was to strengthen the Maharaja's rule and not to undermine it (Chohan 1997: 49).

Maj. Biddulph, who was already familiar with the region on account of his earlier travels in the region, would eventually be appointed as the first British Political Officer to Gilgit. This was not surprising, since this entire sequence of meetings between the Maharaja and the Viceroy, the Madhopur Declaration and his eventual appointment as a Political Officer were a result of his own recommendations. Biddulph was expected to develop relationships with the local tribes in the frontier region, as well as control the access of people, both British and Indians into the frontier regions on political grounds. Biddulph was also expected to provide a weekly diary of intelligence and proceedings about the frontier to Maj. Henderson who was officer on special duty and would form the channel of communication to the GOI (ibid.: 50). Thus, the Gilgit Agency came into existence in 1877, with Maj. Biddulph joining his post in December of that year as an 'Officer on Special Duty'.[18]

THE GILGIT AGENCY

Upon his arrival to the Gilgit Agency, the first crisis which Maj. Biddulph had to deal with was the so called 'Chaprote Affair'. Chaprote, a small village on the west bank of the Indus River occupied a strategically important position between the regions of Hunza, Gilgit and Nagar and was a natural strong point.[19] Historically, Gilgit had claims over Chaprote, however, the village had come under Sikh and later Dogra control in the first half of the nineteenth century. However, in 1848 or 1849, the local garrison was surprised by the Hunza and sold into slavery, with

Chaprote remaining under Hunza control until 1875 (Chohan 1997: 51).

In 1875, Chaprote would fall under the influence of Nagar which, being aligned with the court at Srinagar, requested troops from the state of J&K. Maj. Biddulph found a small number of Kashmir troops to be already stationed in the village. This aspect of deputing Kashmir troops to the village had already been discussed with the Viceroy, during the meetings at Madhopur and had received the assent of the latter.[20]

Mir Ghazan Khan, the ruler of Hunza sent a representation in July 1878, essentially accepting acceding Chaprote to the Kashmir but unwilling to let it remain in the hands of the Nagar ruler Mir Jaffer Khan. For the Government of Kashmir, this was a delicate situation since their garrison in the village was already too small to be viable and any unilateral increase in the garrison number in the could possibly create an unstable situation. After hearing the representation by Ghazan Khan, Biddulph suggested to Henvey in 1879, that it was in the interests of the Kashmir government that Chaprote should be annexed to the territory of Kashmir because of its strategic importance, the unreliable loyalty of the Nagar ruler, Mir Jaffer Khan, and its usefulness for any future military action against Chitral or Yasin. Finally, such a move would result in controlling the road access to Hunza, Nagar and the strategic Ishkoman Pass.[21]

The proposal to take over Chaprote by directly moving a large body of troops there was seconded by Henvey, the OSD in Kashmir, however in doing so he may have gone beyond his mandate. It seems so because when this idea was not supported by the GOI which took the position that it would be more appropriate for the Kashmir Darbar and that the insistence of the British Agent on a particular course of action could have different connotations by the Darbar. Consequently, the GOI advised Biddulph through Henvey, that he should allow the governor of the Darbar in Gilgit to take the initiative on the Chaprote question, while he himself should remain passive and proffer advice only when solicited.[22] Despite instructions to the contrary however, Biddulph in May 1880 would suggest to the Darbar that the strength of the garrison be increased to 250 men from the existing 50. The Darbar accepted this proposal and increased the garrison to 250 men by June. By this time there was information that Nagar and Hunza may attack the village of Chaprote.[23]

Meanwhile, by this time the political situation in the frontier was being shaped increasingly by Anglo-Afghan relations, with the frontier states being essentially forced to choose sides. The ruler of Chitral, which was one of the important frontier states was Aman-ul-Mulk. Traditionally, a state, inimical to Kashmir, Chitral under Aman-ul-Mulk came under increasing pressure from the Emir of Afghanistan after 1877. Aman-ul-Mulk, in response began to move closer towards Kashmir and consequently, in 1877, the Maharaja of Kashmir with the approval of the GOI, offered him a Treaty of Friendship.[24]

Aman-ul-Mulk was trying to maintain a fine balance between his relations with Kashmir and Afghanistan. He, therefore, delayed his response by over a year to January 1879 and changed the terms of the agreement. When this draft treaty as agreed upon by Aman-ul-Mulk, was returned to the Kashmir Darbar, it did not carry Aman-ul-Mulk's signature, only his verbal approval of the terms of the treaty. In fact, Aman-ul-Mulk was trying his best to improve his relationship with Kabul, however since Anglo-Afghan relations at this time were heading towards war, this political stance by Aman-ul-Mulk made matters very difficult for Biddulph.

> Lytton was prepared to turn a blind eye to this, if it would prevent any overt Afghan action against Chitral, but it made things very difficult for Biddulph at Gilgit, especially as Afghan-Indian relations in 1878 were deteriorating towards war. Matters eventually reached such a pitch that Biddulph even doubted whether his projected visit to Chitral in 1878 would serve any purpose at all. On 16 October he reached Yasin. On the 29th, the final ultimatum was despatched to Kabul. On the 31st, several weeks too late, the Indian Government telegraphed to order the postponement of Biddulph's visit. With war about to break out between India and Afghanistan it was impossible to guess which way Aman-ul-Mulk would jump. (Alder 1963: 122)

Consequently, despite the concerns that Biddulph's proposed visit to Chitral and Yasin could be postponed owing to the outbreak of the Anglo-Afghan War, his visit to these two territories did materialize. Biddulph was welcomed in both these states, however their respective rulers did not fail to express to him their displeasure at the Kashmir Darbar.

> Fortunately, Biddulph received a moderately friendly welcome in Yasin and Chitral. Both rulers, however, were loud in their contempt of the Kashmir connection. Pahlwan Bahadur of Yasin claimed that he had met with 'nothing but bad treatment and bad faith from Kashmir; that in consequence he had decided on sending no more vakils to Jammu'. Aman-ul-Mulk was even more contemptuous of the Kashmir subsidy—'I can take a few Kaffir women and sell them for as much', he said and was clearly disappointed that Biddulph had brought with him nothing more than platitudes about the need for friendship with Kashmir. A few days after Biddulph left, despite a very clear warning against it, Aman made fresh overtures to Kabul for a marriage alliance.[25]

It is thus clear that both Chitral and Yasin were hedging their risks and were wary of openly entering into an agreement with any specific side. Chitral was especially wary of Kabul and continued to maintain friendly ties with the latter.[26] Fredrick Henvey, the Kashmir Resident suggested that Aman-ul-Mulk who was an Afghan ally in all but name, should lose his subsidy since Britain was now at war with Afghanistan. This was discouraged by the Viceroy, Lord Lytton on the grounds that India could not prevent the establishment of relations between Chitral and Kabul. This essentially meant the failure of the aptly named 'Madhopur Policy' a personal initiative of Lord Lytton. While Lytton did not want to accept this policy as a failure, his grounds for discouraging Henvey from stopping the subsidy to Aman-ul-Mulk essentially amounted to the same (Alder 1963: 123). Thus it can be concluded that the Maharaja and the British Agent at Gilgit had failed to secure the loyalty and allegiance of Chitral and Yasin rulers.

Clearly, there were strong schools of opinion among British explorers initially regarding the region, over whether it was the best approach for the British to have a policy of friendship with the local kingdoms dotting the region. The geographical inaccessibility and remoteness of the region presented significant logistical problems to any outsider. Leitner* explains this position in his travel accounts titled, *Dardistan in 1866, 1886 and 1893:*

> Now that Abdur-Rahman is suspected, on the flimsiest possible evidence, to have connived at Sher Afzul's invasion of Chitral, we seek to pick a quarrel with him for what a few weeks ago was considered an assertion of his rights. Let it be repeated once for always that if ever Abdur-Rahman or Nizam-ul-Mulk, or the Chief of Hunza or Kashmir or Upper India fall into the arms of Russia, it will be Maxima nostra culpa. I know the Amir Abdur-Rahman, as I knew the Amir Sher Ali, as I know Nizam-ul-Mulk, and of all I can assert that no truer friends to England existed in Asa than these Chiefs.[27]

Leitner here is critical of British involvement in the internal affairs of the princely state of Chitral. He points out that if this frontier region ever, fell under Russian influence, it would be a result of British policies themselves, which Leitner refers to by the Latin phrase *Maxima nostra culpa*—'our greatest fault'. Despite this, the British policy under the Madhopur framework intended to do precisely this albeit in a very indirect and circuitous manner. The British eager to win the friendship of Yasin and Chitral were hesitant to dictate terms directly, instead preferring to act through their Dogra allies. This anfractuous approach, while protecting the British from the antagonism of the frontier states by not being seen as a threat to their rule, also prevented them from using direct military power to implement their objectives. The Dogras, on the other hand, who were essentially acting as British agents to expand their power were seen as the preeminent threat by Chitral and Hunza who used every opportunity to resist Dogra rule. More importantly perhaps, the traditional enmities between the local rulers were acting as a major impediment in bringing these states together under a common suzerain like the Dogras. In doing so, these states were actually undermining British frontier policy which was unable to achieve its objective of controlling the Frontier.

By 1880, this failure began to manifest itself as disturbances on the frontier with Ghazan Khan trying to regain Chaprote by making

* Gottlieb Wilhelm Leitner was a British orientalist who travelled extensively around the world, including in the remote reaches of Dardistan region and wrote accounts of his travels and the people in that region.

a tribal alliance by offering his daughter in marriage to Pahalwan Bahadur, the ruler of Yasin and diplomatic overtures to other local rulers. This was after his earlier attempts to wean Chaprote away from Nagar had failed (Chohan 1997: 60). More importantly perhaps, the massacre of Sir Louis Cavagnari along with the rest of his mission in Kabul on 3 September 1879 had marked a new phase of the second Anglo-Afghan War and an end of Lytton's aggressive policy towards Afghanistan against Russia which had clearly been a failure.

Starting in October 1880, under the leadership of Pahalwan Bahadur of Hunza, a series of ambushes were planned on forts occupied by Dogra troops in Gilgit. Without going into too many details about the attacks themselves, it must be pointed out that during this rebellion, Pahalwan Bahadur had the support of Darelis and promise of support by Mana-ul-Mulk of Chitral at a later date when Cher Kila or Rock Fort located in Punial was captured (Leitner 1996: 60). A series of forts were lost and considering the urgency of the situation, military reinforcements were dispatched. However, Dogra commanders in charge showed remarkable slackness in reaching the besieged soldiers. In view of this general reluctance or military incompetence, Biddulph personally took charge of all Kashmir troops.

By December 1880, a force of roughly 5,000 men had been collected at Gilgit to deal with the rebellion (ibid.: 65). It was at this moment, that Aman-ul-Mulk dispatched his youngest son Nizam-ul-Mulk to arrest Pahalwan and hand him over to the Kashmir authorities.

> As per this communication the Mehtar informed the Maharaja of the steps he had taken, and expressed the hope that Pahlwan would be caught and presented to him (the Maharaja) soon. He also told the Maharaja that, as the troops he had sent to Yasin were strong enough to subdue the insurrection, there was no need for His Highness' troops to undertake the trouble of marching to Yasin. Besides, the presence of a victorious army like the Maharaja's could, in the opinion of the Mehtar, create a commotion in the district of Yasin. He, therefore, requested the Maharaja to countermand the march of troops into Yasin so that the 'ill-advised act of one disaffected person may not result in dire consequences for the entire body of Your Highness' subjects in Yasin'. (ibid.)

Eventually, Nizam-ul-Mulk took Pahalwan Bahadur into custody and finally the latter would be sent away to Afghanistan. As a reward for his actions, Aman-ul-Mulk was rewarded for his actions while Yasin itself was partitioned off as follows:

1. Yasin proper placed under Mir Aman, brother to Gaur Aman and an uncle of Pahlwan.
2. Mastuj placed under Afzul-ul-Mulk, a son of Mehtar Aman-ul-Mulk.
3. Ghizar placed under Mohammed Wali, son of Mir Wali.

The Mehtar stipulated that Pahlwan would not be restored to any part of the territories which he by his misconduct had justly forfeited. He, also undertook to guarantee that his nominees appointed to administer the above three parts of Yasin would behave properly. and would remit annual Nazaranas to the Maharaja. The Maharaja proposed that a part of the subsidy that was to be paid to Aman-ul-Mulk would now directly be paid to the actual rulers of the Yasin territories. These arrangements proposed by the Kashmir Darbar received the assent of the Government of India. (Leitner 1996: 66)

While it seemed that the situation had been brought under control, it was nevertheless, clear that the policy as had been followed so far by Biddulph had been unsuccessful in pacifying the frontier and establishing friendly relations with the local tribes. There had been unsubstantiated allegations that the Maharaja himself interfered with the workings of the British agent in Gilgit:

Treachery was never proved against the Maharaja, but enough was found to show at least 'an unfitness for the functions entrusted to him'. Lytton summed up the ruler unambiguously for his successor as 'a broken instrument which we can neither mend, nor employ again with any safety'. (Alder 1963: 130)

However, apparently, since this alleged treachery was never proved, and the fact that the Maharaja always cooperated with Biddulph, even against his own officials, it seems extremely unlikely that there was any active attempt on the part of the Maharaja to undermine Biddulph. When, according to Henvey, Biddulph made unfounded charges against the Governor of Gilgit, Bhai Ganga and his son Bhai Gurubaksh Singh, the Maharaja immediately recalled them. Similarly, during Biddulph's visit to Yasin and Chitral in 1878, the Maharaja was instrumental in making all the necessary preparations for it including writing a letter to Aman-ul-Mulk to show respect to Biddulph as a friend of the Maharaja and a high-ranking British official.

It seems that there were other reasons for the failure of the British political agent and the Madhopur policy. First, some of the Maharaja's officials did not appreciate an English official presiding over them. Second, the role and position of the agency itself were major factors in its failure, located in the remote frontier of the Indian subcontinent, being cut-off six months in a year[28] and no real authority to advise or intervene in the affairs of the Kashmir Darbar or the frontier states.[29] This remoteness created difficulties in reaching supplies to the region. Third, there were several instances of incorrect assessments of the ground situation by Biddulph himself. He considered Aman-ul-Mulk as unscrupulous and hostile to the Darbar, while believing Pahalwan Bahadur to be trustworthy; however, as events would show, it was Pahalwan who created trouble for the Darbar and Aman-ul-Mulk came to the assistance of the Maharaja. Fifth, the relations between Aman-ul-Mulk and Kashmir were not based on any commonality of interests but rather the force of British influence. Chitral, an overwhelmingly Muslim state naturally gravitated towards Afghanistan with which it had a shared a border and a greater commonality of culture than with Kashmir (Alder 1963: 134). Lastly, it became clear that the initial assessment about the significance of Yasin with respect to the Russian threat had been blown out of proportion and that the passes through Yasin were unimportant. Far more important for the Russian threat was the Baroghil Pass coming through Chitral, and yet Gilgit continued to be the centre of Chitral's defence according to the Madhopur policy (Chohan 1997: 72).

It was in the backdrop of this situation, that it was finally decided to close down the British Agency and recall Biddulph because, while the immediate crisis had been controlled, there was no telling when another uprising might take place. Moreover, a lot of bad blood had been created between Biddulph and the Dogra officials and there was a constant threat to his life. On 11 May 1881, the Political Officer in Gilgit was recalled. The Maharaja, however, said that the GOI still regarded the affairs of the Gilgit frontier with attention and had no desire that His Highness should recede from the position which he had taken up in 1877. On the contrary, His Highness should maintain his influence unimpaired over the frontier Chiefs.[30]

Nevertheless, while the Madhopur policy had failed, the political agent and the Maharaja as a tool of British frontier policy proved to be ineffectual, the underlying objectives of the British policy had not changed. The British expected that after the withdrawal of their agent from Gilgit, the role of providing up to date information on the affairs of the frontier would be fulfilled by the J&K State. However, the British would be disappointed as often, the Maharaja did not provide the same quality of information that was expected; soon enough, Henvey, the British OSD in Kashmir began to complain of the Maharaja's conduct in the conduct of frontier affairs.

Further, the Afghans were increasing their involvement in the frontier states such as Chitral, Swat, Dir, etc., which were traditionally considered as dependencies by the Amir of Afghanistan. Consequently, Abd-ar-Rahman., the Amir of Afghanistan claimed suzerainty over Chitral in a letter dated 20 March 1882. After a veiled threat to him by the GOI to desist from interference in the affairs of Chitral, following which the Amit withdrew. Despite this initial withdrawal, by 1883, the situation would deteriorate to a point that an Afghan invasion into Chitral would be expected at any time and Aman-ul-Mulk was particularly concerned about Afghan intrigues in southern and western parts of Chitral (Alder 1963: 149).

To make matters worse, the Russian moves into the region were quickly gathering steam by the late-1870s. As early as the 1873 Anglo-Russian negotiations, the frontier states as well as other regions in the Upper Oxus had attracted Russian attention. In 1875, the Russian explorer Maiev, discovered new routes from the Russian territories lying to the north towards the Upper Oxus region. The travels of Biddulph in 1876 to the Hindu-Kush would eventually be published by the British Press providing Russians with a wealth of information about the region. In this case, the damage had already been done. Whereas the Russian semi-official work of Terentyef, published in the early 1870s, could only speak of the whole matter of routes across the Indian northern frontier as 'misty and undefined', Kostenko's work of 1880 reported Biddulph's discoveries in full (Alder 1963: 151). Between 1877 and 1879, the Russians occupied Qizil Arvat and came into military contact with the Tekke Turkmen who inflicted a serious military reversal on the Russians in 1879. A major Russian military response came in 1881 under Gen. Mikhail Skobolev which crushed all major Turkmen resistance and the capture of Askhabad.

As a result of this development, only the Merv Oasis remained between the Russian and Afghan borders. The Merv Oasis was thus about to become a point of contention between the British and the Russians, raising alarm bells in Calcutta, Kabul and London.

> England's reaction to this extension of the empire was immediate. On 29 February 1884, the British government protested the annexation of Mari. Russia, to avoid a seemingly inevitable conflict, replied by proposing a joint delimitation of the Afghan frontier, and the two parties agreed on this score. The frontier was fixed for the northern part—from the Amu Darya to Persian Khorasan—in 1887. However, the accord had fixed the frontier only as far as Lake Zarkol; beyond, toward China, nothing had been specified, and England retained access to the Pamirs.[31]

Despite, this attempted demarcation of the frontier, there was nothing concrete which came out of it and in 1885, the Russians occupied Panjdeh which is known in history as the Panjdeh incident. The Panjdeh incident resulted in the significant deterioration of relations between Russia and GB and triggered major British military preparations for the defence of the frontier. The mission to the Hindukush under Col. Lockhart* was a direct response to the Panjdeh incident. The Lockhart expedition made its way through Kashmir and Gilgit to Chitral.[32]

The Lockhart expedition reported its findings that the Baroghil Pass which had been earlier been considered to be 'the easiest route into Gilgit' did not provide any real access required by

* Gen. Sir William Stephen Alexander Lockhart was an officer in the British Indian Army and as a Colonel, led the Lockhart Expedition to survey the Hindu Kush region between 1885-6.

military logistics into Gilgit from Badakhshan; although he did admit that some lightly armed soldiers could cross over to cause trouble into the North-West Frontier (Chohan 1997: 82). By 1888, the Trans-Caspian Railway had been completed linking Samarkand to the Caspian Sea thereby allowing the Russians to not only to carry out trade but also to move large quantities of military equipment to the region. Moreover, in 1887, there were reports of Russian travellers visiting Hunza,[33] followed by the mission under Capt. Gromchevisky.[34]

It was against this backdrop that the then India's Foreign Secretary, Sir Mortimer Durand*, expressed his views regarding the defence of the Indian empire. He proposed that the Gilgit Agency should be re-established under one more English officer supported by Dogras from the local Muslim kingdoms (Chohan 1997: 84). Events would move to support this line of action further when in January 1888, Hunza and Nagar rose up in revolt against the Darbar and Kashmiri soldiers were forced to retreat from their positions in Chalt and Chaprote. Eventually, by the autumn of the same year, this uprising was brought under control and a peace treaty was agreed upon between the Darbar on one side and Hunza and Nagar on the other. It was agreed that Kashmir troops would be allowed to reoccupy Chalt and Chaprote and in turn, Kashmiri reinforcements sent to Gilgit were to return to Srinagar.

Nevertheless, these chain of events both internal and external, brought home the point that the Darbar's policy towards the frontier had failed and that it could not be relied upon to provide the safety and security of the northern frontier of India. Consequently, the then resident of Kashmir, T.C. Plowden seconded Durand's proposal for re-establishing the agency at Gilgit.[35] Capt. Algernon Marion Durand, a cavalry officer of the Central Indian Horse, was sent in the summer of 1888 on a tour of Gilgit, Chitral and other places. Upon his return, he too supported the idea of

* Sir Henry Mortimer Durand was a career British Diplomat and played a major role in policymaking related to the north-western frontier of British India. The frontier between British India and Afghanistan was named the Durand Line after him.

re-constituting the residency and the construction of a road from Peshawar to Chitral.

These recommendations were accepted by the GOI in March 1889, and Capt. Durand himself was appointed as the British Agent in the reconstituted Gilgit Agency. That the Gilgit Agency, was involved with the defence of the Kashmir state as well as that of British India, it was decided that the expenses of the Agency would be shared by both. Durand arrived at Gilgit on 27 July 1889.[36]

One of the first tasks entrusted to Capt. Durand upon arrival, was to make overtures to Hunza and Nagar, thereby counteracting Russian influence there:

> My instructions were that, the moment the sanction of the Secretary of State was received to the proposals of Government, I was to proceed to Gilgit, re-establish the Agency there, visit Hunza and Nagar, and then march to Chitral. If feasible, I was to extend my march, and visit the Khans of Dir and Umra Khan of Jandol.[37]

Durand arrived in Nagar on 19 August 1889 whereupon he was received cordially by its ruler, Raja Jaffer Khan, who expressed his loyalty to the British and accepted the subsidy of Rs. 2,000 per annum as approved for them by the GOI (Chohan 1997: 87-8). Durand proceeded to visit Hunza where he was welcomed by the ruler Raja Safdar Ali Khan. However, upon learning that the Raja was being treated at par with the Nagar ruler, whom he considered below him, his behaviour towards the English representatives underwent a complete change (ibid.: 88). This experience would establish the Hunza ruler as unreliable and untrustworthy in the eyes of the British, even though they initially agreed to his demands. After completing his visit to these two regions, Durand would return to Gilgit, before continuing on his diplomatic mission to Chitral.

The Mehtar of Chitral, would welcome Durand and agree to cooperate in the opening up of the Peshawar-Chitral Road which was one of the original recommendations of Capt. Durand. The Mehtar also agreed to fortify his defences under the guidance of British officers. In return for his cooperation a gift of 500 Snyder carbines was given to the ruler, as a mark of British support for him.[38]

Durand returned to Gilgit on 12 November 1889 and all the neighbouring rulers were invited to mark the formal re-establishment of the Agency. The Gilgit Agency as it existed under Durand, occupied a unique position because he represented British authority in the frontier region and was empowered to carry out foreign relations with the states in the vicinity; this was so even as Gilgit itself, was within the administrative region of the government of the Maharaja and several of the local principalities that the Agency dealt with, were the tributaries of the former. Similarly, the Kashmiri troops within the Gilgit Agency were under the command of the Maharaja's officers, yet no major action involving them could be taken without the consent of the British Agent, and he was really responsible for the discipline and control of the troops.

> I was the representative of the British Government on the frontier, and the external relations with the neighbouring States were under my control. But the rule within the Gilgit border was in the hands of the Kashmir Governor, while the command of the forces rested with the Kashmiri General, with the proviso that no important move of troops should be undertaken without my sanction. It was a difficult position, for every one recognised that, in addition to my own responsibilities, I was really answerable for the proper government and progress of the Gilgit district, and for the discipline and control of the troops. (Durand 1900: 226)

This thorny problem of authority was solved by the establishment of an unofficial Committee of public safety which included the Kashmiri governor of Gilgit, the General of the Kashmiri forces and the Agent who met two to three times a week at the home of the British resident where schemes were finalized in the name of the Darbar (ibid.: 227). At the very outset of taking charge, the first order of business for Durand was to streamline the post and transportation system which was achieved by bringing Kashmir within the Imperial Postal System of India. Under Durand's administration of the supply situation for the Kashmir troops, significant measures were undertaken, including refurbishing the frontier forts, establishing new mule tracks[39] as well as bringing new land under cultivation to provide food for the soldiers stationed there.[40]

Trouble returned to the region when in 1891, Uzar Khan, the eldest son of the Nagar ruler Raja Jaffer Khan murdered his two younger brothers because he was unhappy about the close terms that they enjoyed with the British. After committing this crime, Uzar Khan in collaboration with his father and the Hunza ruler Safdar Ali Khan wrote a letter to Durand acknowledging his act and expressing essentially their aggressive intentions. Further, Col. Durand received information from other sources that Uzar Khan intended to capture Chalt and Chaprote from the Kashmiri troops. On 27 May, the Chalt garrison sent word to Durand that a Nagar force was advancing towards Chalt and another force from Hunza was moving towards a position north of the river known as Nilt (Chohan 1997: 96).

During the organization of the relief expedition, the problems of terrain and logistics once again reared their ugly faces. There was difficulty in moving heavy guns because of poor roads and limits on the quantity of supplies as a result of challenges posed by flimsy rope bridges and fast flowing rivers.

> I gave the order at three in the afternoon, and by dusk two hundred men of the Kashmir Body Guard regiment, little Gurkhas and Dogras, were over the rope bridge and on their way, with their full complement of ammunition and rations. It could not be done quicker, for not more than half a dozen men at most could be on the bridge at one time. (Durand 1900: 96)

During this relief effort, the force under Col. Durand would be joined by Raja Akbar Khan of Punial.[41] The Hunza-Nagar forces had realized that Chalt was now very heavily defended and that it would cost a lot for them to attempt a storming of the fort. After a standoff that lasted approximately ten days, an emissary sent by Safdar Ali Khan of Hunza brought the message of his master's unwavering loyalty to the British and not having any hostile designs on Chalt or Chaprote. A similar message was sent by the Nagar ruler as well.

While Durand was well aware of Azar Khan's ambitions to make himself master of Chalt, he was also anxious to avoid any trouble for the time being. Therefore, he accepted these assurances formally and the crisis was diffused for the time being. However, there were intelligence reports about the Hunza ruler receiving Chinese and Russian officials in his territory (Chohan 1997: 100). Having stabilized the situation, Durand returned to Shimla on 31 August and apprised his superiors about the dangerous situation on the ground. The GOI decided that additional military troops would be sent to reinforce the forces under Durand. This included soldiers from the second Battalion of the 5th Gurkha Regiment as well as modern artillery pieces (ibid.: 101). By November 1891, after experiencing some logistical difficulties on his way back, Durand along with his soldiers had firmly established himself in Chalt with sufficient provisions and supplies for a month.

It was clear to everyone on the frontier that Hunza and Nagar were again arming in preparation for a war. Durand tried to reach out to the chiefs through diplomatic means, however, eventually it was realized that such means had no chance of success. Finally on 29 November, Durand delivered an ultimatum to the chiefs of Hunza and Nagar namely Safdar Ali Khan and Uzar Khan respectively. The British envoy carrying this message was humiliated and threatened with death before being forced to return. However, it was Uzar Khan that seemed to be more eager for a fight than the Hunza ruler whose response was more dignified than that of the former. As per reports, the Hunza wazir had threatened to kill anyone present who suggested an acceptance of British terms. The Hunza reply dubiously claimed possible Russian assistance by the next spring:

> The envoy reported that the enemy had so strengthened Nilt fort (we learnt that they had been at work on it for two years) that they were confident they would have no difficulty in holding it against us until the spring, when the Russians, it was asserted, had promised to come to their assistance with many breechloading guns and a supply of ammunition, if not with Cossacks. (Knight 1905: 381)

Using rather colourful language, the Hunza ruler had even threatened Durand with death:

> 'I have been tributary to China for hundreds of years. Trespass into China if you dare,' he wrote to Col. Durand. 'I will withstand you, if I have to use

bullets of gold. If you venture here, be prepared to fight three nations—Hunza, China, and Russia. We will cut your head off, Col. Durand, and then report you to the Indian Government.' (Knight 1905: 382)

While it is clear that such language made a liberal usage of hyperbole, the invocation of foreign powers like China and especially Russia, certainly had the effect of raising the stakes for the British. Consequently, on 2 December 1891 the composite force under Durand moved into Hunza territory and captured the strategically located fortress of Nilt. During this action, the fortress was captured by a frontal assault by the Gurkha troops and three British officers including Col. Durand himself would be wounded (Chohan 1997: 108).

Spedding, who had accompanied Col. Durand throughout the day as galloper, shortly after this came across the maidan to the bluff. He was the bearer of the bad news that Col. Durand had just been severely wounded. Spedding had received an order to take his Pathans up to the height which the Punialis were holding, as they would be useful in cutting off the retreat of the enemy. (Knight 1905: 397)

Following his injury in the battle, the command was handed over to Capt. L.J.E. Bradshaw of the 35 Bengal Infantry. The British position was still tenuous and without going into too many military details, it was only after some brilliant tactical actions under the leadership of one Lt. Smith on the night of 19 and 20 December that the strong fortress of Mayunin Hunza along with its adjoining positions fell to the British troops. On 21 December, the British troops entered Nagar and the rulers of Hunza and Nagar escaped northwards across the frontier. The defenders of Mayun fled and the entire countryside submitted to the British. By 22 December all military operations had ceased and the focus now shifted to the pursuit of Safdar Ali Khan who had been clearly expecting Russian assistance and was now a wanted man:

It was an open secret that Safdar Ali Khan had counted on help from the north, and had sent an embassy to the Russians, at Tashkent. The Governor-General had refused any assistance, but by all accounts, his staff had held very different language, and Safdar Ali Khan had apparently attached some importance to the reports his messenger brought. In his reply to my ultimatum, he had threatened me with the wrath of the three Empires Hunza, Russia, and China. The help expected had not been forthcoming, and the 'descendant of Alexander' was now an exile. (Durand 1900: 264)

The fighting having now concluded, it was necessary to make arrangements for the administration of Hunza and Nagar. Raja Jaffer Khan of Nagar had apparently been under the influence of his son Uzar Khan, and once the latter had left, Jaffer Khan once again pledged his allegiance to Kashmir, following which he was appointed as the temporary Governor of Nagar. Unlike Nagar, where the ruler had stayed back and pledged his loyalty to the English, it was a very different situation in Hunza. Raja Safdar Ali had essentially led the revolt and following his defeat had fled. Consequently, there remained no political authority in Hunza.

Wazir Humayun was the minister of the former ruler and father of Safdar Ali, Raja Ghazan Khan. Ghazan Khan had been murdered by his son Safdar Ali to take the throne, following which Humayun had been banished. As such Wazir Humayun's loyalty to the Kashmir Darbar could be relied upon. Both these governors of Hunza and Nagar, Humayun and Jaffer Khan respectively were to act under the orders of Capt. Stewart who had been deputed as political officer to Hunza (Chohan 1997: 114).

While this Nagar-Hunza uprising was a relatively minor affair in military terms, it was the last major disturbance caused by these two principalities against the Kashmir Darbar. Nevertheless, this conflict had major implications for the imperial policy in the region going forward. First, the thorough nature of their defeat, by approximately a thousand soldiers of the Maharaja under British command within three weeks of the outbreak of hostilities made sure that these two states would remain loyal to the Darbar for the remaining period of the British rule:

> The country has been opened up. Hunza and Nagar are still tributary to Kashmir, but enjoy almost complete control of their own domestic affairs. Both states have been perfectly loyal since, and, as will be seen presently, rendered valuable service to Col. Kelly in his expedition to relieve Chitral three years later.[42]

Second, men such as Safdar Ali and Uzar Khan had been a scourge to their own people with a history of forcing them to war against their wishes and even destroying their winter supplies before their flight across the frontier. The people of these region therefore, felt relieved that these rulers had left. Third the military forces of the Imperial Service Corps of the Kashmir Darbar which had been built up by the British for actions of precisely this nature, had been battle tested and performed admirably. Fourth, the resources being spent on the subsidy to the former rulers of Hunza and Nagar were now effectively stopped[43] and these resources could now be spent on improving the road infrastructure and public utilities.[44] Finally, the military occupation of Hunza and Nagar, effectively closed any avenues of entry into the region to the Russians:

> The result of the little war may best be summed up in the words of a well-known Russian statesman, who said when he heard of our occupation of Hunza: 'Us nous out fermes la porte au nez' (They have slammed the door in our faces). (Durand 1900: 264)

No sooner had this situation been contained and the region pacified, there was to be a series of other uprisings in the region. In May 1892, Col. Durand who had been injured in the fighting, came down to Shimla from Gilgit. The medical officer of the agency, Dr Robertson had taken over charge as acting agent in his absence. During the absence of Col. Durand, Robertson decided to invite a deputation of Chilas headmen to arrive at a better understanding of frontier issues. The subsequent meeting was held in an amicable environment with promises made by the headmen of future loyalty and obedience.[45] Nevertheless, almost immediately after the deputation had left, there were a couple of raids into the Gilgit district involving several murders. Upon hearing of these disturbances, Col. Durand decided upon returning to Gilgit immediately. When he returned, he discovered that the inhabitants of the Sai Valley as well as Gor headmen were both very apprehensive of Chilasi attacks and demanding security from Kashmir:

> Robertson was very anxious to reciprocate the advances made by the Gor people, and I suggested to the GOI that the wishes of their representative should be acceded to, and that he should visit the country. Sanction was

accorded to the proposal, and early in November Robertson started for Gor. (Durand 1900: 274)

Robertson departed for Gor on 11 November 1892 and upon reaching the boundary of Gor, he was greeted by a Chilasi headman, who had a friendly meeting with Robertson. However, it was soon realized that this was probably a ploy to draw the delegation into an ambush as the Chilasi were preparing for hostilities. Sensing trouble, Robertson together with Maj. Twigg advanced quickly and took control of the village of Thalpen inside Chilas territory, which provided supplies and a strong defensive position (ibid.: 280).

These events in Chilas were the precursors to an uprising among the Indus Valley tribes further to the south. Chilas, being a part of the Indus Valley, was effectively witnessing the associated disturbances which were now threatening the stability of this region. To make matters worse, Durand had a poor logistical situation to supply any troops that might be sent to the rescue of the worsening military condition in the region.

Robertson's position was bad, he could not move his escort with the rapidity of the tribesmen; if he started back hurriedly it would only precipitate matters, and he might after one short march find himself confronted by a strong cliff position held by the tribesmen, and also attacked in rear by a force coming up the valley. (ibid.)

In response, Durand organized reinforcements quickly with every available man in Bunji as well as requisitioning a corps of Balti coolies from Skardu to carry supplies for the troops (ibid.: 279).

Following heavy fighting and a large attack on Thalpen by thousands of tribesmen, the situation began to improve gradually for the surrounded Dr Robertson as reinforcements began to trickle in. About a fortnight after Robertson had entrenched himself in Thalpen, the battle for control over Chilas, ended with Kashmir and British troops firmly entrenched in Chilas. Three hundred men of the Maharaja's bodyguard regiment occupied Chilas while logistics were organized to sustain the position (Chohan 1997: 123).

Soon afterwards, in February 1893, it became clear that a larger force of Indus Valley tribes together with the Darel, Tangir and Chilas was gathering with the intention of making a concerted attack on the British in Chilas (Durand 1900: 283). In the early hours on the day of Eid, there was a major attack on the British in Chilas. Over the following days, after heavy fighting, the attackers were forced to retreat. However, during these heavy clashes the losses on the British side were considerable with twenty-three men killed including a British officer, Maj. Daniell, three Kashmiri officers namely Subedar Man Singh, Subedar Bir Singh and Adjutant Nain Singh and nineteen ranks. Over two hundred of the tribals were killed in this attack and the result was that there was peace in the region for some time (ibid.: 285).

Rumours of a second impending attack, nevertheless persisted. In anticipation of such a move by the tribals, Durand ordered the village near the ruins of Chilas fort to be demolished; for had the village been allowed to stand undisturbed, it would have been used by the attackers as cover:

> I had heard that the ruined fort of Chilas was close to our entrenchment, and also of the village, but I had understood that, as is generally the case in the Hindu Kush, village and fort were one, and I had sent orders to raze the fort. This had been done, but the village allowed to stand, with dire results. A second attack was threatened, and as for various reasons the entrenchment could not be moved, the village should not a second time give cover to the enemy. (ibid.: 286)

Further, Durand arrived personally with reinforcements in Chilas including two hundred men and two mountain guns on 23 March which apparently deterred the attack by the tribesmen, who were gathering below, from taking place (ibid.: 287). There were no further attacks on the British outpost and eventually on 17 August 1893, the Secretary of State for India authorized the British occupation of Chilas, construction of the Kaghan-Chilas road and the construction of a fort there (Chohan 1997: 127).

There was some debate about the morality of British actions in Chilas which had had the effect of entangling the British with the tribes in the Indus Valley. However, it is clear that the Chilasi had become a nuisance in the region, looting and pillaging the neighbouring regions and tribes. The British actions in the region under Durand can therefore, be justified on moral grounds (Chohan 1997: 129-30).

Following these events, Durand left for British India in May 1893, leaving the responsibilities in the hands of Dr Robertson. He spent some weeks at Simla, intending to return to Gilgit in the autumn after a leave of three months. However, Col. Durand would not return to Gilgit:

> In the month of May I left Gilgit for India, as it turned out for good, Robertson, who reached Gilgit a few days after I left, taking over the work of the Agency. My last official act was of a pleasing and peaceful character, and consisted in unlocking with a silver key the gates of the completed Indus Bridge, which was declared open and named after His Highness the Maharaja of Kashmir. (Durand 1900: 290)

Col. Durand's tenure as the British agent at Gilgit was successful, both politically and strategically. Moreover, he was able to achieve this at a relatively low cost both financially and in terms of human lives. His work on the frontier, had transformed the forces of the Kashmir state and changed the security situation on the frontier.

> The changes five years had wrought were great; the Kashmir troops on the frontier, instead of an ill-paid, undisciplined and ill-armed rabble, were an efficient body of troops regularly paid and well fed, who had given their proofs in severe fighting; good roads existed in the place of tracks torturing alike to baggage animals and laden men using them, and the rivers were bridged; extensive irrigation schemes, which were to prove of inestimable value to the people, were in hand; the authority of the Kashmir Government was firmly established on its frontier, and the influence of the British Government was paramount in the tract of country immediately south of the Hindu Kush. (ibid.: 291)

THE CHITRAL CRISIS

While the events had been unfolding in Chilas in late 1892, ground was being prepared for the most significant crisis that would be faced by the Gilgit Agency. Chitral, while not geographically a part of Gilgit or Baltistan, was a critical part of the north-west frontier, a tributary of the Kashmir Darbar and thereby under the responsibility of the Gilgit Agency. The subsequent Chitral crisis of 1895 was a formative event for the region as well as the British policy towards the frontier.

Aman-ul-Mulk who had come to the assistance of the Kashmir Darbar against Pahalwan Bahadur's 1880 uprising in Hunza, passed away on 30 August 1892. Among his several children, the two chief claimants as successors were Afzul-ul-Mulk and Nizam-ul-Mulk.[46] Nizam-ul-Mulk was not present in Chitral, when his father died, being away as Governor in Yasin. Consequently, Afzul-ul-Mulk became the Mehtar or ruler of Chitral. After a few months, Afzul-ul-Mulk was assassinated by his uncle Sher Afzul who had been living in exile in Afghanistan and had attacked the Chitral fort at night.[47]

Upon hearing of this development, Col. Durand gave permission to Nizam-ul-Mulk to try and take control of the seat of power at Chitral. Nizam-ul-Mulk would proceed to Chitral whereupon he would be joined by a large number of supporters in Chitral as well as a force of 1,200 men sent by Sher Afzul to prevent his advance. When Nizam-ul-Mulk had advanced to Mastuj in northern Chitral, Sher Afzul would again escape to Kabul and the former would assume the title of the Mehtar of Chitral. Nizam-ul-Mulk would then request the British government for a political officer for Chitral, while accusing the Amir of Afghanistan of being complicit in the seizure of power by Sher Afzal:

> I have heard that Sher Afzal had full permission and much secret support from the Amir in his attack on Chitral. All these prisoners say that Sher Afzal asked the Amir for help in troops. The Amir refused to give him troops, but ordered all Chitrali slaves in Badakhshan to be given to him, and through the General at Badakhshan supplied money, gold, etc to them. . . . It is a matter of great pity, that at the insistence of Government, so much caution and carefulness have been observed on our side, while the Amir did such immense mischief. My brother has been killed—our whole house ruined. . . . As to meeting you I wrote before. If you cannot come, kindly depute another officer quickly here, because this is absolutely necessary for the settlement of all affairs. I am very much awaiting this.[48]

As has been explained earlier, Chitral had traditionally had a tributary relationship with Afghanistan, and any attempts by the latter to intervene through a favourable agent such as Sher Afzul would not be surprising. However, it seems that the Amir of Afghanistan at the time was not even aware that Sher Afzul had departed for Chitral:

> Although in moving towards Chitral you committed irregularity in having gone towards that place secretly and on your own responsibility without informing our high Government, yet as you intended to proceed to your own and hereditary country and went there it does not much matter. But we are not going to order the troops of the God-granted kingdom of Afghanistan to move a single march to support you in your acts or in your household dissensions which you have amongst yourselves, so you may see to your own affairs and go through what you have undertaken. Our high Government has nothing to do with your affairs.[49]

The British mission as requested by Nizam-ul-Mulk would be led by Sir George Robertson, and include Lt. C.G. Bruce, Lt. J.H. Gordon and Capt. Francis Younghusband accompanied by fifty soldiers of the Sikh Regiment:

> He, like his brother, asked that a political officer might reside in Chitral territory; and Capt. Younghusband, with an escort of Sikhs, was accordingly sent to Mastuj, which is a fort in Upper Chitral sixty-six miles to the north of Chitral itself. (Thomson 1895: 4)

This mission would arrive safely in Chitral on 25 January 1893, thereby strengthening the position of Nizam-ul-Mulk.[50] By September 1893, Capt. Younghusband and Lt. Gordon had withdrawn to Mastuj, 63 miles to the north-east of Chitral. However, Amir-ul-Mulk, one of the surviving sons of Aman-ul-Mulk of about twenty years of age, who had escaped from Chitral following the death of his father, would return to Chitral in 1894. He had fled the country to escape death which was the fate of many of his brothers upon the death of his father and had taken refuge in the small Pashtun principality of Jandul, ruled by Umra Khan. Upon his sudden return, claiming to have escaped the clutches of Umra Khan, Amir-ul-Mulk was welcomed back by Nizam-ul-Mulk. On 1 January 1895, Nizam-ul-Mulk was assassinated by Amir-ul-Mulk during a hunting expedition:

Nizam-ul-Mulk had been murdered on the 1 January by his half-brother, Amir-ul-Mulk, generally believed to be a semi-idiot. . . . About mid-day, when on the point of descending, his turban came unfastened. While an attendant on foot, who had a loaded Snider carbine hidden under his long robe. This wretch, at a sign from his master, who perceived the helplessness of Nizam, pulled out the rifle and shot him in the back. Attendants ran to cut down the assassin, when the real culprit rode calmly forward, and shouted out that the Nizam had been killed by his orders. Whereupon guns were let off in the air for a salute, and he was acknowledged Mehtar as soon as the life ebbed out of the miserable Nizam, who expired with a solitary trembling servant to tend him.[51]

At the time of this incident, Lt. B.E.M. Gurdon was in Chitral. He had succeeded Capt. Younghusband a few weeks earlier as the political officer in Chitral. Amir-ul-Mulk sent a deputation to Gurdon, asking for formal recognition as the Mehtar of Chitral. Gurdon's position was very tenuous; he was in potentially hostile territory, so could not afford to antagonize Amir-ul-Mulk and did not have the authority to grant formal recognition to the latter. He referred the request to the GOI while simultaneously asking for British reinforcements from Mastuj. Once this news reached the Gilgit Agency on 6 January, an additional hundred men were dispatched to Mastuj and two hundred to Ghizer in Chitral, with Robertson himself arriving in Chitral by 1 February with a military escort.

Meanwhile Umra Khan, the ruler of state of Jandul where Amir-ul-Mulk had been in exile, was apparently the mind behind the actions of Amir-ul-Mulk. Nurturing his own aspirations to take over the far larger and important state of Chitral, he was now preparing to intervene in the situation. His intervention, was overtly to support Amir-ul-Mulk, but this was ostensibly done to add Chitral to his own dominions (Chohan 1997: 136).

Despite the Lowarai Pass which divided his dominion from Chitral, being closed with snow at this time of the year, Umra Khan crossed into Chitral at the head of three thousand men. After some initial opposition by the Pathans, who had traditionally been seen as enemies by the Chitralis, the resistance came to an end. This was chiefly a result of their ruler being allied with Umra

Khan and the uncertainty of British support without the direct instructions of the GOI (Younghusband & Younghusband 1910: 20). Umra Khan proceeded to capture and reinforce Kila Drosh on the southern frontier of Chitral.

It was at this most inopportune moment for the British, that Sher Afzul who had been in exile in Afghanistan with a promise by the Amir, to never be allowed to return to Chitral, was apparently allowed to do so (ibid.: 21). It soon became apparent that Sher Afzul and Umra Khan were in league in this action against the British in the frontier with the tacit support of the Amir (ibid.: 22). On 27 February 1895, Sher Afzul contacted Robertson, confidentially asking him to fall back to Mastuj, failing which he threatened military action.

Robertson replied by rejecting these demands and explaining that Chitral was a tributary of the Kashmir Darbar and that no one had the authority to impose a Mehtar on Chitral without the permission of the GOI.[52] Amir-ul-Mulk was taken into custody by the British in the Chitral Fort, and his nine year younger brother Shuja-ul-Mulk was recognized as provisional Mehtar by Robertson pending approval from the GOI. Umra Khan was informed of the imminent use of force to compel him to withdraw from Chitral, if he did not do so of his own accord. Umra Khan, as expected continued to hold on in Chitral, and consequently, the first division of the field army under Maj. Gen. Sir Robert Low was readied for war. While these preparations were going on, Gilgit was experiencing some more developments of a more far-reaching nature.

Gilgit and Chitral were divided from each other by the Shandur Pass. The fortified positions of Gupis and Ghizar were the only two such locations between Gilgit and Mastuj in Chitral. Gupis was located at the begining of the Yasin Valley while Ghizar was located on the Gilgit side of the Shandur Pass. On 16 January 1895 instructions were given to Lt. Fowler to proceed from Gilgit to Gupis where a strong fort had been built as recently in 1894 and after a fortnight, was instructed to proceed to Chitral with Lt. Edwardes of the 2nd Bombay Grenadiers (Thomson 1895: 88).

This party of English soldiers arrived in Mastuj in Chitral after eight days. On 5 March, a party of English soldiers led by Edwardes and Fowler departed Mastuj and arrived in a small village called Reshun in northern Chitral, where they had information that a group of hostile fighters was gathering (Thomson 1895: 89). While on a patrol near the village in a narrow defile, this group came under heavy fire resulting in the death of some sepoys while wounding several others mortally. The soldiers had to withdraw and occupy a defensible position in a nearby village (ibid.: 91). For the next few days, there were a series of assaults, which were repelled from the village, however, the enemy continued to get ever closer:

> After the assault on the 10th the enemy contented themselves with investing the village, and getting gradually closer up to it. This they had no difficulty in doing, for there was plenty of cover-stone walls, and detached houses and trees of which they could avail themselves. (ibid.: 94)

A truce was declared on 13 March by the Chitralis under the leadership of Mahomed Isa Khan who was a foster brother of Sher Afzul. The truce held and on 15 March Isa Khan asked the English officers if they might wish to play a game of polo to which the Englishmen could not refuse. During the course of the game, the English officers were seized, the village was assaulted and captured with most of the defenders being put to death with a few being captured (Younghusband & Younghusband 1910: 57).

These prisoners including the English officers and their Indian sepoys, were taken to Umra Khan at Drosh in Chitral who treated them well. Later they would be transferred to Barwa, the capital of Jandul, where they would be treated well and eventually set free; the English officers being escorted to the camp of Sir Robert Low, who was on his way to relieve Chitral while the Indian soldiers were set free to make their way back home, on their own (Thomson 1895: 102).

Before the ambush at Reshun, Edwardes and Fowler, in anticipation of trouble had sent word to Capt. Ross in Mastuj who had ninety-three men under his command. Capt. Ross left thirty-three men at Buni in Upper Chitral and continued with the remaining sixty men towards Reshun. This group under Ross was also ambushed in a narrow defile near a village named Karagh, midway between Reshun and Buni. During the course of this ambush, the group suffered heavy casualties and its avenues of retreat were cut off. The soldiers under Capt. Ross hid in a cave, waiting for darkness to take their chances at attacking the Sangers (a rudimentary fortification made out of stone work) where the enemy was entrenched.[53]

The attack made at 2 a.m., early morning was successful in clearing out the defenders, but at a heavy cost. Only seventeen of the original sixty soldiers had succeeded in reaching safety along with Lt. Jones who was wounded. Capt. Ross was killed in this daring breakout with a bullet wound on the head (Beynon 1896: 86). Several wounded soldiers could not be extricated and had to be left behind along with about forty rifles which fell into enemy hands. About thirty of such soldiers hid themselves in a cave for a week until they had long run out of food and water, following which they came out on the promise that their lives would be spared (Thomson 1895: 111). However, this promise was broken when most of the prisoners were killed upon laying down their arms.

> They were able to get water, they had no food, and gradually got weaker and weaker. But in spite of hunger and wounds they held out for more than a week, and then only surrendered under a promise that their lives should be spared. This promise, like most Oriental promises given under similar conditions, was not kept. (ibid.)

The remnant of the British force under Jones would withdraw to Buni, where they prepared themselves in anticipation of a Chitrali attack, which never came. A week later on 17 March, Lt. Moberley arrived in Buni from Mastuj with reinforcements, allowing Jones and his surviving men to withdraw to Mastuj with Moberley. Only fourteen men out of the original sixty had survived, and of these ten were wounded (ibid.: 113).

> Lieutenant Moberley arrived on the 17th, exactly a week after, with a hundred and fifty of the Kashmir Rifles, and fifty of the Puniali levies, and they marched back with him to Mastuj, where Capt. Bretherton had been left with only sixty Kashmir Rifles. It was fortunate that the enemy did not attack the fort while Moberley was away. Had they done so, Bretherton would

have had great difficulty in defending it with such a handful of men. (Thomson 1895: 112)

The combined forces of Sher Afzul and Umra Khan would return to Mastuj with an estimated strength of fifteen hundred, surrounding the position and investing it. The consequence of these actions by Sher Afzul, and Umra Khan was that the British government now came to the conclusion that this was essentially an act of war by the former. Moreover, the fates of Capt. Ross, Lt. Edwardes and Lt. Fowler hardened British opinion towards the situation, thereby pressing them to take decisive action to relieve the garrison at Chitral and to further give no quarter to Umra Khan.[54]

There were two primary routes available to the British to send a relief force to Chitral; the first being the Shandur Pass from Gilgit to Chitral and the other being the Malakand Pass connecting Peshawar to Chitral from the south. The route from Gilgit to Chitral was 220 miles and the passes were closed at this time of the year making any relief attempt from this direction unfeasible; on the other hand, the route from Peshawar to Chitral was less than 200 miles and the pass could be traversed by an army. Consequently, the latter was decided as the route of choice for the relief force under Sir Robert Low* (Younghusband & Younghusband 1910: 28).

When Edwardes and Fowler were coming into contact with the enemy around Reshun, Dr Robertson was getting gradually surrounded by the enemy in Chitral. The news arrived at Chitral fort on 3 March, that Sher Afzul was arriving with a large force. Dr Robertson, in anticipation of the impending battle decided to carry out a reconnaissance of the surrounding area:

Two hundred Kashmir Infantry under Capt. Campbell, Townshend, and Baird, and accompanied by the British Agent, Surgeon-Major Robertson, Lieutenant Gurdon, and Surgeon-Capt. Whitchurch, therefore set out from the fort to reconnoitre the Chitrali dispositions. There is no regular town of Chitral, but round the fort, which is merely the residence of the Mehtars, there are scattered over the valley a number of little hamlets, and detached houses, dotted among the cultivated lands which stretch for a distance of about three miles down the valley.[55]

* Gen. Sir Robert Cunliffe Low was an officer of the British Indian Army and the commander-in-chief of the 1895 Chitral expedition.

During the course of this sortie, the force would come under attack by the enemy and Sher Afzul who was supposed to be in the area could not be found. Without going into the extensive details of the operation as given by Capt. and Col. Younghusband in their first-hand account, *The Relief of Chitral*, a brief summary of what happened is as follows. The forces were divided between two sections, one led by Capt. Baird and Lt. Gordon, and the other led by Capt. Colin Campbell and Capt. Charles Townshend. The second group found itself in a disadvantageous position, facing fire from the enemy who occupied the heights, while the first group, led by Capt. Baird was unable to come to their assistance. Umra Khan's troops had been trained and drilled by the pensioners of the Indian army and were equipped with the Snider and Martini-Henry rifles.[56]

As darkness drew near, Townshend found himself in a desperate situation, at which time Campbell arrived to issue instructions to storm the hamlet where the enemy seemed to be entrenched. A bayonet charge was ordered over open ground which failed leading to heavy casualties including Gen. Baj Singh and Maj. Bhikam Singh of the Kashmir forces. It was concluded that a retreat had to be carried out which was done successfully while under heavy enemy attack. During this battle, in addition to the Kashmir state officers, Capt. Baird was killed while Capt. Campbell was wounded and twenty soldiers killed and twenty-eight wounded out of a total of one hundred and fifty. The enemy strength was estimated at a thousand to twelve hundred men including five hundred Jandulis under Umra Khan (Thomson 1895: 43).

The significance of this event lay in the fact that it made the British position in Chitral impossible and almost the entire Chitrali population joined Sher Afzul against the British. Apparently the Chitralis believed that the Amir of Afghanistan had joined the war against the British.

> Our position, though very difficult, was not hopeless till after the disaster of 3 March, but after that unfortunate event, all the Chitralis outside the fort were compelled to join Sher Afzul for fear of their families. They also believed he was supported by the Amir, and that Umra Khan, and the Sipah Salar, and the Mahommedans, had joined in a religious war against us, and that our position was desperate, while they knew that if in time we triumphed, they had still nothing to fear from our vengeance. (ibid.: 44)

On the next day, 4 March, the enemy force began to surround the fort which had insufficient cover for its defenders regarding firearms. The construction of the fort and its location at the bottom of a valley made it extremely vulnerable to enfilading fire from the surrounding mountain edges. Meanwhile Sher Afzul had established himself in the house of the Political Officer. Over the next several days, attacks were made at the water supply of the garrison which was repulsed as well attacks on the fort resulting in heavy losses to the attackers (Thomson 61).

On 15 March, a letter was received from Sher Afzul, mentioning the defeat of the detachment at Reshun, with a letter from Lt. Edwards and Lt. Fowler about their truce. Probably as a result of this information, a truce was made at Chitral for three days which was later to be extended till 23 March. Meanwhile, on 20 March, Edwards and Fowler were brought to Sher Afzul's camp following their capture through treachery earlier at Reshun. Robertson's representative, Munshi Amir Ali was allowed to meet them following which Robertson protested formally against Sher Afzul for the violation of the truce during which the two Englishmen had been captured (ibid.: 62).

The truce came to an end on 23 March after the British rejected Umra Khan's offer of a withdrawal to Peshawar through Jandul. However, upon hearing disturbing news of a large British force moving north from Peshawar towards Chitral, through Swat, Umra Khan quickly went south, over the Lowarai Pass to Dir taking all British prisoners including Edwardes and Fowler with him:

> Edwardes and Fowler in the meantime had been taken down to Drosh, and Umra Khan sent a reply from there, in which he said that he had told the sahibs that if they wished it he would send them back to the fort, but that they had declined to go. It seems that he did really make them this offer, but they asked if their sepoys would be allowed to go with them, and when this was refused, they declined to go back by themselves. (ibid.: 63)

While instructions had been sent to Sir Robert Low to advance from Peshawar, a similar order had also been sent to Col. James Graves Kelly to advance from Gilgit to Chitral over the more difficult Shandur Pass on 21 March. Subsequently, on 23 March

Kelly left with an advance party of two hundred men. This was followed by two hundred more British troops and a hundred more levies from Hunza-Nagar and Punial. Enroute, to the Shandur Pass, the rear guard had, been joined by additional Kashmiri State troops at Gupis (Younghusband & Younghusband 1910: 184).

It would be another week before this group could mover further after reaching Ghizar where it had been snowing for the past five days. Eventually on 1 April 1895 the relief force departed for the Shandur Pass and by 4 April, after a great deal of difficulty in the face of heavy snow and bad weather, the relief force had successfully crossed the pass and had begun to proceed onwards to Laspur on the other side. Col. Kelly and Lt. Beynon joined them on 6 April (Thomson 1895: 127-8). After recuperating and regrouping, this force proceeded on 8 April towards Gasht, 12 miles further in the Laspur Valley, where it arrived unopposed the same day (Younghusband & Younghusband 1910: 196).

Meanwhile, the main body of British troops known as the Chitral Relief Force was advancing ahead from Peshawar under Maj. Gen. Sir Robert Low. This force was a division of 14,000 men and had three main access routes through different passes leading into the Swat Valley. These were moving from the west to east, the Malakand, Shahkot and Mora Passes. All of these passes were now strongly defended by the local tribesmen (ibid.: 84). The British plan was to deceive the tribesmen about the main British thrust and therefore, a brigade encamped near the Shahkot Pass and cavalry moved up to the Mora Pass while the main British force would move towards the Malakand Pass (ibid.: 84).

The main British thrust by the Chitral Relief Force commenced on 3 April and after heavy but decisive fighting, had broken through the Malakand Pass and by 4 April, the division had entered the Swat Valley. The next day, on 5 April, under the leadership of Brig. Gen. Bindon Blood, the British forced their way across the Swat River. On the same day, Umra Khan's brother, Mohammed Shah Khan attacked the British force under Bindon Blood while they were crossing the river, leading to heavy losses for the tribesmen although Mohammed Shah Khan himself escaped (Thomson 1895: 185). Following this debacle, the tribesmen would withdraw to the north, with the next British military objective being Umra Khan's stronghold at Munda in Jandul Valley (Younghusband & Younghusband 1910: 116).

At this time Dr Robertson was still surrounded by Sher Afzul's forces in Mastuj where he was engaged in negotiations. Sher Afzul had threatened to end negotiations and storm the fort. Between 5 and 7 April, there were a series of strong attacks on the garrison in Mastuj which were driven off. On 8 April, the relief expedition under Col. Kelly began to move towards Gasht which is about 13 km from Mastuj where the garrison was besieged. When the relief force arrived at the garrison, it had been under siege for over eighteen days (ibid.: 196). The enemy was then pushed further away from the garrison, but took up a strong position at a place called Nisa Gol, further to the west (ibid.: 206). Over the next several days till 17 April, Umra Khan and his men continued to retreat in the face of advance by Col. Kelly's forces. However their threat to the garrison and Col. Kelly continued.

The Chitralis were getting pushed increasingly, between the Kelly expedition and the large group of British forces led by Gen. Low pushing northwards from the south. On 17 April, Bindon at the head of the British cavalry, had arrived at Umra Khan's stronghold at Munda in Jandul. Here, a message was sent to Umra Khan who was in his stronghold that, he should surrender. However, in his response, Umra Khan indicated his desire to surrender and negotiate but emphasized his constraints in doing so because of his followers who stood to kill him if he did. The following is a translation of the response sent by Umra Khan to Bindon Blood's request for a meeting:

> After greetings, I should greatly like to meet your excellency, and to have a quiet talk with you, whereby the whole affair might be easily settled. But unfortunately, I am surrounded by about 3,000 Ghazis, and these bad men will not hear of my going out to see. You too I notice are accompanied by warriors. Assuredly no quiet conversation can take place under these circumstances. Now I propose that you send away your army and I will send away mine, and then you and I can have our conference alone in the field (Younghusband & Younghusband 1910: 117).

Further, tribesmen continued to collect in the region surrounding Bindon's force which raised further doubts on the intentions of

Umra Khan. Fighting resumed soon as the hostile intentions of the tribesmen became clear and in the face of superior British firepower, the tribesmen were again forced to withdraw. By the next morning, the Munda Fort had been abandoned and Gen. Low's force was free to move on to Chitral itself. The same day on 17 April, Umra Khan fled across the border into Afghanistan (Younghusband & Younghusband 1910: 119). The following is an account of the flight of Umra Khan from Jandul, by H.C. Thompson in his account of the Chitral Campaign:

> On the morning of the 18th Brigadier-General Waterfield with the 2nd Brigade joined me, and the 2nd and 3rd Brigades advanced against Miankila and Mundar. The latter, a fort on the left bank of the Jandol river, was the home of Umra Khan, and it was expected that he would make a final stand at one of these places. Both were, however, deserted, and it was reported that Umra Khan had fled towards Asmar, and had asked for an asylum from the Amir of Kabul. I may add that he has been a fugitive ever since. (Thomson 1895: 235)

The next day, on 18 April, the besieged garrison at Chitral was fully relieved, and by the next day there were no signs of any hostile forces anywhere with Sher Afzul too having fled across the border. Starting from 18 April, the British forces began to withdraw to their base camps with Gen. Low, who had arrived at Chitral on 16 April, departing for Dir on 18 April (ibid.: 238, 240). Sher Afzul, however was captured along with a number of other Chitrali noblemen who were then be taken to Dharamsala in India under custody (Younghusband & Younghusband 1910: 126).

The Chitral Campaign as this came to be known in history, was a watershed event for the region as well as for the Gilgit Agency. It of course highlighted the British superiority in arms and military discipline especially underlined by the stout resistance displayed by the garrison, besieged for forty-six days until rescued by the relief columns (ibid.: 125). Nevertheless, this uprising did raise a question about the appropriateness of British policy with respect to the frontier. Consequently, it raised the issue about the suitability of continued direct British military presence in this part of the frontier. Some contemporary views, such as the one expressed in

Sahachar, a Bengali publication from the time period, pointed out to the British attitudes and responses to the Chitral disturbances as the primary driving factors of this crisis. According to a native journal published in Bengal at the time of the 1895 events, the decision of Dr Robertson, the British agent at Gilgit to send Lt. Gurdon to Chitral was in itself an act of aggression. Moreover, the fact that Amir-ul-Mulk let the British officers who were present in Chitral when Nizam-ul-Mulk was murdered, go unmolested, is indicative of the fact that his intentions towards the British were benign (Chohan 1997: 171).

However, the notion that a British withdrawal in the face of Amir-ul-Mulk's action would have ended further transgression is simplistic at best. Further, the princely state of Chitral was a tributary of the state of J&K which in turn was a subsidiary of the British government in India. A British withdrawal from Chitral at that stage would have had several effects.

First, it would have amounted to a British renunciation of its military obligations towards Kashmir. Second, it would have consequently, undermined British prestige and its military commitments to princely states which would have severe security implications for the British in the frontier regions. The third other effect of such a British withdrawal would be the collapse of the British security structure in the frontier region by further uncentivizing such actions and creating a power vacuum which the Russians would be induced to fill in. Finally, there was the issue of this incident causing direct instability in the adjoining states and the complete collapse of its frontier policy which had built up so painstakingly over the past several years under the Gilgit Agency of which Chitral was a part. It is therefore quite understandable, why the British would be reluctant to withdraw from Chitral when these events unravelled and why Dr Robertson made such decisions.

Once the dust had settled on this major crisis, the British government began to deliberate whether to stay on in Chitral or to withdraw. On 8 May 1895, the British government decided to retain a garrison in Chitral:

On 8 May 1895, the Government of India decided to retain a garrison in Chitral, and, to ensure its safety, proposed the construction of a road from Peshawar through Swat. At the same time the Government of India pointed out that the annals of Chitral were nothing but anarchy, and that Afghan aggression had forced Aman-ul-Mulk to seek the protection of Kashmir.[57]

This did not receive the consent of the Liberal British government at home under Lord Rosebury which rejected the notion of any militarization of Chitral; however, this hesitation was overcome when the conservatives won the 1895 elections under Lord Salisbury.

This decision did not meet with the approval of Lord Rosebury's cabinet and the Liberal government at home. Consequently, on 13 June 1895, instructions were telegraphed to India to the effect that no military force or European agent was to be retained in Chitral; that Chitral was not to be fortified; and that the projected road was not to be constructed. Once more, however, an important imperial problem was to become the sport of English party politics, for this decision was reversed by Lord Salisbury's government in August of the same year. (Davies 1932: 86)

The initial opposition to have a military presence in Chitral was influenced by some of the greatest British military authorities of the time such as Sir Donald Stewart, Sir Neville Chamberlain, Sir John Adye, Sir Charles Gough and Lord Chelmsford. All of these distinguished officers had served in India (and in Chitral) and gave important military justifications, why it was unsuitable to continue a military presence there:

I sum up their opinions, so far as the result which they produced upon my mind and upon the minds of my colleagues, to this effect, that the gigantic natural geographical defences of the northwest frontier render the advance of an invading army practically impossible, and that, having regard to these and other considerations, our position is at the present moment practically impregnable; that Chitral is not a place of considerable importance as a base for military reserves, and that it is not useful as a base for military operations, defensive or offensive; that to lock up troops in Chitral or in the Chitral Valley would be an act of the gravest blundering; and that the construction of a military route to Chitral would, in the event of hostilities, be an advantage to an invading force and a disadvantage to a defending force. (Thomson 1895: 305)

There were other arguments in favour besides the ones mentioned above by Thomson, including that given by Sir Henry Fowler in the House of Commons on fiscal and military grounds:

> Sir Henry Fowler, speaking in the House of Commons, condemned it on military and financial grounds. Running for about 180 miles through hostile Pathan country over the Malakand (4,000 feet) and the Lowarai (11,000 feet), both its construction and protection would entail enormous expenditure, and involve grave military responsibilities. (Davies 1932: 87)

It was further pointed out that the Amir of Afghanistan had by consenting to the 1893 Durand Agreement, was bound to not interfere in Swat, Bajaur or Chitral and therefore, there was no imminent danger from Afghanistan (ibid.). It was however clear that the events of 1895 in Chitral could not have happened without the active involvement of the Amir; as such any promises given by him under the 1893 Agreement could not be relied upon to provide security.

Thus, there were the opposing arguments demanding the militarization of Chitral by the advocates of what would be called the 'forward policy'. This included eminent Englishmen such as Lord Roberts (ibid.) and George Curzon who contended that a British withdrawal would imply a Russian involvement in the region:[58]

> If we left, the Russians, who were now established on the Pamirs, would walk in; and having left it ourselves, we would have poor ground for protesting. And with the Russians in Chitral we would have all the frontier tribes round playing then off against us. There was a fierce controversy going on at home about this, and Mr. George Curzon was in the thick of the fray contending lustily with generals and retired lieutenant-governors. (Younghusband 1927: 76)

Finally, it was the concern that the British would lose face in the region as Russia had successfully extended its frontier to the Hindukush while the British had withdrawn theirs from Chitral.[59] Eventually the balance began to tilt to the latter argument. While it was clear that a large army could not cross the Hindukush, it was certainly possible for smaller bands of soldiers to cross over and cause disturbance. In fact, that is precisely what had happened 1895. Moreover, the town of Chitral itself was located at the junction of several of the passes which connected to the Hindukush which gave it a strategic significance as has been explained by E.F. Knight:

> But the valley of Chitral should be as completely under our control as is that of Gilgit, for it commands some of the lowest and easiest passes across the Hindoo Koosh, and affords a ready road to India from Bokhara vid Badakshan. It is known that the Russian military authorities consider this a favourable route for the invasion of India; it avoids the great natural difficulties presented by the lofty and inhospitable Pamirs, and, moreover, there is an easy and much-used caravan road running direct from Chitral to Peshawar via Bajur. The town of Chitral itself is situated at the junction of several valleys leading to the very passes which an invader would have to attempt, commanding them all. We should certainly maintain an Agency here, as at Gilgit. This has long been meditated, and the late Mehtar himself repeatedly expressed a wish that a resident British officer should be appointed to his State. (Knight 1905: 291-2)

However, these arguments in favour of a British military presence in Chitral could not change the minds of the Liberal government. It was only as a result of its replacement by a Conservative government the same year that George Curzon* would become Under Secretary of State for Foreign Affairs and convince Lord Salisbury the necessity of retaining Chitral (Younghusband 1927: 77). In hind-sight, it would later come to light that the Russians had order to enter Chitral if the British had decided to leave Chitral (ibid.).

Finally, Chitral would be retained by the GOI which established its control over the foreign relations while internal affairs would be left to Shuja-ul-Mulk, the Mehtar of Chitral (Davies 1932: 88). A British political officer was appointed for Chitral who was subordinated to the Gilgit Agency and in doing so harked back to the old British Madhopur policy. The Mehtar of Chitral's position was officially a vassal to Kashmir. Mastuj in Upper Chitral and Yasin was under a separate governor reporting to the Gilgit Agency (Alder 1963: 298). However, next year in 1896, a separate political

*Lord George Curzon was the Viceroy of India from 1899 to 1905 during the Conservative Party government under Prime Minister Robert Salisbury.

agency was established at Malakand which included Dir, Swat and Chitral., thereby separating Chitral from the Gilgit Agency (Alder 1963: 298).

The events in the Gilgit Agency would take a decidedly different route after Chitral was setparated away from the agency because it lost a certain degree of its political importance.

NOTES

1. Alder, G.J., *British India's Northern Frontier 1865-95: A Study in Imperial Policy*, Longmans Green and Co. Ltd., London, 1963, p. 2.
2. A.S. Chohan, *The Gilgit Agency*, Atlantic Publishers and Distributors, New Delhi, 1997, p. 27.
3. A.R. Colquhoun, *Russia against India: The Struggle for Asia*, Harper and Brothers, New York and London, 1900, p. 12.
4. Fred Burnaby, *A Ride to Khiva*, Cassel and Company, London, 1895, p. 250.
5. Government of India, Foreign, Secret-F, July 1874, Nos. 129-30, National Archives of India.
6. Ibid.
7. Ibid., p. 42.
8. Special Report on Kashghar, the Pamirs, and Wakhan by Lt. Col T.E. Gordon, Confidential Report Yarkand Mission by Sri Douglas Forsythe, Government of India, Foreign, Secret, August 1875, Nos. 68-81, National Archives of India, p. 22.
9. Confidential Report Yarkand Mission by Sri Doughlas Forsythe, Government of India, Foreign, Secret, August 1875, Nos. 68-81, National Archives of India, p. 18.
10. Ibid.
11. Ibid.
12. Ibid., p. 40.
13. Ibid., p. 23.
14. Ibid., p. 40.
15. Ibid.
16. S.N. Gadru, (ed.), *Kashmir Papers*, British Intervention in Kashmir, Freethought Literature Company, Srinagar, 1973, p. xxi.
17. Foreign Department Proceedings, Secret, July 1877, No. 39, National Archives of India.

18. Ibid.
19. Biddulph to Henvey, 25 July 1879, No. 149, Government of India, Foreign, Secr., October 1879, Nos. 402-5, National Archives of India.
20. Government of India to Secretary of State for India, No. 4, Frontier, 6 January 1892, Government of India, Foreign, Frontier-A, January 1892. Nos. 15-130. See also Biddulph to Henvey, 25 July 1879, No. 149, Government of India, Foreign, Secret, October 1879, Nos. 402-5, National Archives of India.
21. Biddulph to Henvey, No. 149, 25 July 1879, Government of India, Foreign, Secret, October 1879, Nos. 402-5, National Archives of India. See also A.S. Chohan, *The Gilgit Agency*, Atlantic Publishers and Distributors, New Delhi, 1997, p. 54.
22. A.C. Lyall to F. Henvey, No. 2085 E.P., 8 August 1879, Government of India, Foreign, Secret, October 1879, Nos. 267-310, National Archives of India. See also Secretary of State for India to Government of India, No. 35, Secret, 3 September 1880, Government of India, Foreign, Secret, December 1880, No. 361, National Archives of India.
23. Gilgit Diary No. 107 of 27April 1880, Government of India, Foreign, Secret, December 1880, Nos. 117-66.
24. Aman-ul-Mulk to Maharaja, Government of India, Foreign, Secret, July 1877, Nos. 34-60B, National Archives of India.
25. Ibid., pp. 122-3.
26. F. Henvey to A.C. Lyall, 11 January 1879, Government of India, Foreign, Secret, October 1879, Nos. 267-310, National Archives of India.
27. Leitner, G.W., *Dardistan in 1866, 1886 and 1893*, Asian Educational Services, New Delhi, 1996, Appendix, p. 13.
28. Schomberg, R.C.F., *Between the Oxus and the Indus*, Martin Hopkinson Ltd, London, 1935, pp. 12-13.
29. Government of India to Secretary of State for India, 103, 15 July 1881, Government of India, Foreign, Secret-E, August 1884, Nos. 4-19, National Archives of India.
30. Foreign Department Proceedings, Secret, July 1881, Nos. 314-97, National Archives of India.
31. Edward Allworth, (ed.), *Central Asia: A Century of Russian Rule*, Columbia University Press, New York, 1967, p. 149.
32. Secretary to the Government of India to Col. Lockhart, No. 1043-F, 6 June 1885, Government of India, Foreign, Secret-F, August 1885, Nos. 12-81, National Archives of India.

33. Peshawar Confidential Diary No. 17 of 14 September 1887, Government of India, Foreign, Secret-F, January 1888, Nos. 246-69, National Archives of India.
34. F.E. Younghusband to R. Parry Nisbet, 24 October 1889, Government of India, Foreign, Secret-F, February 1890, Nos. 59-84, National Archives of India.
35. Confidential memo by T.C. Plowden on the new policy for the protection of the north-western frontier of Kashmir, Government of India, Foreign, Sec-F, July 1888, Nos. 63-86, National Archives of India.
36. Government of India, Foreign, Secret-F, September 1889, Nos. 231-52, National Archives of India.
37. A. Durand, *The Making of a Frontier*, John Murray, London, 1900, p. 121.
38. Aman-ul-Mulk to the Viceroy, No. 20, 1889, Government of India, Foreign, Secret-F, February 1890, Nos. 85-113, National Archives of India. See also British Agent to Resident Kashmir, 29 December 1889, Government of India, Foreign, Secret-F, May 1890, Nos. 37-43, National Archives of India.
39. Ibid., pp. 226-32.
40. Ibid.
41. E.F. Knight, *Where Three Empires Meet*, Longmans Green and Co., London, 1905, p. 369.
42. H. Lewis Nevill, *Campaign on the North-West Frontier*, John Murray, London, 1912, p. 144.
43. Government of India, Foreign, Secret-F, March 1892, Nos. 185-94, National Archives of India.
44. Col. Prideaux to Secretary, Government of India, Foreign, No. 59-515, 15 February 1892 (Confidential), Government of India, Foreign, Secret-F, March 1892, Nos. 185-94, National Archives of India.
45. Government of India to Secretary of State for India, No. 142 (Secret-Frontier), 11 July 1893, Government of India, Foreign, Secret-F, August 1893, Nos. 6-34, National Archives of India.
46. George S. Robertson, *Chitral the Story of a Minor Siege*, Methuen & Co., London, 1899, p. 28.
47. H.C. Thomson, *The Chitral Campaign*, William Heinemann, London, 1895, p. 3.
48. Letter from Sardar Nizam-ul-Mulk, to the British Agent at Gilgit, 19 December 1892, Dr G.S. Robertson's Mission to Chitral, Foreign, Secret-F, July 1893, Nos. 571-741, National Archives of India.

49. Translation of a letter from the Amir to Sher Afzul, 29 November 1892, Dr G.S. Robertson's Mission to Chitral, Foreign, Secret-F, July 1893, Nos. 571-741, National Archives of India.
50. G.J. Younghusband, and Francis Younghusband, *The Relief of Chitral*, Macmillan and Co., London, 1910, p. 11.
51. George S. Robertson, *Chitral the Story of a Minor Siege*, Methuen & Co., London, 1899, pp. 53-4.
52. Government of India to H.H. Fowler, No. 66, 17 April 1895, Government of India, Foreign, Secret-F, July 1895, Nos. 1-433, National Archives of India.
53. W.G.L. Beynon, *With Kelly to Chitral*, Edward Arnold, London, 1896, p. 86.
54. Government of India to H.H. Fowler, No. 66, 17 April 1895, Government of India, Foreign, Secret-F, July 1895, Nos. 1-433, National Archives of India.
55. Ibid., p. 130.
56. Ibid., p. 132.
57. Collins C. Davies, *The Problem of the North-West Frontier 1890-1908*, Cambridge University Press, London, 1932, p. 86.
58. Sir Francis Younghusband, *The Light of Experience*, Houghton, Mifflin Company, Boston and New York, 1927, p. 76.
59. Collins C. Davies, *The Problem of the North-West Frontier 1890-1908*, Cambridge University Press, London, 1932, p. 87.

REFERENCES

Alder, Garry J., *British India's Northern Frontier 1865-1895: A Study in Imperial Policy*, Longmans Green and Co Ltd, London, 1963.

Beynon, William G.L., *With Kelly to Chitral*, Edward Arnold, London, 1896.

Burnaby, Fred, *A Ride to Khiva*, Cassel and Company, London, 1895.

Chohan, Amar S., *The Gilgit Agency*, Atlantic Publishers and Distributors, New Delhi, 1997.

Colquhoun, *Archibald R., Russia Against India: The Struggle for Asia*, Harper and Brothers, New York and London, 1900.

Dani, Ahmad H., *History of the Northern Areas of Pakistan*, National Institute of Historical and Cultural Research, Islamabad, 1991.

Davies, Collins C., *The Problem of the North-West Frontier 1890-1908*, Cambridge University Press, London, 1932.

Durand, Algernon, *The Making of a Frontier*, John Murray, London, 1900.

Gadru, S.N. (ed.), *Kashmir Papers: British Intervention in Kashmir*, Freethought Literature Company, Srinagar, 1973.

Knight, Edward F., *Where Three Empires Meet*, Longmans Green and Co, London, 1905.

Leitner, Wilhelm G., *Dardistan in 1866, 1886 and 1893*, Asian Educational Services, New Delhi, 1996.

Thomson, Harry C., *The Chitral Campaign*, William Heinemann, London, 1895.

Younghusband, George J. and Francis Younghusband, *The Relief of Chitral*, Macmillan and Co., London, 1910.

Younghusband, Sir Francis, *The Light of Experience*, Houghton, Mifflin Company, Boston and New York, 1927.

CHAPTER 3

Consolidation of the Frontier

THE CLOSURE OF THE GREAT GAME

The Great Game between Britain and Russia was cooling down towards the end of the nineteenth century. The Chitral crisis and the subsequent British response to it essentially delimitated the frontier between the British and Russian empires. On 11 March 1895 while Dr Robertson was under siege in Chitral fort by Sher Afzul, negotiations were ongoing between the Russians and the British to demarcate the spheres of influence of the two great powers. This was essentially in the form of an exchange of notes by fixing the British area of influence to the east of Lake Sari-Qul; this put the northern boundary of the Wakhan Corridor essentially under British control. Eventually the signing of the Pamir Boundary Commission on 10 September 1895 is understood to have officially ended the Great Game in the nineteenth century between Russia and Britain. Maj. Gen. Gerard headed the British Pamir Boundary Commission who would engage with a Russian Boundary Commission under Gen. Povalo-Shveikovsky, with the primary objective of demarcating the frontier:

> The work of the Commission was compressed into four months, of which two were occupied in marching to and from the Pamirs, and the other two in demarcating about 90 miles of boundary line extending from Lake Victoria in the Great Pamir to the Chinese frontier on the Sarikol range.[1]

The report of this boundary commission clearly points to the fact that the British had sufficient knowledge about the geography of the region to arrive at the conclusion that the region to the east of Badakhshan had relatively few entry routes into India and almost none of them was suitable for military force to cross over. The boundary report goes into extensive details about the routes taken by major invasions of the Indian subcontinent and comes to the conclusion that they were through the mountain passes to the west of the Indus River as they run southwards.

Here, then, historical evidence has been gathered of at least two military irruptions into India, both of which were first forced westward from regions east of the Pamirs, and finally entered India over the Parapomisus, which we now recognise as that part of the Hindu Kush west of Kafiristan which borders the Kabul basin on the north and west. The next great invasion of India from the same direction was that of the Epthalites, or White Huns, about 460 AD, and it followed much the same course.[2]

Timur who crossed the Hindu Kush to Kabul by the 'usual route' in 1398, and who entered India with one column by Banu, whilst his general, Pir Muhammad, crossed the Indus further south with another, is said once to have attempted to cross the Hindu Kush by a pass leading from the Minjan valley in Badakshan into the heart of Kafiristan.[3]

Babur followed almost step by step the route taken by Alexander. He too, crossed the Hindu Kush north of Kabul and established himself securely in the possession of that variable 'key of India' before proceeding to the reduction of the Kunar valley, Bajaur, Jandul, and Swat as a necessary preliminary to the final invasion of India and capture of Delhi and Agra.[4]

It evaluated the various invasion routes into India at various times and came to the conclusion that the primary invasion route into India was through Kabul to the west of Hindukush. Therefore, it concluded that the Gilgit Agency as it remained after 1896 after the separation of Chitral did not sit adjacent to the primary invasion routes into India. It pointed out that while the routes to the north of Gilgit were occasionally used by trade caravans it had never been a primary invasion route.

But this great northern barricade has not been quite so effective in checking commercial intercourse as it has been obstructive to semi-military tribal movements, although none of the passes north of Gilgit and Chitral have ever been utilized as trade routes except on a very small scale. A 'caravan route', which can hardly be other than the Baroghil, is referred to by the Chinese pilgrim Fa Hian; and the Karakorum pass was probably well known also to traders; although the great recognised trade routes of Asia were those which connected east and west along the fertile Oxus valley or on lines north of it.[5]

Further, there was extensive debate in the British establishment as late as 1900 about the shape of frontier administration and whether the Gilgit Agency should continue to be responsible or the responsibility be transferred to other agencies:

There is the scheme partly suggested by Sir George Robertson, of combining the frontier districts, or at any rate those of the Peshawar Division into a 1st class Agency with Kashmir. The only merit of this plan is that Gilgit and Chitral would then be under one officer, but this cannot for a moment weigh against the numerous disadvantages, with which the scheme positively bristles. To mention only a few of them, the work in Kashmir proper has nothing in common with work on the frontier. Kashmir, Gilgit and Kashgar are already sufficient for one man to look after. If the Kashmir Resident were to be the Agent to the Governor-General, this officer would spend 6 months of the year in Srinagar out of reach of the most important part of his charge. One of the drawbacks of the inclusion of Abbottabad in the Peshawar Division is that the Commissioner is for half the year in the Gullies, away from the border. This inconvenience would be intensified if the officer responsible for the frontier were half the year so far away as Srinagar.[6]

Deciding against keeping a unified Agency would mark a fundamental shift in the British attitude towards the Gilgit Agency. The frontier would now be divided between the north-west frontier facing Afghanistan as well as by extension the Russian Empire under the Chitral Agent and the northern frontier facing Qing China under the oversight of the Gilgit Agent. The Gilgit Agency was now therefore, effectively reduced to a secondary theatre and was primarily oriented towards Kashgar in Tibet. The focus hereafter would be on consolidating the Gilgit Agency by establishing new military formations, developing transportation and military infrastructure as well as raising new military formations for defending the frontier.

MEASURES FOR THE DEFENCE OF THE GILGIT AGENCY

When the Gilgit Agency had been established, it consisted merely of four English officers, however, by 1981, their numbers had been increased to fourteen English officers, at the head of two hundred Gurkha soldiers. Initially, this deployment was quite temporary, however, soon, this was changed to a permanent deployment. There were many factors which made it necessary to increase the scale of this deployment. The most important factor driving the British military preparations in the region was naturally the anticipation of a Russian movement across the Pamirs. The Russians had already moved into the Pamir mountains and in doing so, had forced the Chinese and the Afghans out of the region.[7] An instance of such Russian ingress into the northern Pamirs in Tajikistan is described in graphic detail as follows:

> The Afghans had but 15 men and they were encamped on the banks of the Alichur river where it joins the lake just under the bank of the promontory of Surmatash. The Russians had 300 men and six guns. They surrounded the little party of Afghans, and Colonel Yonoff ordered them to lay down their arms. The Afghan officer refused to do so, saying he was sent there by the Amir of Kabul to whom the lake belonged. Colonel Yonoff then ordered his men to make him a prisoner, on which the Afghan officer drew his sword and ran amock into the middle of the Russians, cutting down five men before he was shot with a revolver by one of the Russian officers.[8]

Further, there was an ever-present danger that the rulers or Thums of Hunza and Nagar had antagonistic views towards the Gilgit Agency and the Kashmir State, thereby making increased military preparedness essential to protect against any misadventure on the part of these tributaries (Chohan 1997: 184). To add to these minor states, the larger state of Chitral further to the west, was forever a source of concern for the British. Despite having pledged allegiance to Kashmir in 1878 under the Kashmir-Chitral Treaty of the same year, at the commencement of the Second Anglo-Afghan War, its historical status as an Afghan tributary meant that there was always a possibility of trouble emanating from there especially with Afghan support. This is exactly what would happen in the crisis of 1895 in Chitral which has been covered in the last chapter.

This geopolitical environment and the military experiences of the 1895 campaign in Chitral convinced the British that their military preparedness was insufficient to handle any exigency and this situation needed to be remedied. The experience of the 1895 events in Chitral showed to the British that their investment in the training and equipping of troops of the princely states had yielded rich dividends in their performance during that campaign. However, the officers of these princely units were not up to the mark.[9]

Lastly, the issue of military logistics had to be considered. The difficulty of keeping the military units supplied and ensuring their rapid transportation in the difficult terrain was well known, but the sudden crisis of 1895 and the siege of Dr Robertson, the British agent at Gilgit, drove home the issue of military logistics most keenly. This difficulty would be addressed in two steps. The first would be the attachment of an officer of the Commissariat Department to the Gilgit Agency. The Commissariat Department was a logistical branch of the British Indian Army and was playing an even more important role after 1859.[10] The second step would be a major investment in the road and bridge infrastructure to facilitate the movement of troops and supplies.

There was however, the issue of cost to these military measures that were deemed essential for the Gilgit Agency. In 1896, the troops in the Gilgit Agency consisted of two hundred soldiers of the Kashmir Imperial Service Troops who also acted as the personal bodyguard of the British Agent, a detachment of forty soldiers from the Bengal Sappers, three regiments of six hundred soldiers each of the Kashmir Imperial Service Infantry, one Kashmir Imperial Service Mountain artillery battery and two companies of Kashmir Sappers (Chohan 1997: 187).

The costs of maintaining this military force were quite stupendous and some sort of financial support for this force was essential. However, these forces were spread out over the territory of the Gilgit Agency in nineteen different locations of which twelve were merely communication nodes. The GOI tried to streamline the military logistics by deciding to concentrate the troops in fewer locations and the reorganization of the Kashmir Imperial Service Troops.

Under this new scheme, the troops were to be concentrated at Gilgit and their roles would be taken over by levies in Yasin, Hunza and Nagar, along with reorganizing the six battalions of Kashmir infantry troops into four battalions, each of which had seven hundred and two troops. These changes reduced the Kashmir State's expenditure on the defence of the Gilgit Agency by approximately eighty-four thousand rupees and to British revenues by a further forty-one thousand rupee (Chohan 1997: 188).

As a result of these changes, the number of troops in the Gilgit Agency were brought to two hundred rifles as an escort to the British Agent, a four-gun mountain battery, two battalions of infantry from the Kashmir Imperial Service Troops with a strength of seven hundred and two men each and two companies of Kashmir sappers and miners (ibid.). Going ahead in the year 1900, the expenditure was further reduced by reducing the number of officers at the Agency from fourteen to seven in the light of the reduced strategic and political significance of Gilgit. This reduction of officers together with the withdrawal of the separate complement of the agent's bodyguard, contributed to a further reduction of military expenditure. The agent's security role would hereafter be taken over by the Kashmir Imperial Service Troops in the Agency. However, it must be pointed out that this was in no way indicative of a change in British policy towards the people of the region or towards the state of Kashmir.

Over the next few years, there was extensive debate about increasing the use of Imperial Colonial Troops from various princely states in the defence of the frontier. As early as 1887, the Nizam of Hyderabad displayed interest in investing resources for the defence of the north-western frontier.[11] However, as has been explained earlier, the issue of officers in native military units was realized by the British, during their military experiences on the frontier. Therefore, in 1901, funds were allocated for the construction of the Gilgit-Chitral Road.

> The Secretary of State having intimated that the increase of officers of native regiments may be considered, I would strongly urge that the measure may be regarded as one of urgency and not relegated to a later date for discussion.
>
> Our late experiences have shown us that we require 15 officers per battalion, so as to be in a fit state on mobilization in order to be in a fit state on mobilization in order to officer native regiments up to 12 in the field, and to provide the additional staff for field service.[12]

Further, in 1901 the British would introduce the more modern BL 10 pounder mountain artillery gun in all the mountain artillery regiments with a special focus on the north-west frontier, and earmarked £ 26,833 for this purpose in 1901 alone.[13] As an example of having the involvement of the Kashmir Durbar in 1901, the British expected a contribution of Rs. 75,000 from the former towards the expenses of the Gilgit Agency.

> It is estimated that the probable net extra expenditure chargeable to the Military Department on account of the Gilgit Agency during the ensuing year will be Rs. 2,25,590 as against Rs. 2,55,470 provided in the current year's budget estimates. In the absence of orders as to the concessions to be allowed during 1900-1901, the concessions sanctioned for the current year have been estimated for.
>
> The probable amount that the Kashmir Durbar will be called on to contribute will be roundly Rs. 75,000 which does not include the quarter share of any expenditure on Military Works. Foreign Department may see the file after orders issue regarding budget provision for next year.[14]

All of these measures were indicative of an increasing situation of internal and external stability in the region and consequently a desire for transferring greater security responsibilities to the princely state of Kashmir. Additionally, regulations were introduced in 1901 under which, Imperial troops, under the law could be commanded by British officers while they were on duty as a part of a British military effort within or outside India.

> Whenever the said force or any portion thereof is moved beyond the frontier of the said state the Governor General in Council shall have power to appoint one or more British officers to command the said Imperial Service Troops and such officer or officers shall, by virtue of this agreement, be authorised to administer in respect of the said Imperial Service Troops so serving the military laws and regulations to which they are subject under the law of the said state.[15]

Further, the State of Kashmir was especially expected to provide troops across the 'Frontiers of India'. The following is an extract from the proceedings of a meeting of the J&K State Council held at Jammu on the 2 February 1898, explaining the service parameters of state troops:

The conditions of service of Imperial Service Troops are of four descriptions:

(a) Service in their respective states.
(b) Service in British India in time of peace, e.g., at camps of exercise.
(c) Service in British India in time of war or revolt, and
(d) Active service beyond the frontiers of British India.[16]

This document enumerates the attempts at a standardized system of military discipline across imperial troops which underlines the British attempt to utilize them better in their imperial commitments including these in the frontier. Finally, in this changing military force structure, local levies were to play an important role, to compensate for the reduction in strength of the regular troops. As early as 1892, the GOI was raising local levies for the defence of the Gilgit Agency, which initially numbered three hundred men. The difference between the levies and regular troops was that the levies were raised by the Political Agent and as such did not form part of either the British Indian Army or the Imperial Service Troops. These levies would receive training from British units and Imperial Service Troops (Chohan 1997: 191).

These levies were expected to operate in conditions of glacial snow and the entire cost of their training as well as the expenditure on necessary equipment to operate in this weather was pegged at a sum of Rs. 2,000. These levies were paid Rs. 6 per month while on training and a reduced amount of Rs. 3 per month for the intervening period. The total cost incurred on the pay of the levies was Rs. 13,000 annually to be entirely borne by the Kashmir Darbar (ibid.: 190).

These levies had proven their importance and usefulness in holding the important mountain passes as well as in the campaign in Chitral in 1895 when their support in fighting was extremely significant especially in terms of providing material help. Following the separation of Chitral from Gilgit in 1896, most of the regular troops would be concentrated in the towns of Chitral and Gilgit while the scattering of troops in Yasin, Hunza and Nagar would be replaced by levies. This would raise the number of levies significantly after 1897 resulting in increasing the cost incurred to Rs. 36,000 (ibid.: 191).

This reliance on levies would continue until 1913, when the GOI would create a new force of troops that could be described as paramilitary in character. This was to be the Gilgit Scouts. The Gilgit Scouts was intended to replace the local levies in the Agency. The cost of raising this new military force was to be borne equally by the Kashmir State and the British government. The long reliance on levies from 1892 to 1912 had revealed some of the weaknesses of the system. The levies had lacked the discipline and training of regular troops and it was now being realized that the resource investment on such a system could yield far better results in military terms if regular forces were to be raised instead.

The Political Agent's military assistant was made the commandant of the Gilgit Scouts. The Political Agent was the final authority in all the matters relating to the Gilgit Scouts including those related to appointments and promotions. This close British link with the Gilgit Scouts would have important implications for events that were to transpire later in the region. Since the essential function of the Political Agent was political in nature, it is not surprising that the Gilgit Scouts would take on a political character themselves (Chohan 1997: 193).

In order to impress upon the troops that they were servants of the GOI throughout the year, they were paid a monthly salary of one rupee for a scout and five rupees for a *subedar* for eleven months. For the remaining one month when they were to undergo training, a different rate of pay in addition to their monthly retainer was to be paid. Meanwhile, in addition to paying half the expenditure of the expenses of the Gilgit Scouts which was entirely under British command, the Kashmir Durbar's expenditure on the logistical support for the Gilgit Agency alone would significantly increase. By 1914-15, the Durbar would be called upon to spend Rs. 55,000 on the 'supply and transport arrangements' in the agency.

> For the information of Foreign Department, it may be stated that the amount that the Kashmir Durbar will be called upon to pay during the ensuing official year (1914-15) on account of the Supply and Transport arrangements in the Gilgit Agency is estimated at Rs. 55,000 roundly, exclusive of contribution on Military works expenditure, if any.[17]

This amount was approximately one-fourth of the total expenditure, three-fourth of which amounting to Rs. 1,63,520 was to be provided from the British army budget.[18]

The objectives of raising this new paramilitary force were manifold. First, the raising of such a corps was intended to provide employment to a large number of young men from the region who were eager for employment as well as develop a feeling of greater amiability among the local people towards the British (Chohan 1997: 194). Second, at this time there were significant concerns that the Russians might attempt to move into Kashgar, thus giving impetus to a military restructuring as well, which is discussed in greater detail below, as well as the establishing of a more robust military presence to dissuade any Russian misadventure to the south of the Hindukush. Third, the number of civil levies before the Gilgit Scouts had far exceeded their needs.

Fourth, it was becoming abundantly clear that the Kashmir State troops were increasingly inadequate to meet the emerging challenges of the frontier and had very limited offensive capability. Further, the tribes across the entire Indian frontier were increasingly becoming better armed with modern weapons percolating down to the tribals. This was especially the case in Darel and the adjoining areas. Regular soldiers such as the Kashmir State troops were therefore unsuitable for rapid movement in the mountainous frontier. On the other hand, locally raised troops such as the Gilgit Scouts, were particularly suited to the demands of the local terrain. It was clear that while what the trained veterans that the Kashmir state troops were not able to do, the Scouts, equipped with modern rifles could easily respond to any tribal force that would bear on them (ibid.: 195).

Fifth, all other measures to reduce the cost of the Gilgit Agency had already been expended and it was clear that the role being fulfilled by the levies was absolutely essential to the safety of the frontier. Moreover, keeping in view the mounting security requirements, the only option was to increase the number of levies, which ran counter to the need to reduce costs. Therefore, the best option was to rationalize the security solution by replacing the levies with a more efficient military force.

Finally, an over dependence on the Kashmir troops gave the impression of an occupying military force to the fiercely independent tribals. This led credence to the argument that the British were outsiders who in collusion with the Kashmir State had bought this region under military occupation. This perception made the region vulnerable to external political activity by hostile powers such as Afghanistan or Russia to provoke uprisings. This is exactly what had happened in the events in Chitral in 1895. It was therefore concluded that the best way to change this perception was to make the local inhabitant, a stakeholder in the defence of his own territory and the most appropriate way forward was the creation of an indigenous military unit like the Gilgit Scouts.[19]

CHANGES IN GEOSTRATEGIC PERCEPTIONS

The internal and external geopolitical situation had significantly changed since the beginning of the twentieth century. The intensity of the Great Game had withered away after the delimitation of the boundary between the Russian and British empires at the end of the nineteenth century and the de facto status of Afghanistan as a neutral buffer state between the two empires. Further, the defeat of Russia in the Russo-Japanese War in 1904-5 would contribute to a political realignment between Britain and Russia with the realization in Britain that Germany was a far more significant military and strategic threat with imperial ambitions. This political realignment would manifest itself as the Anglo-Russian Entente of 1907. Nevertheless, while Britain was binding itself to Russia as part of an alliance against Germany and Austria-Hungary, it was clear that the old strategic vulnerabilities and concerns simply continued to persist.

In 1903, it was considered doubtful if the British would be able to reach Kabul before the Russians in the event of a war. Doing so was essential for British military plans in the eventuality of a military conflict with Russia. There were several challenges before the British which inhibited their ability to carry this out. First, the frontier tribes had repeatedly exhibited their ferocity in battle and their uncertain loyalty ensured that the British had to continuously maintain troops in the inhospitable terrain. Second, the Indian army as it existed at the turn of the twentieth century was in dire need of modernization and it was well understood that in any event of war with Russia, it would need to be heavily reinforced. The concern, however was that the army might not withstand the fighting before it could be reinforced, chiefly due to the great distances of the forward positions from the railheads. These fundamental problems were what made the Indian army unprepared for war and made the strategic condition bleak for the English.

Therefore, the defence of the Indian frontier rested on three important factors. First, the loyalty of the Amir and the frontier tribes. Second, development and maintenance of transportation infrastructure, particularly railways in the frontier and third, a promise of military reinforcements to support military units already present. It was as an extension of pacifying and engaging the local tribes that paramilitary units like the Chitral and Gilgit Scouts were raised.

Under Lord Kitchener* a series of military reforms were to be undertaken with a chief emphasis on making the British Indian Army capable of missions relating to India's defence without an immediate need of reinforcements from overseas. An important element of this restructuring was to create divisions focused on a particular frontier and those would be trained and equipped accordingly.

> Kitchener set out four main principles: that the Army's chief role was the defence of the North-West Frontier against external aggression; that its organisation should be the same in peace as in war; that the internal security role was secondary and chiefly the task of the police, in whose support troops might nevertheless have to act at times; and that all units should have experience and training on the terrain where they might be called upon to perform in their chief role, the Frontier.[20]

* Field Marshal Horatio Kitchener was a British Army officer who played prominent roles in the Sudanese Mahdist War, Boer War and later during First World War. Lord Kitchener was appointed as the Commander-in-Chief of the British Indian Army from 1902 to 1907.

Therefore, Kitchener in 1904 would introduce his 'Scheme for the Redistribution of the Army of India and the Preparation of the Army in India for War', a document which articulated his ideas about the reforms necessary for the defence of India.[21] These reforms were structured around linking all of the major cities in India with railway lines to allow rapid internal movement of troops. Further, each division of the army was to be allocated a specific area of operations and was to be by and large 'homogeneous' or consisting mostly of soldiers drawn from the local population. These divisions were to be oriented primarily towards the defence of the north-western frontier (Wyatt 2011: 97).

There were of course powerful incentives for these changes. The Russian superiority in logistics with the completion of the Orenburg-Tashkent Railway allowed them to move larger numbers of soldiers to the Afghan border and keep them provisioned. The other major concern was that if the Afghan Army joined in with the local frontier tribesmen then the Indian Army would find itself in significant difficulty (ibid.: 98).

An alternate point of view was that was put across by Sir George Clarke* who was critical of the changes being implemented under Lord Kitchener. Proponents of this view such as Clarke himself, would point out that the assumptions about the progress of Russian railway buildup were conjectural and that Kabul was far closer to British India than to Russia which put the British at a significant advantage during any conflict. In this context, the enormous costs involved in these reforms were simply unjustifiable and redundant. Eventually, owing to the prohibitive cost, a compromise solution would be agreed upon and by 1909, the British Indian Army would be largely reorganized along British lines.

Finally, in 1904, in order to ensure the allegiance of the Amir of Afghanistan, the Dane Mission would be sent to Afghanistan. Led by Sir Louis William Dane,** the mission was intended to

*Col. Sir George Clarke was British Army officer of the Royal Engineers and served in India as Governor of Bombay from 1907 to 1913.

**Sir Louis Dane was Indian Civil Service officer of the 1876 batch. He became the foreign secretary to the Government of India in 1903 and led the Dane Mission to Afghanistan in 1904.

give British officials privileges in Afghanistan, thus allowing them to carry out geographical surveys of the territory and allow British subjects safe entry into Afghanistan for purposes of trade. Further, the Amir was permitted to import arms from the British and the British would give him eighteen and a half lakh rupees as an annual subsidy (Wyatt 2011: 119).

In return, the Amir promised to conduct his foreign policy exclusively through the British and indicated his expectation of being provided military support against the Russians if so required:

> The Amir reiterated his willingness to conduct all political relations with foreign powers through British mediation and said he would ask from his friend such help as he could receive without damaging his honor and religious prestige. The Amir saw the danger from Russia as being much greater now than during the time of his father, and he promised to give a written expression of his views on Dane's suggestions.[22]

The Amir of Afghanistan would become increasingly eager after his initial discussions with Dane for some sort of an official treaty with the British, formalizing British military support against any Russian advances, however, the Indian government under Curzon believed that this was undesirable. Further, it was convinced that this Afghan eagerness for a British military guarantee was because of a poor handling of the diplomatic initiative by Dane.

> Once the Government of India heard the news, they were critical of Dane's handling of the negotiations with the Amir. E.H.S. Clarke, the Assistant Secretary to the Foreign Department, argued that the early emphasis on the military question was counterproductive as it constrained British freedom of movement. (ibid.: 120)

The primary concern here was that the Amir, having got a grasp of the British desire for a buffer against the Russians would essentially dictate terms of the treaty to the British. The British on the other hand, saw the treaty primarily as a warning to the Russians that any violation of Afghan territory by the latter would be seen as a *casus belli* by the British (ibid.).

Eventually, after many discussions and negotiations, the treaty between Britain and Afghanistan would finally be signed on

21 March 1905 which effectively gave Afghanistan British military support in the event of war; however, this was at the cost of the Amir dictating terms to the British, something that the British had been wary of from the very outset. For example, Dane was unable to secure a prohibition on Russian trade which continued even as Dane was signing the treaty.

The overall assessment of the treaty by Curzon was that of pessimism. The treaty had essentially been pushed ahead by the Home Government because it was desirous of a treaty with Afghanistan. However, Curzon was of the view that the treaty had not improved the security situation on the Indian frontier tribes materially.

> He saw progress with the Amir as not forthcoming on several military issues connected with the frontier tribes, as was clear regarding British plans for railways running through tribal territory. Curzon also distrusted the Amir's stated willingness to refrain from intrigues with the tribes, particularly the Afridis, and wrote that 'we cannot feel very sanguine as to the future'. (Wyatt 2011: 138)

While these diplomatic means to secure India's frontiers were afoot, the Russo-Japanese War was raging in the far east. Buttressed by the protection offered by the Anglo-Japanese Alliance against any French support to the Russians, the Japanese went on the offensive against the Russians in East Asia. The Japanese victory in the war had two important security implications for the British. The first was that the Russians, had now lost their status as the third largest naval power in the world after the Battle of Tsushima and their prestige by their loss to a much smaller power. This, in turn, reduced the British threat perception from Russia towards their Indian empire. Second, the British began to consider the Japanese as a strong ally in Asia against other European Imperial interests including the Russians.

While the initial Anglo-Japanese alliance of 30 January 1902 was focused mostly on China and Korea, it would have security ramifications for India after the 1905 Russo-Japanese War. In a proposed renewal of the 1902 Anglo-Japanese alliance in 1905, a draft treaty was submitted on 26 May 1905 to Hayashi, the

Japanese ambassador in London (Wyatt 2011: 142-3). After some initial discussions, a new draft treaty was submitted to the Japanese side on 10 June, and the most striking aspect of this treaty was Note B:

> It is agreed that Japan will, in the event of war, provide and maintain a force which shall be equal to the force of British troops from time to time in India up to a limit of ,000.[23]

However, during the course of the Russo-Japanese War, the Japanese victories at Mukden and Port Arthur had led to Japan being seen as the champion of Asian nationalism against European imperialism. This gave rise to the question as to whether, Japanese troops were even desirable on Indian soil since they would then encourage the feeling that independence could be achieved (ibid.: 145). Consequently, by February 1906, the conclusion had been reached that there would be no British troops being deployed to Manchuria or Japanese troops to the North-West Frontier of India with the common agreement of both the new Viceroy Lord Minto and Lord Kitchener (ibid.).

The next year, in 1907, the Anglo-Russian Entente would be signed, thereby, bringing the two countries diplomatically closer. Nevertheless, this did not completely eliminate the thorny issue of the frontier while there were attempts at greater cooperation to resolve the issue. In 1908, the outbreak of the Jamshedi crisis would again raise tensions between the two allies. Syed Ahmed Beg, the leader of the Jamshedi tribesmen, along with ten thousand of his followers, apparently left for Russia from their homes in northern Afghanistan, with Syed Ahmed Beg himself having based himself in Samarkand (ibid.: 194). This was initially seen as Russian connivance with the Jamshedi against Afghan and British interests. It, however, soon became clear that this was not the case. The Jamshedi earned the scorn of the local Turkomans who considered the presence of the former as an infringement of their traditional grazing lands.

The Russians were quite unhappy with the situation themselves as a result of the local intrigues of the Jamshedi and their attempts at extorting money from the Russians. The resulting irritability of the Russian administration and the hostility of the local Turkoman population disillusioned the Jamshedi tribesmen, most of whom returned to Afghanistan. During most of this crisis the Russian Imperial government demonstrated maximum restraint and 'observed the provisions of the Anglo-Russian convention as though they were in force' (Wyatt 2011: 195). By the end of February 1906, this crisis had come to an end and by 1910, the Great Game, which had been driving the traditional Anglo-Russian rivalry over the frontier came to an effective end until the establishment of the Bolsheviks in Russia.

This aspect of the frontier geopolitics is important to understand the implementation of British policies in Gilgit-Baltistan in the aftermath of the 1907 Anglo-Russian Entente. With the frontier now relatively secure politically from the Russian threat, the primary axis of focus for Gilgit would be the Kashgar region in western Tibet.

THE PAN-ISLAMIST THREAT ON THE FRONTIER

The second decade of the twentieth century marked a definite shift from a Russia focused threat to another, based around Pan-Islamism emanating from Central Asia. The primary drive behind this threat was the idea that the European Christian powers were antagonistic to the Muslim Ottoman Empire on religious grounds. The situation in the frontier was more tense than ever because the Afghans and the tribals on the frontier were convinced that there was an alliance between the British and the Russians to bring about the downfall of the Ottoman Empire and the Caliphate.

As such, there was the even-greater danger, not so much of a Russian invasion or incursion on the frontier, but rather, of a threat emanating from Afghanistan. This transformed the nature of the threat and the security requirements on the frontier. No longer was a military force capable of dealing with the Russian army required:

With the Russian threat gone, Sir Charles Hardinge, made Viceroy in 1910, stated: 'at present what we have to look forward to is possible trouble from

Afghanistan'. He wrote again, five months later, that: 'On the North-West Frontier we require an Army to keep the Afghans in check, but not to meet a modern Russian Army'. At this time, Muslim feeling in India was also growing, particularly in the north and Bengal. Hardinge reported that 'Mahommedan feeling has never been so intense'. This was heightened by the possibility of war with Turkey over tensions in the Persian Gulf. (Wyatt 2011: 196)

This shift in military requirements in the frontier was the underlying driving factor in addition to the reasons mentioned earlier leading to the move towards abandoning the system of levies in favour of the Gilgit Scouts. In fact, the Frontier Constabulary in the North-West Frontier was another such paramilitary force established to cater for the changed strategic situation.

However, despite the Gilgit Agency having been relieved of its charge over Chitral and the north-western passes, the boundary which separated the Agency from the north-western frontier had not yet been defined. This boundary demarcation exercise was carried out in 1914, chiefly by defining the boundaries of Dir, Swat and Chitral as follows:

(a) *Dir:* The eastern boundary of Dir is the watershed of the Panjkora and Swat rivers from the Tal Pass through the Badgwai and Zhandrai Passes to the head of the Shar Darra: thence the boundary runs through the Kar Pass to the Shagoderai peak and down the spur which forms the southern watershed of the Daral stream to the Swat River, which it meets at a spot between the villages of Tirat and Baranial. The boundary thereafter is the Swat River. The north-western and northern boundary is the crest of the Lawarai range.

(b) *Swat:* For geographical purposes, can be described as consisting of the valley of the upper portion of the Swat River, south of Baranial; and its western boundary, below that point, may be regarded as the watershed of that river. But, politically, the western watershed of that river. But, politically, the western watershed area, below Baranial, belongs to Dir, having been conquered and annexed in 1897 (vide page 72 of Volume XI of Aitchison's Treaties) and to give Swat its geographical boundary would cut off an integral part of Dir territory. It therefore seems expedient to restrict Swat, as a separate entity, to the area south of Baranial and east and south of the Swat River.

(c) *Chitral:* The north-western and northern boundary of Dir, indicated above, forms the southern and south-eastern boundary of Chitral. The eastern boundary, as shown on the blue print, is correct.[24]

The above document mentions certain corrections to the boundary between Gilgit and the north-western frontier by introducing certain corrections by Col. Roger Lloyd Kennion to an earlier letter from the Government of India, Foreign and Political Department to the Survey of India Department dated 12 March 1914.[25]

While these boundary demarcations and military rationalization of the frontier was being carried out, the Great War had broken out in Europe, thus diverting the entire focus to Europe. The Ottoman Empire was aligned with the Central Powers, against the Entente. The frontier and Afghanistan especially had enormous latent sympathy for the Ottomans, which had been further heightened because of conspiracy theories of a Christian plot against the Caliph. By 1914, the Amir's control over Afghanistan was weakening, partly because of his pro-British position (Wyatt 2011: 199).

The primary British concern at the start of the Great War, was regarding the response of the large Muslim population at the frontier with clear loyalties to the Ottomans. After the outbreak of the war, the Amir, keeping in line with his traditional stance, continued to remain neutral against the British despite large sections of the population and powerful factions at his court desiring otherwise.

> The Amir stood resolute in his neutrality and was 'keeping his head in the face of surrounding excitement'. He also 'suppressed' a native Kabul paper [the Siraj al-Akhbar] which threatened to become dangerous by its warlike attitude'. Despite this, public opinion in Afghanistan was still strongly pro-Turkish and it was both difficult and unpopular for the Amir to restrain his subjects. Some Afghans defied the wrath of the Amir and attacked the Miram Shah Post in the Tochi Valley. (ibid.: 203)

However, things were being made more complicated because of Ottoman agents and seditionists being sent into Afghanistan through Persia to stir up 'Pan-Islamic anti-British sentiment' (ibid.: 203). Such actions were however not unique to the

Ottomans as the British too had sent agents such as Maj. Thomas Lawrence to Arabia with the purpose of raising the Arab tribes in revolt against the Ottomans. The following account explains the degree of seriousness with which the British took the discontent among the Muslim population on the frontier by attacking Iran:

Day before yesterday the Turkish troops were still at Bisaitin, and such a small force is hardly likely to risk isolation or show Persia such active hostility as to advance to Karun themselves. It is more likely that they will content themselves by inciting Beni Los and the disaffected tribesmen of Shaikh of Muhammerah to threaten Ahwaz. The shaikh of Muhammerah is still anxious about the effect of the Jihad movement, but as regards Ahwaz, fanatics have been deprived of their main objective by the withdrawal of European and British subjects, and it is hoped that, pending the arrival of the 12th Brigade, loyalty of the tribesmen of the Shaikh's own clan, whom he has dispatched from Muhammerah, will suffice to prevent any serious raid on Ahwaz.[26]

Nevertheless, it did mean that the British had to allocate greater resources to the frontier, which they were already short of.

I am very strongly of opinion as regards the nature of the reinforcement, that India should now receive back from Egypt one of our two divisions that are there and which, had we known the demands which would be made of us in the Gulf, would not have been allowed to go. No more regular troops can be spared from India, and it would be madness for the Territorial Troops to be sent to the North-west Frontier. I may mention that, in my opinion and that of the Commander-in-Chief, the last lot of Territorials sent to India, the Wessex Reserve Division, have very small military value.[27]

Further, there were reports of desertions among Indian Army units consisting of Muslims, especially from Pathans hailing from the frontier:

There is some fanatical talk across border, and a rumour of conversion of the Kaiser to Islam meets with general belief. Appearance of a gang which was led by Hindustani fanatics on Hazara border, made it necessary to strengthen Oghi with troops. Mohmands and Utman Khel are showing signs of restlessness but former are contemplating coming in and settling cases which are outstanding. Afridis are quietly awaiting a reply to their petition for enhanced allowances in connection with duplication of road. Their future attitude is a crucial factor on frontier and will depend largely on result of petition. Dissensions among Khost tribes have resulted from failure at Spina Khaisora. On Kurram border gathering of Mangals have been negotiating with Political Agent. Caravan traffic is reported to be more or less in a normal state. . . . Though some recruiting has been reported, there is no information of abnormal military movements or war preparations in Afghanistan. There is no change to report in tone of Muhammedan press. The number of desertions that have taken place, which also include abstentations on the part of the reservists in the Indian Army, have been excessive since the beginning of the war. From Pathans highest of all classes but from Muhammedan classes not higher from Hindu classes. The Trans-frontier Pathans are undoubtedly affected by war now being waged with Turkey. Cis-frontier Pathans are also affected but to a lesser extent. Punjabi Mussalmans are apparently only very slightly affected if at all. Whilst we have no direct evidence, the inference is that the preaching of 'Jihad' is a contributory cause of desertion amongst Sepoys of the Muhammedan faith.[28]

Additionally, there was also a marked reduction in the number of recruits from among the Pathans on the frontier:

Signs are not wanting that trans-frontier Pathans are ceasing to come in, preaching of Jihad is probably accountable for this.[29]

It was during the time of these concerning reports in February 1915, that the Germans were attempting to make overtures to the Afghans, an example of which was the Niedermayer-Hentig Mission.* Once this mission entered Afghanistan, it arrived in Kabul on 28 September 1915 (Wyatt 2011: 205). Once the mission had reached Kabul, it was isolated from everyone to prevent the pro-Ottoman factions in the court from getting access to it. The mission was also made to wait till 16 October to meet the Amir. Niedermayer went on to promise the Amir German military aid including troops and weapons if he agreed to wage war against the British as well as stretching territory as far south as Bombay and till Samarkand in the north (ibid.: 205).

*The Niedermayer-Hentig Expedition was a Central Powers' diplomatic expedition to Afghanistan led German Army officers Oskar Niedermayer and Werner Otto von Hentig.

However, to the dismay of the mission, the Amir, reportedly explained his intention of remaining neutral in the war and not break off diplomatic relations with the British on his own initiative. The Amir had taken this position at a great personal risk and cost to his popularity in the countryside. Nasrullah, his younger brother had publicly declared that he would not abide by the British treaties if he came to power. In doing so he appealed to the anti-British factions in the country as well in the Afghan army (ibid.: 206).

When Niedermayer eventually came to the conclusion that the Amir would not support their appeals for an alliance of some sort, there were ideas that there would be a coup:

> The truth of this dawned on Niedermayer and Hentig and they reached the conclusion that the Amir would not support them. They briefly entertained the notion of a coup and wrote a letter to this effect to the German Minister in Tehran. This, too, was intercepted by the British and they then forwarded it to the Amir to poison the relationship with the Germans. (ibid.: 206-7)

This event led to the dismissal of the Niedermayer mission from Afghanistan on 22 May 1916. While, Amir Habibullah prevailed in this struggle between different factions in his court to the benefit of the British during the remainder of the war, the unpopularity of his policies among the army personnel eventually proved to be his undoing. Habibullah was assassinated while he was out on a hunting trip on 19 February 1919 in the Laghman Valley. While it is not clear who was behind the assassination, it is generally believed to be the Amir's third son Amanullah (ibid.: 212). Nasrullah, the Amir's second son immediately declared himself the ruler, however, he was denounced for their father's murder by Amanullah who then had him arrested and imprisoned after ruling for a week. Amanullah who was adamantly opposed to British control over Afghan foreign policy, then crowned himself the Amir. This essentially set the stage for the Third Anglo-Afghan War of 1919.

The end of the Third Anglo-Afghan War resulted in the Treaty of Rawalpindi of 1919, wherein the British recognized the independence of Afghanistan and that the British frontier would not extend across the Khyber Pass. Henceforth the British also stopped their subsidies to Afghanistan.[30] This conflict and the resulting treaty set the stage for a renewal of the Great Game with Afghanistan no longer a British bulwark on the frontier against Russia.

Another, consequence of the Third Anglo-Afghan War was that many local princes and rulers began to pledge the services of their state troops to the British in the defence of the frontier regions. This included the state troops of the princely state of J&K which owing to its geographical proximity to the troubled Afghan frontier, was a natural choice:

> His Highness the Maharaja of Kashmir in addition to placing his Imperial Service Troops and resources of his State at the disposal of Government desires also to offer his personal services.[31]

Nevertheless, the British government politely refused his offer of help on the grounds of his age but did request clarification on whether Gilgit borders on Afghan territory or not, to which the resident at Kashmir, G.D. Ogilvie clarified that Chitral and the states of Hunza and Nagar on the north-west separated the territory of Kashmir from Afghanistan.[32] This clearly shows that the boundary demarcation of the Gilgit Agency which had been carried out earlier in 1914 was still not clearly understood.

Meanwhile, the 1917 Russian Revolution had triggered the Russian Civil War and British troops were a part of the international expedition sent to fight the Bolsheviks in Russia. The Wakhan region, a narrow sliver of land to the north of Yasin in Gilgit separating British territory from that of Communist Russia regained strategic significance which had reduced since 1910.

GILGIT AND THE BOLSHEVIK SCARE

It was clear that a reorientation of the Gilgit frontier was taking place towards China and to address possible unrest being created by Bolshevik Russia. This became quite evident in the following telegram from Kashgar:

I received on the 13th instant a telegram via China from the Foreign Office to the effect, that according to news from the War Office, there should be German agents working at Uliassutai, Maimaicheng, Kiakhta and Urga with the object if establishing an independent republic in Manchuria, and of fomenting trouble in Tibet and Afghanistan; also that the Bolsheviks were attempting to send agents to disturb India and Tibet.[33]

This communication referring to such potentially hostile activities in Central Asia towards the end of the Great War, clarified that these communications could not be reliably sent via Beijing because of the unreliable telegram system there which resulted in the corruption of the cipher code:

It happens to explain that a telegram is sufficiently understood to render the asking of a repetition unnecessary, whilst its real meaning remains uncertain. If you see no objection, would you in future cause the figures to be forwarded to me by post so that, if necessary, telegrams may be re-deciphered? This applies only to telegrams via China which undergo probably a dozen successive transmissions before they reach Kashgar, and errors go on accumulating with each transmission.[34]

In response to the Consulate General Kashgar's plight over the corruption of the cipher telegram, the Viceroy of India took the following decision to send all telegram cipher from Kashgar to India via Gilgit:

Telegrams to Consul General Kashgar from India are now being addressed 'C/o Political Agent Gilgit' owing to mutilation of cypher figures and delays over Chinese lines. Political Agent transmits them by speediest available method. It is supported by Macartney that Foreign Office should adopt similar procedure.[35]

This problem in communications was essentially owing to the political unrest in China, however, this orientation of the Gilgit region towards China and Kashgar was a harbinger of things to come. The Gilgit Agency continued to receive investments in the form of land and additional budgets from the British government which reflected its continued strategic importance. The period between 1919 and 1935, essentially reflected the two processes of military consolidation and reorientation towards concerns in

Chinese Turkestan through the mechanism of the Political Agent in Gilgit.

In order to address the issues of military logistics, a significant part of which involved moving large quantities of food to the troops in the agency. A partial solution to this problem was to grow crops and trees locally for fuel. By the end of the second decade of the twentieth century there had been an enormous destruction of forest cover which had further exacerbated the fuel crisis in Gilgit.

The Political Agent in Gilgit had in 1917, requested the assistance of Lt. S.W. Steane who was a forest officer with the Gilgit Agency. Between 1919 and 1926, on the recommendations of Lt. Steane, thousands of young willow and other quick growing trees to provide fuelwood had been planted in the region. However, this was unable to completely resolve the fuel situation at Gilgit.[36]

Further in 1926, significant resources were allocated to the purchase of equipment and stores for the Gilgit Scouts, and that expenditure was higher than expected:

Military Stores for the Gilgit Corps of Scouts

In the Budget estimates a sum of Rs. 4,850 has been allocated under this head. But owing to an increase in the price of ball ammunition and the additional and entirely new demand for Customs and Departmental charges the actual expenditure which is settled by Book-debit accounts with the Arsenal Rawalpindi has exceeded the grant by Rs. 1,100.

Web-equipment for the Gilgit Corps of Scouts

A grant of Rs. 13,200 was sanctioned by Government in the year 1924 for the purchase of Web-equipment for the Gilgit Corps of Scouts (vide your Memorandum No. 99-F., dated 28 November 1924). The equipment did not reach Gilgit until the summer of 1925 and consequently the grant was not operated upon and lapsed at the close of the financial year.[37]

This seems to have been a regular feature ever since the British had established the Agency and more recently, after the establishment of the Gilgit Scouts that the actual expenditure on the military maintenance would exceed the allocated amount. Additionally, certain military posts were removed, while others were earmarked for closure under a process of financial rationalization:

Tangir Blockade: A sum of Rs. 16,000 was sanctioned for this purpose for six months during the current year (vide telegram No. 551-S., dated the 16 May 1925, from the Foreign and Political Department). Two of the three posts have now been removed but the post at Thor still continues. Its continuance has been sanctioned in Foreign and Political Department telegram No.1307-S., dated the 19 October 1925. The actual expenditure on the three posts has, so far, amounted to about Rs.12,865. Certain charges for renewals of Kit have not yet been made and expenditure on the Thor post for the remainder of the year are to be met. The total expenditure will be within the full grant of Rs. 16,000.

The Political Agent, Gilgit has now intimated that he has so far been able to recover Rs. 640 by the sale of property belonging to Tangiris and this amount has been credited to Government as a departmental receipt.[38]

In addition to these investments in the Gilgit Agency, there were other financial requirements of the Agency of a diplomatic nature such as sending gifts to the Kashmir Darbar, as explained by the Gilgit Resident which required higher investment:

I have the honour to state that the Imperial allotment of Rs. 2,000 for 'Darbar Presents' of this Agency has not been sufficient for many years and although no very great increase has been asked for in reappropriation and every effort has been made to portion out the amount to cover the whole year and presents have been kept low in order to keep within the allotment. Owing to the general rise in prices it has only been possible to give very inferior presents entirely inadequate for the purpose.

Annual khillats for the Mirs of Hunza and Nagar are Rs. 300 each and those of the Governors about Rs. 200 each only. The articles purchased for presentation for the above amounts are very inferior and, in my opinion, compare very unfavourably with those I have seen presented elsewhere and with them it is increasingly difficult to satisfy local opinion.

I therefore request that sanction of the Government of India for increase in their contribution to the above grant making it equal to that of His Highness' Government, viz. Rs. 3,500 be obtained for next financial year.[39]

In response, the GOI agreed to increase the monetary allocation to the Gilgit Agent for such monetary expenditure:

The Resident in Kashmir has supported a request from the Political Agent, Gilgit, for the enhancement of his annual grant for 'Durbar Presents' from Rs. 2000 to Rs. 3,500.

Papers showing the original grant on this account are not traceable. The provision under the head 'Durbar Presents' appears to have been fixed at Rs. 2,000 in the Gilgit Agency budget for the year 1898-99 (the amount having been Rs. 1,000 prior to that year) from when it appears to have remained unaltered. This represented that prices have risen since then and more is now required in the way of hospitality to official travellers etc. than when the grant was fixed and this may easily be admitted. When compared with the British Trade Agent, Gyantse's allotment of Rs. 4,000 for a similar purpose the request for an increase in the Gilgit Agency allotment does not appear to be unreasonable. The principles mentioned at (1) and (2) of para. 2 of the P.U.C. also carry weight although we need not necessarily follow the Kashmir State in this respect. The proposal may accordingly be recommended to the Finance Department for favourable consideration.[40]

That, the request for the increase in the Darbar grant was given favourable approval and the demand was considered reasonable, was evidence that even till the late 1920s, the requirements of the agency were given due weightage. Further, this was an example of the Gilgit Agent continuing to wield significant geopolitical clout and influence on grounds of the diplomatic significance of his position.

As mentioned earlier, in the aftermath of the Third Anglo-Afghan War, the Gilgit Agency was getting reoriented towards the events in Chinese Turkestan with the diversion of cipher traffic from Kashgar to India via the Gilgit Agent. The Russian Revolution would raise concerns about the spread of communism to China, especially in Chinese Turkestan or Sinkiang. The civil war in China had led to political instability in the country and by 1927, the GOI was becoming increasingly concerned about the spread of 'Bolshevism' into Sinkiang. This is clearly reflected in the following, very detailed report on Chinese Turkestan by Col. Schomberg*:

* Col. Reginald Charles Schomberg was an officer in the British Indian Army and travelled extensively in Central Asia.

The following notes were taken during a journey made in July, August and September 1926, in Chinese Turkestan. The area visited included the Pamirs in Chinese Territory as far North as Bulunkul, the towns of Kashgar, Yarkand and Yangi Hissar, and the adjacent country. No opportunity was lost to collect such information as might be useful.

It will be observed that the report refers frequently to the activities of the Russian Bolshevists: and lays stress on the undoubtedly anti-British nature of the activities of the Soviet.

How far the hostile propaganda of this organisation constitutes a menace, or how much reliance may be laid on the threats of this anti-British camarilla would be beyond the province of this report to discuss. It is manifest, however, that in Chinese Turkestan, the officials of the U.S.S.R. both openly as well as by agents, neglect no chance of showing their dislike of Great Britain, or of vilifying in the eyes of a simple and uneducated race all acts of the British authorities, whether locally, in India, or elsewhere.[41]

The report goes on to explain the loss of Russian prestige including the loss of extra-territorial privileges in China which prevent the Soviet government from regaining its Czarist political role in the region:

Though heirs to the domains and policy of the Romanoffs, and though avid to regain the power and prestige of pre-war Russia, the Bolshevists have wholly failed to establish themselves in the confidence of either the inhabitants of Chinese Turkestan or of the Chinese officials. Apart from the general ill-repute of the Soviet, there are four local factors which hamper the Russians in regaining their former position:

(a) The loss of extra territoriality

This privilege was voluntarily relinquished by the U.S.S.R. and their nationals in China suffer in consequence. No Russian subject is safe from the primitive methods of Chinese administration, and action is even taken against members of the Soviet Consulates.

Formerly no Chinese official dare touch any Russian subject.

(b) The absence of a Consular Guard

In the old days Kashgar was practically in Russian occupation There were some 500 troops and at times more, as a guard to the Consul General. Now there is no guard over the consulate as the Soviet has lost its right to one. The

British have preserved their right although for reasons of economy, advantage has not been taken of it. The contrast however, is less great than in the case of Russia whose display of armed force used to overawe the Chinese in pre-war times.

(c) The Russian Imperial rouble note

There is hardly anyone in Chinese Turkestan that does not possess these notes. The Government as such, has large numbers. Merchants have quantities. Indeed traders were accustomed deliberately to get rid of their gold as the Russian note was less conspicuous and more portable.

The whole country now finds that this paper is valueless. The resentment is considerable and the Chinese authorities often urge the Bolshevists to recognize the old notes, even at a discount.

This the Soviet consistently declines to do. Thus there is a fruitful source of friction, as the Turkis and Chinese cannot stomach the loss of the large sums held by them in Imperial paper. The fact too, that the Bolshevist are always pushing their own notes, further exasperates the people of Sinkiang.

(d) The personnel of the Consulate

The Russians at the bolshevist Consulates appear ill-mannered and boorish, and make a lot of enemies wholly unnecessarily as Orientals set great store by good manners, here conspicuously absent.

These four causes are a handicap to Soviet activities. So much so that it does not pay to be a Russian subject nowadays in Sinkiang. The Soviet, however, strive to regain the old Russian influence and use methods that the imperial regime would never have tolerated. Thus, Russia is trying to establish herself by intrigue, bribery and misrepresentation which make action against her difficult.

This report shows some of the means that the U.S.S.R. adopts to destroy Britain as a rival and leave a clear field for Bolshevist enterprise.[42]

This rather detailed perspective of the contemporary conditions in Kashgar by Col. Schomberg goes on to express concerns that the Bolsheviks' attempt to influence populations much closer to the Indian frontier near the Wakhan corridor:

The Bolshevists are said to be anxious to win over the Moulai sect of Shiah Mohamedans. These people inhabit the Chinese Pamirs South of Tashkurghan, the state of Hunza in the Gilgit Agency, the extreme Northern end of Afghan Wakhan, and some areas in Russian Territory—viz. Shighnan. The Spiritual head of this sect is H.H. the Aga Khan.[43]

More importantly, is that the principal body through which this sensitive region was being monitored and accessed was the Gilgit Agency. This clear elaborated in the following paragraph from the document:

> There is no European doctor nearer than Gilgit: communication with India is by Chinese wireless only as the telegraph at Misgar is ten days away runner and there are no amenities to counterbalance the remoteness and isolation of the Consulate. Mail communication with India is by runner to Gilgit: and from its nature is not reliable. The Kashgar mail bag is made up in Gilgit. A sealed bag of mail for Kashgar should be prepared to Srinagar, Kashmir, and correspondence from Gilgit sent in a supplementary bag. (Note on Chinese Turkistan by Colonel Schomberg, Government of India, Foreign and Political, External, No. 583-X, Secret, 1927).

The Russian currency did not have any worth, the Russian traders were bereft of their preferential trading rights and the Russian people stripped of their extraterritorial privileges and this led to collapse of trade in Central Asia. This was clearly seen as an opportunity which had to be leveraged to the benefit of British interests, and Gilgit was seen as the most suitable node for this purpose owing to its geographical position.

> The most important point, and the one point on which all depends is the opening of the route via Gilgit and the Pamirs. At present it takes 65 days via Leh for goods to reach Kashgar from railhead: and this under favourable conditions. Via Gilgit goods could reach Kashgar from Havelian (N.W. Railway) in 40 days, with only two passes as against six to cross.[44]

Col. Schomberg had asserted in his report, that the GOI had as a matter of policy closed the route via Gilgit for military-strategic reasons which had affected trade to Kashgar adversely. In response, the Gilgit Agent clarified that the Gilgit route was not closed for trade, but that the decision had been taken to not develop the road infrastructure for strategic reasons:

> The Gilgit route to Sinkiang is open to traders, the rules restricting the number who use this route referring only to European travellers and sportsmen. The insuperable obstacle to trade has always been considered to be natural difficulties of the route and for this reason probably, it was decided to encourage trade via the Leh Yarkand route, vide Treaty No. CXXXVI (Aitchison's Treaties).

Furthermore, it has been the policy of the Government of India not to improve communications along the Gilgit Frontier. The route beyond Baltit is only a mountain track, maintained by the Mir of Hunza, for which he receives a subsidy of Rs. 1,000 per annum.[45]

In the course of his response, the Political Agent further made reference to an earlier 1896 report by Capt. S.H. Godfrey on the Gilgit Agency regarding trade to Central Asia:

Please also refer to Captain Godfrey's Report on the Gilgit Agency, 1896-7, revised by Major B.E.M. Gurdon, Political Agent in Gilgit, 1906, page 132 where under the heading 'Trade' he writes as follows:

The route leading from Hunza to Chinese Turkistan is not popular with traders owing to the difficult nature of the country.

Captain Godfrey noted in 1896 that 'there seems to be a great opening for the development of Central Asian Trade', but it has been deemed inadvisable on political grounds to improve communications in little Gujhal, and it is extremely doubtful whether much progress will ever be made in this direction. The country is probably, one of the most difficult in the whole world, and, even if the existing tracks were improved, the almost entire absence of grazing would prevent an insuperable obstacle to the passage of large caravans.[46]

The GOI had, by the mid-1920s, taken a policy decision to support the then government in Sinkiang to prevent Bolshevism from taking hold. In order to accomplish this and the given poor conditions of the roads from Gilgit to Kashgar. The GOI had to carry out a suitability assessment of the various routes to Kashgar from India:

So it is in India's interest to support the existing regime in Sinkiang, which appears to be the only alternative. . . . Our best policy would appear to be to foster the trade connection by improvement of the trade routes. This can be done on the Indian side; on the Chinese nothing will be done. The improvement of communications will facilitate both attack and defence, but the advantage will still lie with the defence.

The Karakoram route (A) is incapable of much improvement: it is destitute of supplies, physically very difficult, and of the most difficult portion much lies in Chinese territory.

There are two other possible routes: (B) from railhead at Dargai through Dir and Chitral to the Baroghil and Wakhjir passes and thence via Tashkurghan to Kashgar and Yarkand; (C) from railhead at Havelian (possibly before long at Mansehra) over the Bahusar pass to Gilgit and thence via the Hunza valley and Kilik pass to Tashkurghan, etc.[47]

Further, there was a major debate over the closure of the route from Gilgit to Kashgar via Hunza owing to 'strategic' or military reasons, for the concern that any improvement in road infrastructure for the purpose of trade would increase the military vulnerability of the region to a future attack by the Union of Soviet Socialist Republics (USSR):

> As regards the strategical importance of not improving this road, as far as I have been able to ascertain since I have been in Gilgit, military authorities seem to be of opinion that no improvements that are at all feasible would ever induce an enemy to consider that route. Apart from the state of the road there are other insuperable difficulties such as climate, shortness of the open season, distance from base-scarcity of local supplies-ease with which a force could be held up.[48]

Nevertheless, after significant discussions, it was decided that supply issues would make the route via Gilgit unsuitable for trade with Kashgar especially owing to most of the supplies being used up by the military garrison in Gilgit itself:

> If the Indian trader in Kashgar considered that they still have a chance of retaining their position in certain articles and if our commercial standing there is of considerable importance, then I think there would be no harm whatever in modifying the policy of 1902 to a certain extent.
>
> Apart from the strategical policy there are other difficulties which have prevented an expansion of trade by this route. The chief perhaps is that of supplies.
>
> In Gilgit there is a considerable garrison which consumes most of the local supplies up to the Nagir border. From Hunza and Nagir nothing except a few sheep are purchased.[49]

In response, the GOI to Resident of Kashmir, Lt Col. G.D. Ogilvie,* communicated its concurrence, that the expenditure necessary to throw open the route through Gilgit would not be advisable and that the route through Leh in Ladakh, of which Baltistan is a contiguous extension of, would offer better possibilities for a trade route to Kashgar:

*Lt Col. Sir George Drummond Ogilvie was an officer in the British Indian Army and also served in the Indian Political Service as Chief Commissioner and Agent of the Governor General in Rajputana.

The Government of India concur in the view that the expenditure which would be necessary to throw open the Abbottabad-Babusar-Chilas-Gilgit route to regular trade would not be justified by results, and that the best method to assist Indian trade with Sinkiang is to improve the Leh-Karakoram route in the manner suggested by Howell to the Kashmir Darbar. They also agree that, if the Mirs are willing to provide the necessary facilities, the experiment might be tried of permitting traders desirous of using the Gilgit route in its present condition to do so.[50]

While the issue of trade was taking primacy, another important issue that was raised by the Chinese Governor of Chinese Turkistan and Col. Schomberg was the supply of arms and ammunition to Sinkiang. This was another facet of a new rivalry between Britain and the USSR, the other being the newly emerging trade competition between Britain and USSR in Central Asia. These geopolitical rivalries, were the early markers of a new Cold War between the West and the USSR, more than a decade before the commencement of the Second World War. Examples of these early tensions between the east and west are clearly visible in this official communication from the Consul Gen. at Kashgar:

Schomber had two very friendly interviews with him (new Governor, Chinese Turkistan) in both of which he raised the question of the arms and ammunition which were asked for by his predecessor two years ago [Serial Nos. (39) and (40) in File No. 364-X of 1925].

In his first letter, dated the 21 September, he says: 'We discussed several things (1) Rifles. He is most anxious to obtain rifles which his predecessor asked for. He said he had seen the correspondence, and that there was no reason why he should not be supplied with them. The country was not at war. There was nothing in the supply of these arms against the league of Nations or international law. He prefaced his remarks by saying that he had been offered arms and small arms and ammunition by the U.S.S.R. He had declined the offer, and I see no reason to doubt the truth of what he said. He was most anxious and emphatic about these guns. He asks that delivery be made at Yarkand and that on no account should any arms be sent to or via Kashgar'.

The reason of his not wishing the arms to come to Kashgar is that the Taoyin is a Tungan, of whom the Chinese are at present very much afraid. The Governor clearly is not prepared to trust the Taoyin very far.[51]

The Taoyin, was an administrative official, meaning 'Civil Administrator' of the city of Kashgar;[52] the term 'Tungan' or 'Dungan' refers to Chinese Muslims from north-western Sinkiang. This requirement to provide arms to Sinkiang before the Soviets again brought to the fore the strategic significance of the Gilgit Agency as well as Leh, both of which were oriented towards Sinkiang. Further, there were concerns, if some of the rifles being delivered might find their way back to Gilgit, thereby complicating the military situation for the British:

For the Governor has made a bare-faced attempt to bounce us into giving more than twice as much as we said we would, and if we resist that, he is more likely to feel resentment than gratitude. Apart from that the Russians have almost as much right to feel the same way about this action on our part, as we should if they sent the same quantity of munitions to Sistan. And, a comparatively minor matter, if the rifles find their way into Hunza and Nagar, as might well happen, we should find the Gilgit Agency a very much harder place to manage than it is now.[53]

Nevertheless, there were difficult challenges involved in transporting heavy goods through Gilgit, which in the absence of any rail or road network, had to be carried out using draft animals:

Wakefield told me some interesting facts communicated to him by General Janak Singh who was in Gilgit at the time of the troubles in Swat in 1897. At that time there was a Rajput regiment of Indian infantry at Gilgit and Government thought it necessary to send up considerable quantities of additional rifles and ammunition to them. Owing to the crushing nature of loads composed of such heavy things, the ponies which were carrying these perished in large numbers and the whole road was dotted with clumps of sepoys on guard over portions of the consignment which could not be moved until fresh ponies had been obtained.[54]

Finally, the GOI agreed to use the route through Gilgit in addition to primary route through Leh to supply Sinkiang:

The Government of India would be glad to be furnished with your views as to the possibility of dispatching a second possible smaller consignment of arms and ammunition by Gilgit route this year. Such a course if practicable would relieve the strain on transport on the Karakoram route and would probably be cheaper.[55]

Further, in addition to playing a central role in any trade and transport to Sinkiang, the Gilgit Agency was to play an important function in an exploration expedition beyond Leh, led by Mr. P.C. Visser and accompanied by Lt. G.C. Clark and Maj. Thomas William Corbett in 1928. This exploratory visit to Sinkiang was reminiscent of such 'exploratory expeditions' which were undertaken to the Indian frontier and beyond in the late nineteenth century by British explorers. It is certainly no coincidence that these visits coincide with periods of intense geopolitical competition in the region which was now again beginning to flare up with the fear of Bolshevik expansion into the region. The GOI advised the expedition to use the Gilgit route for this trip because this trip involved permissions from the Afghan government, which made the Gilgit route more appropriate:

Please see G.S. Branch note on page 1 ante. We may inform the G.S. Branch that we do not anticipate any difficulty in procuring Chinese passports and permits to carry arms for the officers in question. As they will have to be obtained through H.M.'s Minister, Peking, however, after the views of the Consul Genl. Kashgar and Resident, Kashmir, have been obtained, the only question is of their being received in time.

The following applications to visit Chinese Turkestan during the year 1929 have so far been received:

(i) Mr. P.C. Visser wishing to lead an expedition in the early part of 1929 via Leh and the Karakorum Pass to Chinese Turkestan in order to explore unknown or little-known regions in the Karakorum, the Aghil mountains and the Kuen-Len.
(ii) Lt. G.C. Clark R.E., K.G.O., Bengal S.&M., Roorkee, accompanied by Major T.W. Corbett of Hudson's Horse, Kohat.
(iii) Mr. Frank Ludlow, I.E.S. (Retd.)

In addition to the above, the Spoleto expedition will also be using the Leh route. (F.No. 31-X of 1928). As regards (i), please see Sr. Nos. (1), (2), (8), (9) and (12) in F.No.170-X/28. The reply from the Secy. of State as to whether Visser's party have been able to secure the necessary permission from the Chinese Govt. is still awaited.

As regards (ii), both Major Corbett and Lt. Clark who are travelling together prefer to go by the Gilgit (Hunza) route and come back by the Wakhan-Chitral route. As the use of the latter route involves obtaining the Afghan Govt.'s permission these officers should stick to the Gilgit route both ways. Lt. Clark has not furnished details of the arms he proposes to take.

As regards (iii), the object of the visit is given in para 2 of Mr. Frank Ludlow's application. He wishes to go by the Karakorum route but would like to return by the Gilgit route reaching Srinagar about the middle of Sept. 1930. The Resident, Kashmir, has no objection to the proposed journey.[56]

However, the two accompanying British officers explained their visit officially as a hunting trip:

I am intending to do the trip in company with another British officer Major T.W. Corbett, of Hodson's Horse.

We hope to get three months leave, during the period 15 July to 15 October 1929, in which to proceed to the Pamirs.

The object of the trip is shikar.[57]

Naturally, such expeditions and the selection of the appropriate routes for the same was done after carefully assessing the political and logistical suitability of the route concerned. It is also abundantly clear, that while the Gilgit Agency had lost its direct connectivity with the more strategically active north-western frontier after the Chitral imbroglio, it continued to play an active role in the defence of British India and providing access to Central Asia. The level of activity in the Gilgit Agency would ebb or intensify with the change in the political scenario in Central Asia, it is undeniable that the Gilgit Agency and Ladakh would remain strategically sensitive territories. It is because of Gilgit's strategic significance gaining strength only because of the increasing Soviet presence in the neighbourhood as well as Japanese actions in Manchuria, that the British administration was desirous of maintaining a more direct control over the region than had been possible through just a Political Agent.

THE DOMESTIC SITUATION IN KASHMIR

Following the demise of Pratap Singh in 1925, his nephew Hari Singh, son of Amar Singh ascended the throne at the age of 35 as per the expectations of the British. The scenario started to change soon and the British realized that Hari Singh could not be easily managed. Maharaja Hari Singh started asserting his authority, becoming a bone of contention for the British. Hari Singh replaced

British Indian Army troops in Gilgit Agency with state troops and restored the jurisdiction of state courts over state subjects and Indian visitors. The British and the Maharaja were in a confrontation.[58] Not only this, he pushed for a series of social, agricultural, administrative and judicial reforms which could be considered progressive for his time. To mention some, his reforms included setting up a minimum age for marriage, prohibiting the practice of older men marrying much younger girls, removing the ban on remarriage for young Hindu widows, providing untouchables with access to public services and public places, especially state-owned temples and eradicating the infanticide of girls, which was particularly prevalent among Rajputs. Reforms in education included reservations for Muslims, scholarships to make education more affordable, an increase in the number of primary schools, and compulsory education for children.[59]

Hari Singh imposed restrictions on non-hereditary state subjects regarding the acquisition of real estate and the appointment to jobs in the civil service was also significant. Hereditary state subjects were those who had moved to J&K before 1885, according to legal definitions from 1927. The Englishmen perceived this as a setback that would eventually lead to them losing job possibilities at the higher levels of public service (Kaul 2009: 352). His acts of defiance were mostly symbolic, but they led to quite significant confrontations with the British. In a climactic moment, Hari Singh delivered an address on the future Constitution of India to the First Round Table Conference in London in 1930, in which he identified himself as sharing the aspirations of the Indian people:

> As Indians and loyal to the land whence we derive our birth and infant nurture, we stand as solidly as the rest of our countrymen for our land's enjoyment of a position of honour and equality in the British Commonwealth of Nations.[60]

Throughout the address, Hari Singh stressed 'the communal harmony in his state as a living example of how Hindus and Muslims could live peacefully as brethren'.[61] By this point, the British goal was to exert enough pressure on the Maharaja to make him relinquish his rule over all of Gilgit. Nevertheless, in July

1931 communal riots broke out in Srinagar. It is a debated topic as to what exactly triggered the conflict. As per Maharaj Kaul, this was British orchestrated but an equally divisive role was played by the Islamic extremists in it. He writes under the heading 'British Engineered Communal Violence':

> With an uncooperative Maharaja, the British found it difficult to achieve their goals easily in Gilgit. They, therefore, chose to use the communal weapon, having already effectively employed it in the Provinces of British India to disrupt the freedom movement led by the Congress party. In their efforts, they found a willing ally named Sheikh Mohammed Abdullah. (Kaul 2009: 353)

An extensive and fierce propaganda campaign against the Maharaja's rule was let loose from Lahore and other cities of Punjab by the Muslim press. Leaflets and journals containing stories of the deliberate suppression of Muslims in the state were distributed in thousands among the people, instigating them to rise against the Maharaja who, it was alleged, was dominated by his Hindu officers—The state government, according to the authors of the propaganda literature. was entirely Hindu and determined to keep the Muslim majority in perpetual serfdom. The Anglo-Indian press joined the chorus of denunciation of the Maharaja and his government. Jammu being nearer to Punjab was the first to be affected by this propaganda.

In December 1930, the All-Kashmir Muslim Conference founded a few years earlier, held the annual session in Lahore which was attended by some young men from Jammu who, on their return to the state, embarked upon a campaign of agitation against the government. This excited the Muslim residents of Jammu city and adjoining villages. A few unfortunate incidents pertaining to the reading of the Khutba by a Maulvi and the disrespect shown to the holy Quran by a police constable were seized upon by the agitators and the cry 'Islam in danger' was raised.[62] Inflammatory posters were prepared by the Jammu-based Young Men's Muslim Association; the Muslim Reading Room in Srinagar lent additional support to their activities. After completing his MSc degree from Aligarh Muslim University Sheikh Abdullah returned to Kashmir in 1930. As an active member of the Reading Room Party, Sheikh Abdullah was responsible for organizing mammoth meetings of Muslims in various mosques and delivering fiery speeches exposing the hardships and the depressed condition of the people. Communal tension reached the flash point and it needed only a spark to explode. The spark was supplied by the arrest and trial in Srinagar of one Abdul Qadir an agent provocateur, who had come to Kashmir in the service of a European visitor as a cook.

On 21 June 1931, he made a speech at a meeting held in the precincts of the *khanaqah* of Shah Hamadan. The speech was considered by the government as seditious. He was arrested and his trial in the court of the Sessions Judge provoked the Muslim public greatly and huge crowds assembled in and outside the court on the days of the hearing. Consequently, it was decided to hold the trial in the Srinagar Central Jail. While the court was in session, a crowd of 4,000-5,000 people that had collected outside the jail, raised slogans demanding the withdrawal of the case against Qadir and made a rush to the gate of the jail. Their progress was halted by a posse of police. Angered at this the crowd pelted the police with stones. Meanwhile, the prisoners in the jail became restive. Telephone wires were cut. The district magistrate thereupon ordered the armed police to open fire on the crowd. Twenty-one persons died and many more were wounded (Bamzai 1994: 731).

The news of this incident spread like a forest fire. Hari Singh additionally retaliated with draconian arrests, detentions, floggings and, in some cases, additional shootings. Pro-Muslim organizations also demonstrated in Jammu Province as the discontent spread there. To support the Maharaj and re-establish law and order, the British dispatched three companies of armed troops (a total of about 500 soldiers). The rebellion in 1931 had intensified.[63] Indeed, it 'was possibly the most serious communal outbreak in India between the Moplah rebellion (in southern India) of 1921 and the Calcutta riots of 1946'.[64] Maharaj Kaul argues that this communal conflict was engineered by the British to destabilize the rule of Maharaja Hari Singh, tarnish his credibility and compel him to approach the British Indian government for help. And this is what happened.

THE PROBLEMS OF 'DUAL CONTROL'

The internal and external situation with respect to the Gilgit Frontier was increasingly making taking decisions more challenging. On the advice of the Government of India, the Maharaja had appointed Col. E.J.D. Colvin, an officer of the Government of India, the prime minister of the state. E.J.D. Colvin had multiple motives while becoming the prime minister of the state on 22 February 1932. Two more officials of the Indian Civil Service had been inducted into the state ministry and put in charge of the home affairs and finance. Colvin was a committed civil service official. He had been sent to fulfil more than one commission in the state. Besides being deputed to tighten the control over the administration of the Maharaja and stabilize the political situation in the state, he was entrusted with the arduous task of securing British control over Gilgit and the rest of the northern frontier of the state. The fast-changing patterns of relationships in Asia, particularly after the invasion of Manchuria by the Japanese, had given the northern frontier of the state, the importance it never had before. The Russian frontiers which sprawled menacingly close to the borders of the state continued to pose a serious threat to the British Colonial interests in India. Gilgit and its adjoining territories remained undefended, and it was in this backdrop, that Colvin succeeded in persuading the Maharaja to hand over Gilgit to the British.[65]

By 1933, the British had implemented numerous changes, including those in the social, educational, and administrative fields, while still allowing the former princely regions to run their affairs without interference. It was during this time that the Soviet Union's influence continued to expand in Central Asia. Earlier in 1926, monetary allowances were added and the rations were slightly increased for the Gilgit Scouts so that they could purchase shoes, but more importantly to counter the increasingly growing Bolshevik influence in the frontier regions. The Soviet socialist model, which the Russians were using to attempt and influence people from the other side of the Hindu Kush Range had already got a significant foothold in Central Asia such as Sinkiang as has already been explained earlier.

The Gilgit territory was technically a part of the princely state of J&K and while the Political Agent was a British official there, the Kashmir state had its own official known as the Wazir-i-Wazarat who did not report to the Agent but rather to the Maharaja of Kashmir. As such, they represented a parallel system of authority (Chohan 1997: 218). Naturally, this did nothing to strengthen British freedom of action in the Agency and by the 1930s, the arrangement had become inconvenient, especially for the Kashmir Darbar who while having parallel officials in the territory, found themselves unable to challenge any British decisions.[66] On the official level, there were conversations about how to develop a more effective plan to eliminate dual control. A letter from Lt. Col. Elliot James Dowell Colvin, the then prime minister of J&K, to L.E. Lang, the Resident in Kashmir, conveyed the change in the situation.

The Agency had continued to be completely under the control of the Political Agent during the early decades of the twentieth century and he was responsible to the GOI through the British Resident in Kashmir, while Gilgit remained under the control of state officials. Gilgit Wazarat included a portion of the right bank of the Indus River that extended to the south of the Gilgit and Hunza rivers and included Gilgit Tehsil, whose civil administration was managed by state officials. A strange and at times complex configuration called 'dual control' evolved due to this sharing of responsibilities between the state and the British Indian government and it grew rather intricate.

This issue of 'dual control' was undoubtedly worrying the Political Agent, and he desired to get rid of the state governments in the light of the 'Russian menace'. He wrotes:

> The imperial considerations relating to the safety of India as a whole which necessitated the establishment of the Agency in Gilgit in the latter half of the last century have materially changed and the danger of a foreign invasion of India from that direction has been considerably minimized, or, indeed, ceased to exist.[67]

Due to the formation of the Soviet Union in 1922, the British were concerned about the Soviet Expansion into South-east and Central Asia. Regions of present-day countries like Uzbekistan, Kyrgyzstan (then Kirghiz), and Tajikistan were parts of the USSR and it brought USSR very close to the Gilgit Baltistan region, which was and is still considered an essential strategic position as a doorway to Central Asia and South Asia through the Wakhan corridor.

Consequently, the Kashmir Darbar gave two proposals to the GOI to resolve this difficult situation. The first was that the British administration under the Political Agent be withdrawn from the Gilgit Frontier and the responsibility for the military defence and the civilian administration of the Agency be transferred to the State of J&K. The second proposal was that the entire civilian administrative establishment of the princely state and its troops be entirely withdrawn from the frontier and these responsibilities, in turn, be taken over by the GOI. The British government in this scenario would have to establish its political and military control over the districts and portions of the Gilgit Wazarat which was to the north of the Indus River.

It was believed, that by adopting any of these two proposals, the difficulties arising out of dual control would be eliminated (Dani 1991: 216). In response to these proposals, the Resident of Kashmir, asked the Political Officer in Gilgit about his views regarding these two proposals. The Political Officer responded by saying that it would be extremely difficult to ensure the submission of the Mirs of Hunza and Nagar as long as the Kashmir officials were present and continued to interfere in the working of the agency. The continued submission of these two territories was essential to the British frontier policy and any withdrawal of the British authority would ensure some nature of disturbance on this frontier.

Consequently, it was the recommendation of the agent that the second option of including the trans-Indus portion of the Gilgit-Wazarat under the direct control of the Agency and the removal of all the Kashmir state troops from the region was the preferable course of action. This would essentially eliminate all problems arising out of dual control and interference from the Darbar in the political affairs of the Mirs and other minor frontier principalities. The Resident of Kashmir extended his support to this suggestion by the Gilgit Agent and this recommendation was then forwarded to the Government of India.[68]

Finally, a conference was held on 22 September 1934 at the Residency in Srinagar, where Metcalfe, the Secretary to the Government of India, Foreign Department, the Resident in Kashmir and Majors Gillan and Kirkbride, who were the former and future Political Agents of the Gilgit Agency, were present. At this conference, it was decided that the GOI would take over the trans-Indus portion of the Gilgit Wazarat and that there would be a formal agreement to this effect with the Kashmir government (Chohan 1997: 219).

The agreement was signed on 26 March 1935 by the then Maharaja of Kashmir, Hari Singh and the Resident in Kashmir Col. L.E. Lang. This agreement would subsequently be ratified on 3 April 1935 by Lord Willingdon who was the Viceroy and Governor Gen. of India. Under this agreement, the British were given a 60-year lease over the territory of the entire state which was on the north of the Indus River, until 1995. The state then withdrew all of the Imperial Service personnel stationed in the Agency and gave the Scouts control of the defence and security of the Agency. The State Flag had to be flown over the leased out region, though the area was still part of the state. In addition, the British pledged to honour the Maharaja on special occasions like his birthday. But the state still held the rights to the mines.[69]

On 1 August 1935 at Gilgit, the Wazir-e-Wazarat, Rao Rattan Singh, handed over control of the leased area to the Political Agent, Maj. Kirkbride, following the de-induction of all state forces, including the Imperial Service Troops, from the region. Currently, Bunji was home to the closest post of the state forces. Direct British control over the territory would make the Gilgit Scouts far more important in the defence of the northern frontier, now that state troops had been entirely withdrawn from the territory. Therefore, the government instructed Col. C.E.T.

Erskine, inspecting officer of the Frontier Corps, to examine the Scouts in October 1935 and report on them along with any suggestions for improvement. Although the officer's report was critical, many of the recommendations he made later resulted in the reorganization of the Scouts. The companies were disbanded and a platoon-based organizational structure was implemented in 1937. Fifty men made up each platoon, which was led by a *subedar* who was a local. There were 11 platoons in total, and each soldier was equipped with a rifle. Additionally, each platoon was equipped with automatic firearms. Again, a native and regarded as the Commandant's closest counsellor, the Subedar Major oversaw the headquarter platoon of the Scouts. Aside from these individuals, the headquarters also featured a Jemadar Adjutant, Jemadar Quarter Master, drill instructors, a signals detachment, bandsmen, buglers, radio personnel, orderlies and a small number of civilian employees. The Scouts engaged in their first armed encounter in September 1938 when they killed four members of a hostile tribe without suffering any fatalities. Despite the action having a military component, every effort was taken to maintain the status of the force as a civilian armed force. The Political Agent was also in charge of the promotions of the Scouts and other similar procedures.

THE STATUS OF GILGIT AFTER THE LEASE

Meanwhile, the Government of India, having taken direct control of the region as a leased territory, began to refer to it as a 'centrally administered area'. However, this soon began to cause difficulties, because technically the ownership of the territory lay with the State of J&K which was the lessor, while the British government was the lessee. This was clarified by the following decision by the Government of India:

> Political Department are of opinion that the term 'Centrally administered areas' must now be confined to areas under the control of the Central Government, which does not include the Crown Representative. All administered areas in Indian States are controlled by the Crown Representative.[70]

Further, it was elaborated that:

> The above decision is for D.S.F.'s information. It is understood that the Gilgit Agency is an administered area in the State of J&K and is controlled by the Crown Representative. The fact that on considerations of administrative convenience and practical necessity the External Affairs Department of the Central Government have been authorised to exercise in it the functions of the Crown Representative does not bring it within the purview of the term 'Centrally administered areas'. The Political Department may, however, be asked kindly to confirm this.[71]

After the GOI Act of 1935, the Indian princely states were given the option of joining the Indian Federation, if they so opted to. It is quite clear from the available documents that there was already concern in the GOI about the implications for the British Frontier policy, if the princely state of J&K chose to join the Indian Federation. The British were particularly concerned about their control over the region of Hunza, Chilas, Nagar, Koh Ghizar, Ishkuman and Yasin in such an event:

> I understand that not long-ago Kashmir made over to us the complete administration of Gilgit for a period of 60 years. This administration falls since 1st April 1937 to the Crown Representative but he has authorised the External Affairs Department to act as his agents.
>
> I think we should ask the External Affairs Department to let us have their views on the question of a declaration under section 294 (1). The effect of such a declaration is clear from the terms of the section, but we may explain that if no declaration is made the effect will be that while the Crown Representative will by virtue of the existing agreement with Kashmir retain exclusive legislative and administrative authority in non-federal matters and exclusive Civil and Criminal jurisdiction in all matters, federal and non-federal, he will lose his existing legislative and administrative authority in federal matters. This will go to the Federation but the Ruler of Kashmir will or may have concurrent powers in this field which could be outside by the Federation only and not by the Crown Representative. Administrative functions conferred upon the Ruler and his officers under Section 124 or Section 124 or section 125 of the Act with respect to a federal law would or might extend to the administration of that law in the Gilgit Agency and the Crown Representative could not interfere.[72]

The British were therefore concerned, that the legal consequences of a decision by the princely state of J&K might impede their control over the frontier. It is also important to observe that this document attempts to explain how parts of the territory on lease to the British are actually not a part of the princely state of J&K:

The constitutional position of these tracts seem as follows:

(a) is an administered area in an Indian State the Civil and Military Administration of which has been taken over by the Paramount Power for a period of 60 years from 1935;
(b) though under the suzerainty of Kashmir the powers and jurisdiction in these countries, with the exception of Hunza and Nagar who manage their own affairs, vests in the Political Officers of the Paramount Power;
(c) though Darel has paid an annual tribute to Kashmir the Tangir has no relations with it.[73]

The payment of tribute was used as the principle of acceptance of suzerainty of J&K by the minor principalities. Nevertheless, this note explains that despite Darel, which was a part of the Tangir region in south-western Gilgit paying an annual tribute to the Kashmir Darbar, was not a part of J&K. However, later in a different note from the same document, Mr. Griffin from the Political Department, named various territories of J&K which gave an annual tribute to the Kashmir Darbar and were therefore under the suzerainty of J&K, but emphasized that they were not territories of J&K:

The position in regard to the political Districts of Hunza, Nagar, Chilas, Koh Ghizar, Yasin, Ashkuman and Punial does not appear to be quite clear for the purpose of a declaration under section 294 (1). It is stated in previous discussions, that though these areas are under the suzerainty of Kashmir, (Kashmir Durbar receive annual tributes from all these areas except Punial) they are not territories of the Kashmir State and State officials are not permitted to interfere in the internal administration of these territories. Criminal jurisdiction in these areas with the exception of Hunza and Nagar vests in the Political Agent in Gilgit and his Assistants. With regards to Hunza and Nagar it was stated that these two areas though under the suzerainty of Kashmir managed their affairs most admirably, it was not proposed that the Political Agent or his Assistant should exercise criminal jurisdiction within their borders.[74]

Earlier, Mr Hay from the External Affairs Department (EAD) had highlighted the absolute strategic importance of the Gilgit frontier and by implication had revealed the British interests in the territory:

The Gilgit agency is a vulnerable position of India adjoining the Russian, Chinese and Afghan borders. It has now no regulars and therefore depends on locals for its defence. It is essential therefore that in peace time the Political Agent should have actual authority, where in war-time he will have responsibility, in order that he may be able to gain the confidence of the people, to establish and maintain a standard of administration which will ensure their loyalty and to acquire control over the resources of the country. In order to attain this desideratum, it seems necessary to retain its existing administrative arrangements. How such desiderata can best be secured for us vis-a-vis the new constitutional changes in India is for the Political Department to decide.[75]

At this stage it would be appropriate to point out that Darel and Tangir, bordered the North-Western Frontier Province in the south and south-west. Further, it was pointed out in the same note of 29 February 1938 from the Political Department that Darel and Tangir should be classified as 'tribal territories', thereby allowing them to be classified as separate territory from that of J&K:

Darel and Tangir do not appear to be within the dominions of Kashmir, but probably in view of the fact that a small tribute is received by the Kashmir Durbar annually from Darel through the Raja of Punial and the Political Agent, Gilgit, the Durbar considers this territory to be under their suzerainty. The External Affairs Department, however, are of the opinion that Darel and Tangir having been definitely held, to be tribal territories, no declaration with regard to them should be made. We may agree.[76]

The Political Department, was also very particular to make sure, that the territories north of the Indus in the Gilgit Agency and those classified as 'tribal territories' should not be considered under section 294 (1) of the GOI Act, 1935, even though it would be acceptable for the remaining parts of the princely state of J&K to be considered under it:

We agree that a declaration under section 294 (1) of the Government of India Act, 1935 at any rate so far as the Gilgit Sub-Division is concerned, will be desirable if Kashmir accedes to the Federation. With regard to the remaining parts of the Agency, it is considered that great care will have to be exercised as any declaration made in respect of them will amount to an acknowledgement that they form part of Kashmir. With regard to Darel and Tangir in connection with the preparation of a map the Political Department agreed that they should be regarded as tribal territory, vide para. 1 of their note at page 5 on File No. 432-G.37. Presumably therefore they should be treated as tribal areas under the Government of India Act, 1935 and should not be mentioned in any declaration under section 294 (1).[77]

The reason that so much caution was being warned against classifying the mentioned regions under section 294 (1) of the 1935 Act and all effort was being made to make sure that politico-legal grounds be prepared to show these regions as not being a part of J&K State, would be clearer once one looks at the necessary section:

294. (1) Neither the executive authority of the jurisdiction. Federation nor the legislative power of the Federal Legislature shall extend to any area in a Federated State which His Majesty in signifying his acceptance of the Instrument of Accession of that State may declare to be an area theretofore administered by or on behalf of His Majesty to which it is expedient that the provisions of this subsection should apply, and references in this Act to a Federated State shall not be construed as including references to any such area:

Provided that—

(a) a declaration shall not be made under this subsection with respect to any area unless, before the execution by the Ruler of the Instrument of Accession, notice has been given to him of His Majesty's intention to make that declaration;
(b) if His Majesty with the assent of the Ruler of the State relinquishes his powers and jurisdiction in relation to any such area or any part of any

> such area, the foregoing provisions of this subsection shall cease to apply to that area or part, and the executive authority of the Federation and the legislative power of the Federal Legislature shall extend thereto in respect of such matters and subject to such limitations as may be specified in a supplementary Instrument of Accession for the State.[78]

It is therefore, clear that any reference to the trans-Indus portion of the Gilgit Agency along with other regions of interest for British frontier policy, if made under section 294 (1) of the GOI Act, 1935 would have weakened British attempts to maintain any role in the internal administration of the concerned territory. Having already prepared ground for the exclusion of the necessary territory from the territorial definition of the 'Kashmir State', it was decided as a matter of policy by the Political Department to maintain purposeful ambiguity in the wordings of the instrument of accession of J&K to the Federation of India:

> If Kashmir accedes to the Federation its accession will, according to what has so far been decided, be in the following terms:
>
> 'I (i.e., the Maharaja of Jammu and Kashmir), hereby declare that I accede to the Federation of India . . . with the intent that His Majesty the King, the Governor-General of India, the Federal Legislature, etc., shall exercise in relation to the State of Jammu and Kashmir such functions as may be invested in them by or under the Act.'
>
> There will be no mention of what is meant by the State of Jammu and Kashmir. I do not think that it is beyond the bounds of possibility that some one (not necessarily the Kashmir Darbar) might take it into his head to bring before a court the issue whether Chitral was a result of Kashmir's accession included in Federal India.[79]

The British concern, moreover, became quite evident when they realized that the argument of the frontier territories of the Gilgit Agency, not being a part of the princely state of J&K, held little ground in a court of law. This became clear from the following:

> But there can be little doubt that the Ruler of Jammu and Kashmir having acceded to the Federation for the State of Jammu and Kashmir, if the issue were brought before a Court, by the Kashmir Durbar or

otherwise, whether Chitral was as a result of Kashmir's accession included with Kashmir in Federal India, the court would, on the strength of the definition of 'Indian State' contained in Section 311 (1), hold that it was.[80]

Further, Mr Griffin from the EAD, explained that if the British did not actively get involved in Chilas, Yasin, Koh Ghizar and Ishkuman, there was a danger that the administrative machinery of the Kashmir state might make greater inroads into the regions to the detriment of British interests:

As regards Chilas, Yasin, Koh Ghizar and Ashkuman, there are other courses to be considered besides that indicated in paragraph 5 of the enclosure. One is to take action in regards to them at all. The result would be that they would automatically come into the Federation as apart of Kashmir and that a federated Kashmir, exempt in these respects from control by paramountcy, would enjoy in these areas legislative and executive authority concurrently with the Federation in matters accepted by Kashmir as federal and could exercise these such federal administrative functions as fell to it under section 124 or 125 of the Act. It is not considered desirable to allow this intrusion of Kashmir's authority and the second course would be to make a declaration under Section 294 (1) in respect of these areas. It would seem that they fulfil the criterion of areas 'theretofore administered by or on behalf of His Majesty' and that this is therefore the proper and most simple course to take. Its only disadvantage is that these areas will thus be permanently debarred from qualifying for membership of the Federation as States separate from Kashmir and the question of adopting instead the course indicated in paragraph 5 of the enclosure only arises if it is considered that these areas are at all likely in course of time to qualify for such membership in their own right.[81]

While the External and Political departments were supporting a segregation of the frontier territories from Kashmir state strongly, the British Resident at the Kashmir Darbar was of the view that these territories should be considered a part of Kashmir:

The Kashmir Government have not interfered for many years in the administration of Chilas, Yasin, Koh Ghizar and Ishkuman. The Governors—the post is not hereditary—(with the exception of Chilas which nowadays has no Governor, administer these areas subject the approval of

> the Political Agent, Gilgit, who exercises criminal jurisdiction, under the Frontier Crimes Regulation. . . . I am therefore of the opinion that, if the Kashmir State accepts Federation, all the country north of the Indus-Chilas, Yasin, Koh Ghizar—Ishkuman and Punial should be included in the boundaries of the State for the purposes of computing population, mineral rights, etc., but that for the purposes of administration control Section 294 (1) of the Government of India Act of 1935 should be applied to these areas.[82]

To summarize, the evidence available indicates that the British were concerned that they may lose their direct control of the frontier if the princely state of J&K acceded to the Federation or the issue was put to a legal test. The territory in question would include not only those areas in the Gilgit Agency but also the tributary state of Chitral which had been separated from the control of the Gilgit Agency after 1896. While, however, the princely state of Chitral had not been under lease to the British and had been separated administratively from Kashmir State for over forty years, the remaining northern territories had not been so separated. In order to ensure that British interests remained unchallenged and unimpeded, the British decided to adopt an official policy under which the frontier territories north of the Indus under the Agency would be interpreted on dubious grounds as not being a part of the territory demarcated as part of J&K State. The very fact that this region had been obtained on lease for sixty years from J&K state went contrary to the notion of Yasin, Chilas, Koh Ghizar and Ishkuman not being a part of the territory of the former.

However, there were also genuine concerns that such subjective interpretation of minor tributary principalities as not being a part of an Indian princely state could have larger connotations for other princely states in India which also had such subsidiary relations with local principalities. There could be a potential political crisis with several princely states if there were concerns that the British were trying to take over state territory based on dubious legal and historical interpretations. Consequently, a clarification was issued to princely states:

I am directed to invite your attention to the definition of 'Indian State' contained in sub-section (1) of section 311 of the Government of India Act, 1935. As a result of this definition it might well be that an Instrument of Accession executed without qualification by His Highness the Maharaja for the State of Kashmir would be held automatically to have brought the State of Chitral into the Federation on the ground that Chitral is under the suzerainty of the Ruler of Kashmir. This suzerainty is little more than nominal, Chitral being in reality independent of Kashmir, but it is a recognised fact. An acknowledgement of it will be found in condition 1 of the agreement executed by the Mehtar of Chitral on the 2 April 1914 (printed on page 428 of Aitchison's Treaties, Fifth Edition, Volume XI). Thus, in accordance with the definition the 'Indian State' of Kashmir can be held to include the State of Chitral which is under the suzerainty of His Majesty. The population of Chitral is not included in the figure of population shown against Kashmir in the Table of Seats appended to Part II of the First Schedule of the Act and the inclusion of Chitral in the scope of Kashmir's accession, which would result in a federated Kashmir enjoying in Chitral legislative and executive authority concurrently with the Federation in matters accepted as federal and also exercising there administrative functions under Section 124 or Section 125 of the Act, was of course never intended.[83]

Therefore, it becomes clear that a section of the British administration was interested in separating the frontier from the jurisdiction of the Kashmir State for maintaining direct control over the strategically important frontier, even though other British officials did not necessarily agree.

Eventually, in 1941, the Government of Kashmir referred to a Court of Arbitration, the issue of official maps not reflecting the territories of Hunza, Nagir, Chilas, Koh Ghizar, Ishkoman and Yasin as a part of Kashmir:

All turns on the decision not to notify the Kashmir Government, or the Resident, of the Secretary of State's orders regarding the relationship of Hunza, Nagir and the political Districts with Kashmir. This decision was taken on Sir B. Glancy's recommendation, and was based on the need, as he saw it, for not discouraging the Kashmir Government's war effort.[84]

It is important to observe, that in order to not discourage the contribution of the state to the British war effort during the ongoing Second World War, it was suggested that the Kashmir government and the British Resident be kept uninformed about the policy of the GOI regarding the territories of Hunza, Nagir, Chilas, Koh Ghizar, Ishkuman and Yasin. However, three days later, Mr Caroe, who wrote the above note, came to the conclusion that it had now become necessary to communicate the British position to the Kashmir Darbar.[85] He further added that:

> The fundamental question here does not relate to separate tabulation of census figures, but to the territories which do and do not form part of the Kashmir State, and that is a matter on which, as I conceive, no Court could arbitrate.[86]

This statement was an acceptance of the fact that the earlier rationale given in 1938 that a separate population census of the region meant that these regions did not comprise the territory of J&K, and this determined that the territory in question were not owned by the state. Other questions which now arose were that when this decision was communicated to the Darbar, first, would it be considered *ex parte* by the Darbar and second, would the Darbar have the right to appeal against the authority informing them of the decision. Regarding the first issue, the following was the British perspective:

> The question as to whether our decision can be construed by the Kashmir Government to be ex parte would seem to depend on whether the decision is to be communicated to them as that of the Crown Representative. If the former course is adopted they can reasonably argue that it has been arrived ex parte. If, however, it is communicated as the Crown Representative's conclusion (as the intention seems to have been) it is very doubtful whether, in view of the opportunity afforded to them to submit their point of view, they could very well put forward this plea.[87]

Regarding the second issue of arbitration, clarity was hereby provided in the following note:

The Kashmir Government cannot ask for a Court of Arbitration against a decision of the Secretary of State, if for no other reason than that it is the Secretary of State himself who is the authority to whom final appeals against decisions of such court can be made. In this connection attention is also invited to side-lined portions of notes page 8 and Correspondence page 142 in I.B. April 1921, No. 298. There seems to be no such objection, however, to a request for arbitration against the Crown Representative's decision, but even here, the discretion to accede to such a request will, under the Resolution of 1920 [S.R., September 1921. Nos 5/21], rest entirely with the Crown Representative himself. It is therefore for consideration whether the request, if and when made, should be granted.[88]

It is therefore, clear that the Darbar in reality had no recourses to challenge the unilateral British decision regarding its territorial boundaries. If the decision was communicated to the Darbar by the Crown Representative, thereby, allowing the former to challenge the British decision, it would eventually rest before the Secretary of State who could be expected to uphold the position of the Government of India.

The Government of J&K, unaware that a decision had already been reached by the British on the issue, had put across its arguments in a lengthy document prepared in 1939, as to why it had claims over the contentious, unsettled frontier districts. The rather lengthy report prepared by Mr Ram Chandra Kak, the then Chief Secretary of the J&K government, included pertinent historical and rational arguments, which at the culmination of the report were distilled in the following points:

(a) The Sikh Government of Lahore exercised some influence and control over Hunza, Nagar and the adjacent territories through their Military Commandant at Gilgit.
(b) Whatever rights the Sikhs had over these territories were transferred to Maharaja Gulabsinghji by the Treaty of Amritsar together with the territories concerned.
(c) Maharaja Gulabsinghji and his son and successor, Maharaja Ranbirsinghji extended and consolidated their territories by peaceful penetration and military conquest long before the British Government sent their officers for intelligence work to Gilgit in 1878.

(d) The extension and consolidation of the authority of the State was done without any reference to or assistance from the British Government who were bound by treaty to assist the State only in repelling external enemies.

(e) Where the extension of the State's sphere of influence beyond the territories implicitly or explicitly transferred to Maharaja Gulabsinghji by the Treaty of Amritsar was concerned, as in the case of Chitral, Dir, Bajour, Wakhan, Shignan, the Maharaja consulted the Viceroy, but he made no reference whatever to him with regard to Hunza, Nagar, etc.

(f) Not only did the State exercise direct administrative control over what are the component parts of the Gilgit Agency, but it exercised considerable administrative authority over even Chitral.

(g) The first time the Agency was established at Gilgit it was established with the Maharaja's consent and was intended purely for intelligence work.

(h) The second time the Agency was established, the object was primarily to organise the defence of the frontier in view of the Russian menace. The rebellion of Hunza and Nagar, which followed the tightening up of the control on the frontier, was put down by the State troops commanded by State officers who in many cases were accompanied and advised by British officers, though in some cases they achieved victory alone. The British officers were there for the purpose of organising the defence of the frontier which was that of the Indian Empire as well as of the State.

(i) The disturbance caused by Hunza and Nagar was in the nature of a rebellion and not of an invasion by a foreign enemy.

(j) From the date of the re-establishment of the Gilgit Agency in 1889, the prestige of this State on the frontier declined and the control of the State over the unsettled districts, including even Punial, which was not originally treated as an unsettled district, was gradually eliminated and an ex parte ruling was given in 1901—but never communicated to the State, if we omit a reference to it in a communication on a different subject in 1905—to the effect that Hunza and Nagar were not part of the State territory, though they owned the suzerainty of the State. The State did not accept this position though during the regime of Maharaja Pratap Singh no direct protest was made against the ruling, but the State continued to contribute towards the cost of the maintenance of the Agency. A protest was made by the present Ruler soon after he ascended the Gaddi, with the result that the Resident with the informal approval of the Government of India made a proposal for the abolition of the Gilgit Agency and the complete re-transfer of the civil and military administration of the districts comprised in the Agency to the State, thus reverting in the main to the conditions preceding the re-establishment of the Gilgit Agency in 1889.

(k) From 1889 upto 1935, the State has paid about three crores of rupees towards the maintenance of the Agency. This the State did because it always considered and treated the Agency districts as its own territory. Otherwise there would have been no occasion for it to accept such a heavy liability. The liability' was not only for purposes of defence but also on account of medical aid, education, construction of roads, etc., besides political subsidies. This expenditure would not devolve on the State, if its relationship with these districts was only one of nominal suzerainty.

(l) When His Highness' Government objected to the procedure relating to the political Jalsa and the method of administration generally in Gilgit neither the Resident nor the Government of India referred to the 1901 ruling, but agreed to the abolition of the Agency and the transfer of full control to the State.

(m) When the match excise pool was entered into, the Government of India continued to pay the State its share in proportion to its entire population, including the population of Hunza and Nagar. This was done even after the agreement of 1935. The population of Hunza and Nagar has been excluded for this purpose only during the last two years, though His Highness' Government have questioned the propriety of such exclusion.

(n) Whatever rights of administration which the Government of India exercise or have ever exercised over the Chiefships and territories comprising the Agency are derived directly or indirectly from and through the Jammu and Kashmir State in whose name and on whose behalf they exercise those rights, the State having already been in effective possession of those rights prior to the establishment of the Agency.

From the foregoing note and the summary of conclusions it is clear that the unsettled districts comprising the Political Agency of Gilgit are and have been an integral part of the territories of the Jammu and Kashmir State and even though no mention of them is made in the Gilgit Agreement of 1935, His Highness' Government were in their draft Instrument of

Accession justified in including them in the territories to which the provisions of sub-section 1 of Section 294 of the Government of India Act should be made applicable.[89]

In this backdrop, the Resident of Kashmir, Lt. Col. S.M. Fraser, expressed his anguish because of his inability to explain to the Government of J&K, the reason for the GOI's position regarding the frontier territories in this confidential demi-official letter:

1941 Census in the Gilgit Agency

1. Will you kindly refer to my official letter No. F.-510/38, dated the 21 September 1940, on the above subject, in which I described the difficulty I was experiencing in explaining to the Kashmir Government the decision to exclude the Census figures of Hunza, Nagir and the Political Districts from the Kashmir State Census Tables.
2. In reply to this letter I was asked (vide memorandum from the External Affairs Department No. F.-805-G./40, dated the 28 October 1940) to inform the Kashmir Government that the status of the Political Districts and Hunza and Nagir being in dispute, it has been decided to show their population under the Census separately. This I did, and I have now received a personal and confidential letter from the Prime Minister the gist of which is as follows.
3. He complains that it seems hardly fair that without attempting to answer any of his arguments (which I have passed on to you in various letters) it should simply be laid down that it has been decided to show the population of these Districts separately. By 'separately' he presumes is meant separate from the state figures altogether, for in any case when these are embodied in the Census Report of the State they would be shown separately for those areas in the report.
4. He is amazed that the political Agent has been instructed by Census Commissioner for India to send his report to be tabulated and written up by the Census Superintendent of the North-West Frontier Province, and cannot understand why the figures for these Districts, which have been linked with the Census of the State for the last half century, should now be linked with the North-West Frontier Province.
5. He considers this controversy so important that he will, although reluctantly, feel compelled to advise His Highness to consider the question of having this dispute between the State and the Government of India referred to His Excellency the Crown Representative for

decision to a Tribunal of Arbitration under the terms of Foreign and Political Department Resolution No. 427-R., dated 29 October 1920.[90]

In response to Fraser's Demi-official letter, the Political Department responded on 5 June 1941, by rejecting the arguments of the Kashmir government forwarded by the former. The response was as follows:

With reference to the correspondence resting with your demi-official letter No. F.25-O. (2)/38, dated the 31 August 1939, I am desired to inform you that notwithstanding the authoritative pronouncements which have been made in the past, the position has been fully re-examined in the light of all the material available. The Crown Representative regrets that he is unable to agree with all the conclusions reached in the note of the Kashmir Government forwarded with your letter and has been pleased to decide as follows:

(i) Hunza and Nagir: Though these are under the suzerainty of the Kashmir State, they are not part of Kashmir but are separate States.
(ii) Chilas, Koh Ghizar, Ishkoman and Yasin: Though these too are under the suzerainty of the Kashmir State, they are not part of Kashmir but are tribal areas.[91]

Therefore, the GOI, rejected all claims of the Kashmir government on the frontier territories under the Gilgit Agency, and thereby laying down the framework for a future territorial dispute in the region. In 1943, a British officer Capt. William Brown, who was to play a major role in future events, took over as Assistant Commandant or Adjutant of the Gilgit Scouts.

He decided to follow the charter, which called for paramilitary duties such as defending against small-scale aggressions, upholding local law and order, escorting the convoys, and controlling the area and was highly critical of the previous officers' attempts to train the Scouts like military units. In his memoirs, he claimed that prior Commandants had made the same efforts, which resulted in the Scouts being sent out to suppress native tribes, humiliating the Political Agent. A pair of brown leather sandals, a pair of *khaki* shorts, a leather belt, a grey shirt, a leather bandolier, and a brown *koi* were all part of the Scouts' basic uniform that was approved in 1943. A silver badge featuring an ibex was displayed on the *koi.* The shorts were replaced with serge in the winter and a woollen jumper was added. There was a linen band beneath the *koi*, part of which could be seen just below the emblem on the fish. The uniform of each lineage was distinguished by a different colour, such as plain black for the Gilgit people, light green for the Hunza scouts, scarlet for the Nagar warriors, yellow for Punial, blue for Yasin, maroon for the Kuh Ghizr, and dark green for the headquarters staff. In November 1946, Maj. Brown was assigned to the Tochi Scouts in Waziristan (NWFP). He made a close connection with Capt. Jock Mathieson was there after meeting him for the first time (Raina & Singh 2021: 60-1).

While Capt. Brown was reorienting the Gilgit Scouts, Col. Schomberg wrote confidential letters to Sir Evan Jenkins, who was the private secretary to the incumbent Viceroy of India, highlighting the pitiable state of administration in the Gilgit Agency.

May I ask if H.E. the Viceroy would let me bring to his personal notice the lamentable state of the Gilgit Agency, where maladministration is rife and where consequently much misery and hardship exist?

I have just returned from that Agency (which I know intimately) and I can vouch for my facts. It is I fear, a waste of time to invoke the aid or interest of the External Affairs Department, although, it is responsible for present conditions. Indeed, I wrote to the Secretary and Deputy Secretary in June 1945, but neither gentleman saw fit to reply.[92]

Col. Schomberg wished to visit the Agency before he returned to Britain; further, he seemed to have a reputation as an eccentric.

Please refer to your endorsement No.D.5618-G/45 of the 24th October forwarding a copy of a letter from Schomberg about the state of the Gilgit Agency. This letter is very much in tune with Schomberg's character and I have no doubt that it is greatly exaggerated.[93]

However, his requests to visit the Agency were refused after his letter. Schomberg was convinced that this refusal came about as a result of his highlighting the administrative deficiencies in the Agencies.

The Resident in Kashmir has just refused my request for leave to visit the Gilgit Agency where I wished to climb before leaving India for good at the end of this year.

The inference is obvious. I am to suffer because I brought to the private notice of the Viceroy the abuses prevalent in the Agency.

I ask that this refusal be cancelled. There can be no justification for it, and any suggestion that I make mischief is untrue.[94]

However, the EAD later clarified that the reasons for refusing entry to Col. Schomberg were not related to his criticism of the administration, but rather because of his past conduct in the Agency.

Please refer to your office endorsements No.1195/G/43 and No.767-S of the 23rd March, about the refusal of permission to Schomberg to enter the Gilgit Agency. As stated in my letter No.2274-CA/46 of the 25th March, the reason for this refusal was not that Schomberg complained about the administration but because his activities in the Agency gave cause for complaint against him.

We have had detailed replies from the Political Agent to each of Schomberg's criticisms but for the purposes of a reply to Clauson it will probably suffice to say that Bacon, the present Political Agent in Gilgit, has reported that the Mirs of Hunza and Nagir spontaneously and without any prompting from himself asked confidentially that if possible Schomberg should be prevented from visiting their states again. In particular the Mir of Hunza considered that Schomberg was responsible for causing difficulties for him both within his own State and with his neighbour, Nagir. Bacon adds that Schomberg's interference in the administration of the Agency tends to undermine the authority of the Political Agent, and he thinks that Schomberg was mainly responsible also for bad feelings between Cobb, the former Political Agent, and the Commandant of the Gilgit Scouts.[95]

It is therefore, important to point out that Col. Schomberg's presence was considered undesirable by the Mirs of Hunza and Nagir. Further, since he had a history of undermining the relationship between the erstwhile Political Agent and the Commandant of the Gilgit Scouts, it can be safely concluded that he had not endeared himself to the administrative leadership of the Gilgit Agency. Finally, this incident brings to the fore a certain congruence of interests between the frontier feudatory states of J&K under the Gilgit Agency and the British officials in the Agency including the Gilgit Scouts. Taken in the context of the earlier British position regarding the legal status of the frontier territories vis-à-vis J&K states and the British interests in keeping a direct control over the frontier, this set the stage for the series of fateful events in Gilgit in the wake of India's independence.

NOTES

1. University of Nebraska Digital Commons.edu, 'Report on the proceedings of the Pamir Boundary Commission' by M.G, Gerard, 1896, p. 12, accessed on 9 December 2022. https://digitalcommons.unomaha.edu/afghandocsreports/8/
2. Ibid., p. 31.
3. Ibid.
4. Ibid., p. 32.
5. Ibid.
6. Proposed formation of a North-West Frontier Agency, Minute by his Excellency the Viceroy, Government of India, Proceedings, Foreign, Secret-F, September 1900, No. 37, National Archives of India.
7. Government of India to Secretary of State for India, No. 192, 19 October 1892, Government of India, Foreign, Secret-F, December 1892, Nos. 430-41, National Archives of India.
8. Report on the Pamirs by The Earl of Dunmore, External, Confidential, 1892, National Archives of India, p. 6.
9. Ibid.
10. Kaushik Roy, 'Feeding the Leviathan: Supplying the British-Indian Army, 1859-1913', *Journal of the Society for Army Historical Research*, vol. 80, Summer 2002, pp. 144-61.
11. Stuart Beatson, *A History of the Imperial Service Troops of Native States*, Office of the Superintendent of Government Printing, Calcutta, 1903, p. ii.
12. Schedule of Proposals Involving Considerable Military Expenditure for 1902-3, September 1901, Government of India, Military Department,

Accounts Budget-A, Proceedings, November 1901, Nos. 42-3, National Archives of India.

13. Ibid.
14. Inclusion of Rs. 2,25,590 in the military budget estimates for 1900-1901 on account of the Gilgit Agency, Government of India, Military Department, Accounts Budget-A, Proceedings, April 1900, No. 30-36, National Archives of India.
15. Measures for the Effective Control and Discipline of the Imperial Service Troops Under All Conditions of Service, Government of India, Military Department, Special and Miscellaneous, Political-B, August 1901, Nos. 256-64, National Archives of India.
16. Ibid.
17. B.W. Marlow, *Estimate of the Kashmir Durbar share of expenditure during 1914-15*, Government of India, Foreign Department, Establishment-B, January 1914, Nos. 176-7, National Archives of India.
18. Ibid.
19. Political Agent to Resident Kashmir, No. 402-T, Government of India, Foreign, Secret-F, May 1913, Nos. 95-102, National Archives of India.
20. Michael Barthorp, *Afghan Wars and the North-West Frontier 1839-1947*, Cassell, London, 2002, pp. 142-3.
21. Christopher M. Wyatt, *Afghanistan and the Defence of Empire*, I.B. Taurus, London, 2011, pp. 95.
22. Ludwig W. Adamec, *Afghanistan, 1900-1923*, University of California Press, Los Angeles, 1967, p. 51.
23. Ian H. Nish, *The Anglo-Japanese Alliance*, The Athlone Press, University of London, 1966, p. 325.
24. S.E. Pears to A.H. Grant, Proposed boundary between the North-West Frontier Province and the Gilgit Agency, 1914, Government of India, Foreign and Political Department, Frontier-A, August 1914, Nos. 1-2, National Archives of India.
25. Ibid.
26. Telegram from Private Secretary to the Viceroy to Secretary to the Government of India, 1 February 1915, General War Diary, Army Headquarters, India (F.S.R., Part II, Section 140; and Staff Manual, War, Section 20), Confidential, Foreign and Political Department, 1915, Volume 14, National Archives of India.
27. Ibid.
28. Ibid., Telegram from the Secretary to the Government of India, Foreign and Political Department to Private Secretary to the Viceroy, 1 February 1915.

29. Ibid., Telegram from The Viceroy, to the Secretary of State for India, 4 February 1915.
30. Anglo-Afghan Treaty of 1919, accessed on 25 December 2022. https://eudocs.lib.byu.edu/index.php/Anglo-Afghan_Treaties#Anglo-Afghan_Treaty_of_1919
31. Telegram from the Resident of Kashmir, No. 2053, 26 May 1919, Offers of services, gifts and assistance made by Ruling Princes and Chiefs and private individuals in connection with the war with Afghanistan, Government of India, Foreign and Political Department, Internal-A, Proceedings January 1920, Nos. 1-230, National Archives of India.
32. Ibid.
33. British Consulate General, Kashgar to Sir A.H. Grant dated 19 February 1918, Corruption of Cypher telegram to Kashgar, Government of India, Foreign and Political Department, 1919, Nos. 45, National Archives of India.
34. Ibid.
35. Ibid., Viceroy of India, Simla to Secretary of State for India, London, dated 20 May 1918,
36. Government of India, Foreign and Political, External, No. 612-X, Secret, 1927, Nos. 1-2. See also A.S. Chohan, *The Gilgit Agency*, Atlantic Publishers and Distributors, New Delhi, 1997, p. 202, National Archives of India.
37. Memorandum No. 369 from J.B. Wood, Resident Kashmir to the Political Secretary to the Government of India dated 28 January 1926, Additional Grant in the Gilgit Agency, Government of India, Foreign Department, Accounts, No. 55-A, 1926, Nos. 18, National Archives of India.
38. Application for an additional grant of Rs. 41,960 to meet excess expenditure incurred or to be incurred in the budget estimates of the Gilgit Agency for the year 1925-6, Additional Grant in the Gilgit Agency, Government of India, Foreign Department, Accounts, No. 55-A, 1926, No. 18, Additional Grant in the Gilgit Agency, Foreign Department, 1926, No. 18, National Archives of India.
39. Memorandum from the Resident at Kashmir, No. F. 317/27, dated the 30 March 1928, Increase in the 'Darbar Presents' grant of the Gilgit Agency, Government of India, Foreign and Political Department, Accounts, 1928, No. 88-A, National Archives of India.
40. Ibid.
41. Note on Chinese Turkistan by Colonel Schomberg, Government of India, Foreign and Political, External, No. 583-X, Secret, 1927, National Archives of India.

42. Ibid.
43. Ibid.
44. Ibid.
45. Copy of a letter from the Political Agent, Gilgit, No. 36-S/16-X, dated 30 April 1928, to the Resident in Kashmir, India's concern with Sinkiang, Government of India, Foreign and Political Department, File No. 37-X, Secret, 1928, Nos. 1-12, National Archives of India.
46. Ibid.
47. Ibid.
48. Ibid., Copy of a Demi-official letter from the Political Agent, Gilgit, No. 91-S/X-16, dated 20 September 1928.
49. Ibid.
50. Ibid., Demi-official letter to Lieutenant Colonel G.D. Ogilvie, C.I.E., Resident in Kashmir, No F. 37-X/28, Simla, 3 May 1929.
51. Extract from demi-official letter from Mr. Williamson, H.B.M.'s Consul-General, Kashgar, 18 October 1928 (Original in File No. 145-X of 1928), Supply of arms and ammunition to the Governor of Sinkiang, Government of India, Foreign and Political Department, File No. 248-X, Secret, 1928, Nos. 1-217, National Archives of India.
52. Daniel C. Waugh, *Etherton at Kashgar: Rhetoric and Reality in the History of the 'Great Game'*, Bactrian Press, Seattle, 2007, p. 18.
53. Communication from F.V. Wylie dated 15 January 1930, Supply of arms and ammunition to the Governor of Sinkiang, Government of India, Foreign and Political Department, File No. 248-X, Secret, 1928, Nos. 1-217, National Archives of India.
54. Ibid., Demi-official letter from J.C. Walton, Esq., C.B., M.C., India Office, to Lieutenant-Colonel R.C.F. Schomberg, D.S.O., Chasewood Lodge, Ross, Herefordshire, No. P. 1391/30. Dated 4 March 1930.
55. Ibid., Express letter to the Resident in Kashmir, No. F.-248-X/28, Simla, 21 July 1930.
56. Dy. No. 4733-X/28, Visit to Chinese Turkestan in 1929, Government of India, Foreign and Political Department, File No. 115 (3)-X, External, 1928, Nos. 1-52, National Archives of India.
57. Ibid., Major T.W. Corbett to the Deputy Secretary (Foreign), Foreign and Political Department, Delhi, dated 5 November 1928.
58. Maharaj Kaul, *Essays in Inequality and Social Justice (Essays in honor of Ved Prakash Vatuk)*, Edited by Kira Hall, Archana Publications, Meerut, India, 2009, p. 351.
59. Mohini Qasba Raina, *Kashur The Kashmiri Speaking People*, Patridge, Singapore, 2014, p. 305.

60. H.L. Saxena, *The Tragedy of Kashmir*, Nationalist Publishers, New Delhi, 1975, p. 110.
61. N.N. Raina, *Kashmir Politics and Imperialist Manoeuvres: 1846-1980*, Patriot Publishers, New Delhi, 1988, p. 73.
62. P.N.K. Bamzai, *Culture and Political History of Kashmir*, Volume 3*: Modern Kashmir*, M.D. Publication Pvt. Ltd., New Delhi, 1994, p. 730.
63. Christopher Snedden, *Understanding Kashmir and Kashmiris*, Oxford University Press, 2015, p. 125.
64. Ian Copland, *Islam and Political Mobilization in Kashmir, 1931-34*, Pacific Affairs, vol. 54, No. 2, Summer 1981, pp. 228-9.
65. Mohan Krishen Teng, et al., *Kashmir: Constitutional History and Documents*, Light & Life Publishers, New Delhi, 1977, p. 88.
66. Prime Minister Jammu and Kashmir State to Resident Kashmir, No. S.P.-I. C/D.O, 20 March 1933, Government of India, Foreign and Political, Secret, File No. 401-X, 1933, Nos. 1-57, National Archives of India.
67. Ahmad H. Dani, *History of the Northern Areas of Pakistan*, National Institute of Historical and Cultural Research, Islamabad, 1991, p. 296.
68. Resident Kashmir to Government of India, No. F-l-C/31, 28 November 1934, Government of India, Foreign and Political, Secret, File No. 401-X of 1933, Nos. 1-57, National Archives of India.
69. Ajay K. Raina and Rajendra Singh, *Treachery & Gallantry*, Sabre & Quill Publishers, New Delhi, 2021, p. 59.
70. Extract from notes in F.No. 326-Genl. by C.L. Corfield dated 12 April 1937, Decision that Gilgit is an administered area in an Indian state and therefore cannot be described as a 'Centrally Administered Area' Government of India, External Affairs Department, External, File No. 130-X, 1937, Nos. 19.
71. Ibid.
72. Note from L.C.L. Griffin to C. Latimer dated 6 November 1937, Position of Hunza, Nagir, Chilas, Koh Ghizar, Ishkuman and Yasin in the event of Kashmir acceding to the Federation, Government of India, External Affairs Department, External Branch, Secret, 1937, File No. 676-X/37, Nos. 1-9, National Archives of India.
73. Ibid., Note from W.R. Hay, dated 19 November 1937.
74. Ibid., Note from L.C.L. Griffin, dated 29 February 1938.
75. Ibid., Note from W.R. Hay, dated 19 November 1937.
76. Ibid., Note from L.C.L. Griffin, dated 29 February 1938.
77. Ibid., Note from W.R. Hay, dated 2 February 1938.

78. Legislation.gov.uk, Government of India Act 1935, accessed on 14 January 2023.https://www.legislation.gov.uk/ukpga/Geo5and1Edw8/26/2/contents/enacted
79. Note from L.C.L. Griffin dated 29 March 1938, Position of Hunza, Nagir, Chilas, Koh Ghizar, Ishkuman and Yasin in the event of Kashmir acceding to the Federation, Government of India, External Affairs Department, External Branch, Secret, 1937, File No. 676-X/37, Nos. 1-9, National Archives of India.
80. Ibid., Demi-official letter, from L.C.L. Griffin, External Affairs Department to P.J. Patrick, C.S.I., India Office, No. F.24-Fed.IX'38, dated 21July 1938.
81. Ibid., Note from L.C.L. Griffin, dated 6 August 1938.
82. Ibid., Letter from the Resident, Kashmir, No F. 25-C.X'38, Srinagar, 30 September 1938.
83. Ibid., Letter from the Secretary to His Excellency the Crown Representative to the Residents of Indian Princely States, No. F. 24-Fed.IX'38, Simla, 21 July 193.
84. Note from O.K. Caroe dated 27 January 1941, Status of Hunza and Nagir and Political Districts of Chilas, Koh Ghizar, Ishkoman and Yasin vis-à-vis the Kashmir State, Government of India, Political Department, Secret, 1941, File No. 112-P, Nos. 1-5, National Archives of India.
85. Ibid., Note from O.K. Caroe, dated 30 January 1941.
86. Ibid.
87. Ibid., Note from Political Department, dated 21 February 1941.
88. Ibid.
89. Ibid., A Note on the nature of the relationship between the Jammu & Kashmir State and the Chief ships and Territories comprised in the Gilgit Political Agency prepared by His Highness' Government, Jammu & Kashmir, Ram Chandra Kak, Jammu, 10 March.
90. Ibid., Confidential demi-official letter from Lieut.-Colonel D. de M.S. Fraser, C.I.E., Resident in Kashmir, No. F.-610/38, dated 21 January 1941.
91. Ibid., Letter to Lieut.-Colonel D. de M. S. Fraser, C.I.E., Resident in Kashmir, No. D.-276-P. (Camp)/41, dated 5 June 1941.
92. Confidential letter from Colonel R.C.F. Schomberg to Sir Evans Jenkins dated 20 October 1945, Colonel R.C.F. Schomberg's complaint about maladministration in Gilgit Agency, and consequent misery and hardship among the people of Gilgit, Government of India, Office of the P.S.V., General Branch, 1945, File No. 1195-G/43, National Archives of India.

93. Ibid., Letter from Sir Olaf Carroe to Sir Evans Jenkins, dated 26 October 1945.
94. Ibid., Letter from Colonel R.C.F. Schomberg to G.E.B. Abell, dated 18 February 1946.
95. Ibid., Letter from External Affairs Department to G.E.B. Abell, dated 4 April 1946.

REFERENCES

Bamzai, Prithvi N.K., *Culture and Political History of Kashmir,* Volume 3: *Modern Kashmir*, MD Publication, New Delhi, 1994.

Chohan, Amar S., *The Gilgit Agency*, Atlantic Publishers and Distributors, New Delhi, 1997.

Dani, Ahmad H., *History of the Northern Areas of Pakistan*, National Institute of Historical and Cultural Research, Islamabad, 1991.

Kaul, Maharaj, *Essays in Inequality and Social Justice* (Essays in Honor of Ved Prakash Vatuk), ed. Kira Hall, Archana Publications, Meerut, India, 2009.

Raina, Niranjan N., *Kashmir Politics and Imperialist Manoeuvres: 1846-1980*, Patriot Publishers, New Delhi, 1988.

Wyatt, Christopher M., *Afghanistan and the Defence of Empire*, I.B. Taurus, London, 2011.

CHAPTER 4

Partition and the Territorial Dispute

INDEPENDENCE, INVASION AND ACCESSION

By 1947, the British had come to the conclusion that they could no longer hold India in thraldom, and on Viceroy Lord Mountbatten's recommendation, they announced a plan for the Partition of India. The Indian Independence Act, which was passed on 18 July 1947, stated that the British would relinquish their rule over India on 15 August 1947, at which point India would become an independent nation. East and West Pakistan were to be established as autonomous, sovereign states in a portion of its borders that had a predominance of Muslims.[1] It was decided that the region of Gilgit Agency which the British had taken on lease would be handed over to the Maharaja. The date to transfer the territory was decided to be 1 August 1947.

Initially, the Maharaja of J&K was willing to maintain the status of the princely state as independent but he soon realized that after a certain point, it was not going to be possible. Even then he presented a 'Standstill Agreement' to both the dominions of India and Pakistan. Pakistan immediately signed it, but India did not exhibit any haste in doing so and wanted to examine its implications. Maharaja Hari Singh was quite puzzled by this time. He was a Hindu ruler of a region with a majority Muslim population, with some regions like Jammu and Ladakh being the clusters of Hindu and Buddhist demography respectively. The communal riots before Indian Independence further acted as a catalyst for the Maharaja's anxiety. V.P. Menon* writes in his book:

*Vappala Pangunni Menon was a civil servant in the Government of India and acted as the Secretary to the Government of India in the Ministry of the States from 1947-51.

In fairness to Maharajah Hari Singh, it must be said that situated as he was in, it was not easy for him to come to a decision. If he acceded to Pakistan, the non-Muslims of Jammu and Ladakh as well as considerable sections of Muslims led by the National Conference (NC) would have resented such action. On the other hand, accession to India would have provoked adverse reactions in Gilgit and certain areas contiguous to Pakistan.[2]

Some scholars are of opinion that the Maharaja had made up his mind that the accession of J&K along with Gilgit-Baltistan was going to take place with the Indian dominion and this was the reason why he dismissed the Pakistan-inclined PM Ram Chandra Kak* on 11 August 1947 and appointed a former officer of J&K State Forces, Maj. Gen. Janak Singh as temporary PM of the state.[3]

After Col. Baldev Singh Pathania reportedly turned down the offer, the Dogra cousin of the Maharaja was appointed governor of Gilgit. However, as one can see from Brig. Ghansar Singh's** own account, his appointment was fraught with complications because he didn't have the support of Ram Chandra Kak, the then prime minister of J&K (Dani 1991: 315). In many works, the name of Brig. Ghansar Singh is also mentioned as Brig. Ghansara Singh though the correct name was as mentioned above. First, according to him, then PM Pandit R.C. Kak wanted a different person to replace the Governor. Second, the PM disregarded his advice to oppose the continuance of British officers in the Gilgit Scouts. Third, the PM instructed the Governor to get there by foot or pony in two days because Gilgit's airlift could not be arranged between 21 and 24 July 1947. Travelling more than 200 km in that terrain was simply too much to ask. Maj Gen. Henry Lawrence Scott intervened and alerted the Maharaja who instructed the PM to organize a plane (Raina & Singh 2021: 70).

The chief of staff of the J&K state forces, Maj Gen. Scott, and Brig. Ghansar Singh flew in on July 30 to finish the legalities of

*Ram Chandra Kak served as the prime minister of Jammu & Kashmir under Maharaja Gulab Singh from 1945-7.

**Brig. Ghansar Singh was the last governor of Jammu & Kashmir to Gilgit-Baltistan, having taken charge in August 1947 from the Lt. Col. Bacon, who was the last British Political Agent to the territory.

taking command on July 31. While another officer from the state forces (5 J&K Infantry), Capt. Mohd. Sayeed, joined the scouts. Following the collapse of British paramountcy on 1 August 1947, the area was given back to the Jammu & Kashmir Princely State and Brig. Ghansar Singh was appointed the first governor of Gilgit Agency and Gilgit Wazarat by Hari Singh (Raina & Singh 2021: 69).

Maj. William Brown* started calling all the native Junior Commissioned Officers (JCOs) one by one at his residence in the name of discussing the developments but it had the ulterior motive of injecting the feeling in them that Gilgit was best under British rule. For this, he even summoned the most influential JCO Subedar Maj. Mohammed Baber Khan and set a course on his mission without wasting any time. There was a point when Maj. Brown wrote in his book that he mentioned the following:

> Did not trust (Baber Khan), but nothing could be done about it. Any attempt to get rid of him would give grounds for grave suspicion and might have regrettable consequences.[4]

Maj. Brown's accounts make it clear that prior to this day, he and JCO Baber Khan did not have a cordial relationship.

Gen. Janak Singh was succeeded soon by Mehr Chand Mahajan as prime minister on 15 October 1947 (Menon 1961: 272). Although Pakistan had signed the Standstill Agreement, it was still pressurizing Hari Singh adamantly and violating the terms of the agreement to compel J&K for accession to Pakistan. The object of the Standstill Agreement, drafted by the British Indian government (Political Department) on 3 June 1947, in the context of J&K, was to provide for the continuance of economic and administrative relations between J&K and the two neighbours on the same basis as had existed before the creation of the new dominions and normal amenities of life such as supplies, post office, communication, etc. could be maintained.[5] It had been mentioned that the Standstill Agreement would guarantee, that

*Maj. William Brown was a British Army Officer who was the Acting Commandant of the Gilgit Scouts in 1947. He played a central role in the fateful Gilgit Scouts uprising of 1947.

till new agreements were made, all existing agreements and administrative provisions would continue. In case of any dispute in this regard, it would be settled by arbitration.

It may be noted that due to a hazardous 300 km long dirt road connecting Jammu with Srinagar over the Banihal Pass and a mule track connecting Ladakh with Himachal, as well as with Kashmir, the main supplies of cloth, ammunition, fuels and lubricants for vehicles and machinery in Kashmir were traditionally brought in via the Domel-Kohala route that entered the state astride the Jhelum River. The Jammu region had its supplies arriving via Sialkot to Jammu and via Jhelum to Mirpur. From Srinagar, the main supply route ran through Bandipora-Gurez-Burzil Pass-Bunji and onwards to the other parts of the Gilgit-Baltistan region (Raina & Singh 2021: 77). Even after the execution of the Standstill Agreement, the relations between Kashmir and Pakistan were far from cordial. The Government of J&K complained that to coerce the state into acceding, the Pakistan authorities had cut-off the supply of food, petrol and other essential commodities, and hindered the free transit of travellers between Kashmir and Pakistan.

At this time the Government of J&K requested the Government of India for 5,000 gallons of petrol which Pakistan had been unable to provide. India sent only 500 gallons to meet the immediate necessity of preventing a complete breakdown of transport in Srinagar.[6] Mehr Chand Mahajan talks about the visit of Maj. Shah, one of the prominent secretaries to the Pakistan government to Srinagar, in the following words:

> The Standstill Agreement notwithstanding, an economic blockade—and a very effective one—had been started and no stuff of any kind was allowed to come inside the State. The object was to starve the population and cause an uprising. Major Shah, son-in-law of my erstwhile Chief Justice in Lahore, who was one of the important Secretaries of the Pak Government, was in Srinagar with a whip and a sword in one hand and a letter of accession in the other.[7]

Even before the Partition, Maj. Akbar Khan mentioned in his book *Raiders in Kashmir* that the proponents of Pakistan were confident that the region of Kashmir would accede to Pakistan. He gave several arguments in favour of this:

Since the British declaration about the forthcoming partition, we had assumed that Kashmir would naturally join Pakistan. In fact, the very concept of Pakistan had included it as an integral part, the letter K in the name Pakistan standing for Kashmir. The sub-continent was to be divided on the basis of a Muslim-majority area for Pakistan and a non-Muslim majority area for India. Kashmir had to be in Pakistan because three/fourths of its four million inhabitants were Muslims, and its territory of 84,500 square miles had no effective road, river or rail links, nor direct economic ties, with India.[8]

He further wrote that the Quaid-e-Azam (M.A. Jinnah) of Pakistan had assured a delegation some weeks after the British declaration and a few days before the actual Partition that Kashmir would join Pakistan despite the reluctance of Maharaja and the rise of the popularity of Sheikh Abdullah, who had previously opposed the concept of Pakistan (Khan 1970: 5). Jinnah's confidence rested on the figures of the Muslim majority and the connectivity of Kashmir with the proposed Pakistan territory via two major roads. He received the first blow when the actual lines of demarcations were defined between India and Pakistan, days after independence under the Radcliff Award. These defined boundaries gave India an option to develop good connectivity with the region from Jammu to Kathua. Akbar Khan commented:

One glance at the map was enough to show that Pakistan's military security would be seriously jeopardised if Indian troops came to be stationed along Kashmir's western border. Once India got the chance, she could establish such stations anywhere within a few miles of the 180 miles long vital road and rail route between Lahore and Pindi. In the event of war, these stations would be a dangerous threat to our most important civil and military lines of communication. (ibid.)

The economic dependency of Pakistan's agricultural sector on the perennial rivers coming from Kashmir, further acted as a catalyst for the desperation of Pakistan's leadership. These points clarify why the Muslim League anxiously wanted Kashmir to join Pakistan and why they planned an attack on Kashmir even when the Standstill Agreement of 12 August 1947 was still in place. Akbar Khan (then director of weapons and equipment) went to Muree for two weeks after the Partition in September 1947. There he was introduced to Sardar Ibrahim, who was to become the first President of Azad Kashmir. Ibrahim believed that the time for 'peaceful negotiations was gone' and if 'they wanted to prevent the Maharaja from handing Kashmir over to India, they needed weapons'. For a start, Sardar Ibrahim asked for five hundred rifles to begin with, which according to Akbar Khan was too modest an estimate.

> A large part of our share of the reserve stocks of weapons and ammunition was still lying in India. Even if these stocks were in Pakistan there would be no possibility of giving any for Kashmir unless the Government ordered the Commander-in-Chief to do so. Since he was not to be taken into confidence; some other way had to be found to get hold of some rifles. (Khan 1970: 12)

In his book *Raiders in Kashmir*, Maj. Gen. Akbar Khan provided a compelling narrative of the invasion of J&K. He noted that Sardar Ibrahim was not prominent enough to be known in Pakistan. Since the Pakistani army and Muslim conference were unable to find a Kashmiri-speaking leader, Ibrahim was used to execute the plan of tribal invasion and instigate the people in Poonch. As per Pakistani records, Poonch was in a state of revolt. The title of Akbar Khan's book itself makes it clear that there was no indigenous rebellion during the unrest that broke out in the princely state of J&K immediately after the Partition. It wasn't just a tribal invasion either.

The leadership of the Muslim League, which at the time held the top positions in Pakistan, organized the operation. Pakistan did not want to have a direct confrontation with the Indian army. In order to discuss the preparation and execution of the operation, Prime Minister Liaquat Ali Khan and Gen. Akbar Khan met at least four times, according to Gen. Akbar Khan, who was then a colonel in the Pakistani army. Akbar Khan made a plan to divert a portion of the order of 4,000 rifles by the Punjab Police for the plan in Kashmir.[9] It was noted by Justice Muhammad Yusuf Saraf, a Muslim Conference activist at the time, that such a significant operation could not have been carried out without Jinnah's knowledge and consent. Sardar Ibrahim mentioned that on 20 August 1947 he and Shaukat Ali, general secretary of the Muslim Conference went to see some Pakistani friends in Gulmarg. A long follow-up meeting was also held in Srinagar at the residence of Dr. Mohammad Din Tasir. During this meeting, it was decided that Sardar Ibrahim had to leave for Pakistan to re-enter Poonch and lead the movement there. For this, he received a letter of authority from a senior leader of the Muslim Conference. This important letter is presented in Ibrahim's accounts:

Srinagar,
17 September 1947

My dear Sardar Muhammad Ibrahim Khan, we have started the civil disobedience movement here, and I have addressed a number of mass meetings. I may be arrested at any moment. Therefore, in consultation with the available members of the working committee, I am constrained to appoint you as my successor. As such, you will be perfectly competent to receive and deliver goods on behalf of the Muslim Conference. You can negotiate with any party or organisation, and arrive at any understanding you deem fit and proper. The Muslim Conference will be bound by your acts and words. In my and my colleagues' opinion, you are utterly worthy of the trust reposed in you. I hope and trust you will, as usual, discharge your heavy responsibilities with zeal and enthusiasm, and our community will surely profit by your able guidance. You will please appoint your successor whenever the prospect of your arrest arise.

May God bless you,
Yours sincerely,
(Sd/-) HAMIDULLAH KHAN,
Acting President,
All-J&K Muslim Conference.

N.B. It may please be noted that, as long as I am not arrested, you are, even now, quite competent to act on my behalf outside the State.

Sd/- HAMIDULLAH KHAN.[10]

Sardar Ibrahim left for Lahore where he met Mian Iftikharuddin, a senior leader of the Muslim League which is mentioned in Akbar Khan's accounts as well. Iftikharuddin met Akbar Khan in Muree and said:

He had been deputed to go to Srinagar to contact the Kashmiri Leaders and to assess the chances of Kashmir's accession to Pakistan. He also said that if the people of Kashmir were not likely to have the chance of freely exercise their choice—the Muslim League may have to take some action to help the Kashmiri Muslims and to prevent the State's accession to India. He did not seem particularly optimistic about the outcome of his mission but thought that his visit would at least clear their doubts about the necessity of taking action. He would be away for about a week and, in case the situation was not promising, he had to take back with him to Lahore a plan of action. He asked me to prepare a plan for him.

The plan which Akbar Khan forged has been titled as 'Armed Revolt in Kashmir' in his book (Khan 1970: 14). The 'Standstill Agreement', which Pakistan and Maharaja Hari Singh's government signed on 12 August 1947, was still in effect when the attack was planned and carried out. As for the decision to resort to arms, Sardar Ibrahim mentioned that he had taken that decision without discussing it with any leaders of the Muslim Conference. He disussed it with the officers of the Pakistan army (Khan, Ibrahim 1965: 71).

The Pakistani army and Muslim League had been unable to find a Kashmiri-speaking leader who could support their initiatives. Justice M.Y. Saraf illustrated in the first volume of his book that M.A. Jinnah realized very early that unless the party was able to approach Kashmiri-speaking Muslims through a leader who could speak to them in their mother tongue, it was not possible to hold up the organization. During his stay in Srinagar Jinnah asked Chaudhari Ghulam Abbas Khan to search for a presentable Kashmiri-speaking person, who could be launched as their leader.[11] The struggle to find an ordinary Kashmiri to become the face of pro-Pakistan uprising in Kashmir was a long one and for the most part, unsuccessful. There came a point when Jinnah advised Chaudhari Ghulam Abbas Khan to learn the Kashmiri language because in his view the party could otherwise make no effort (Saraf 2015: 640).

CONTINUING BRITISH INTERESTS IN THE FRONTIER

The frontier region of Gilgit had however, not ceased to be a region of strategic interests for the British as was clear by the British steps to consolidate its control over the frontier first by taking over the region on lease and then by denying that the region was ever a part of the princely state of J&K. This has been clearly brought out in the preceding chapter. When the British decided to transfer power to the Indians, it would gradually become clear that their strategic interests in the territory were clearly still alive. In his letter dated 10 October 1947, just prior to the unfolding of the fateful events in J&K State, the former Assistant Political Agent of the Gilgit Agency and ICS, F.P. Mainprice reasserted the old British position that on moral and administrative reasons the Gilgit Agency should not be returned to J&K State and instead some 'new' political arrangements be made for Gilgit Agency:

> Theoretically the 60-year lease of this area round Gilgit which was acknowledged as part of Kashmir State was to be terminated prematurely, and the sub-division should have reverted to pre-1935 State administration on the termination of paramountcy. But in fact all the reasons which had caused the Central Govt. to take over its administration in 1935 still held good, and the people, who had experienced an infinitely better administration for 12 years, strongly opposed putting the clock back and restoring the alien regime of those whose inefficiency and neglect were only equalled by their contempt for the local people and their aspirations. . . . Following the treatment of Hyderabad and Kalat claims to Berar and Quetta, a very strong case could be made out for the retention of Central Govt. administration in Gilgit Sub-Division; its retrocession to Kashmir, though a highly retrogressive and unpopular step, was not however in itself incompatible with satisfactory new political and strategic arrangements for the Gilgit Agency as a whole.[12]

Further Mainprice went on to explain, why Chilas, Darel and Tangir, could and should never be a part of J&K:

> Neither Chilas nor the two unadministered territories were even part of Kashmir State, though Chilas had a small garrison of State troops before 1935 and the Darel Jirga paid a small annual tribute to the Darbar through the Political agent (as well as a small annual tribute direct to the Raja of Punial). Tangir had no outside obligations, though it had historical connections with what is now the Governorship of Yasin. None of these three territories was united, but each was a loose collection of mutually hostile and feuding families and villages which had never evolved a satisfactory indigenous political structure.[13]

It must be pointed out that most or all of these reasons could be applied to any number of small principalities that had existed across British India on the eve of Independence, however the British concern regarding these minor states on the frontier region is striking. Further, that the British had already transferred power technically by the time this note was written, this preoccupation with these territories simply because of the nature of their local political histories or the concern with the well-being of the local populations seem to be quite out of place. However, the deeper motivations behind these suggestions unfold, as the note reveals itself:

> The defence of India and Pakistan (including Kashmir itself) and of the British Commonwealth's only common frontier with the Soviet Union seen to demand the immediate re-establishment of the Central (now Pakistan) Govt's Political Agency at Gilgit in overriding control of the border states with control over the Gilgit Scouts and any other forces in the Agency, and with sole responsibility for maintenance of the international frontier, intelligence, internal stability and in fact all the responsibilities of the old Political Agency of the Central Government. As on the purely political plane this might be difficult it could no doubt best be effected through the Joint Defence Council, and it might be desirable to change the designations of the Central Government's representatives in Gilgit. Lt. Col. Bacon at Peshawar, Major Redpath at Kabul and perhaps Lt. Col. Cooke until recently at Peshawar are former officers of the Indian Political Service with Gilgit experience who are serving on in Pakistan. Either in Baluchistan or the N.W.F.P. have Frontier Agencies been withdrawn. Gilgit was as much a Frontier Agency as the Khyber or the Malakand, and not a Political Agency in Indian States like Bhopal or Simla, and was under the External Affairs Dept, not the Political Dept, in recognition of this fact. Here, in a situation fraught with such internal and external dangers and where both dominions have the same vital interest in a firm inviolable international frontier backed by a stable political structure, would seem to be an opportunity for friendly cooperation by Pakistan, which is primarily responsible, and India, which is equally interested, having due regard to the wishes and interests of the peoples of the Gilgit Agency and to Kashmir's as well as the Central Govt's rights in that area. If something is not done properly, Gilgit may be the first breach in the former frontiers of India, and the thin end of a Soviet wedge.[14]

In the light of these views, it is clear that there was a strong view in the British policy circles at the time of India's Independence that this frontier territory should rather be under Pakistani control as the latter was the main bulwark against any Soviet expansion into India. It is also clear that any question of the status of the region as a territorial part of J&K state or the welfare of the people, was merely a smokescreen for the British policy of having direct or indirect control over the frontier. It is uncannily eerie, how the events that would unfold over the next fortnight would be similar to the proposals made in this note.

TRIBAL INVASION OF KASHMIR, OPERATION GULMARG

The Pakistani invasion of the Kashmir Valley in 1947, was well-planned and showed significant strategic and tactical expertise. First, the army of the state was to be divided into small groups by hit-and-run raids along the extensive border with Pakistan. The defensive army was required to disperse into garrisons of platoon strength that were extremely thinly spaced throughout the whole southern boundary in order to control these attacks, which appeared to be disorganized. The state army was divided up into countless little garrisons due to the steep terrain and poor connections, which meant that it was no longer a powerful, coherent force that could defend the place against any strong invader anywhere along the boundary.

As a result, the defensive force was severely hindered. At the same time, vicious sectarian propaganda was directed squarely at the state, inspiring the Muslims living in frontier regions and serving in the state army to revolt against the Hindu Maharaja and slaughter their neighbours who belonged to the minority group. The motive behind the Pakistani invasion of J&K is not difficult to guess:

> When the British transferred power, one of the problems left unsolved by them was that of the tribal people, and Pakistan had to tackle it. Crores of rupees were spent by the British out of Indian revenues to appease these people, but the newly-born State of Pakistan could ill afford to spend so much money on them. Besides, the leaders of Pakistan have made Islam the basis of

modern nationality, and all their high-sounding words would lose meaning if they treated the tribal people, their co-religionists, in the British way. There was again another menace growing rapidly in the NWF Province. Badshah Khan (Khan Abdul Ghaffar Khan) started his Pathanýstan Movement—autonomy for the Pathans—and they were afraid lest it should disrupt Pakistan It had to be nipped in the bud before the movement lured the Pathans both of the NWF. Province and the tribal areas into one hostile camp. The urgent need felt by Pakistan to force the issue of Kashmir, and secure its speedy accession to Pakistan contained the possibility of a solution of more than one problem. To hold out to the poor tribal people the alluring promise of land and plenty in Kashmir, to give them a lurid description of the supposed atrocities done to Muslims so that they might be worked up to fever pitch, and allow them a free run of the beautiful valley—why, this would secure Kashmir, solve the problem of the tribal people, kill the Pathanistan Movement and secure Pakistan's safety and prosperity—all at one stroke.[15]

Passions on fire, lawlessness raging, and authority paralysed, the raiders attacked. Numerous tribal warriors surged across the border and then spread like a great flood across the state along every bridle path and mountain trail. The major invasion, known as 'Operation Gulmarg', was explicitly set out by the Pakistani Army Headquarters.

Within a few days after the creation of Pakistan, orders were given via demi-official (DO) letters that were signed personally by the British Commander-in-Chief of the Pakistan Army and stamped Personal/Top Secret. The first important source of these rapidly unfolding events was Maj. Onkar Singh Kalkat, who later held the position of Brigade Major at the headquarters of the Bannu Frontier Brigade Group. Maj. Kalkat received and opened an envelope marked Personal/Top Secret on 20 August 1947, when his Brigade commander was absent at the outpost of Miral. Inside was a letter from the Chief of Staff of the Pakistan Army outlining the specifics of 'Operation Gulmarg'. Kalkat hurriedly dialled his Brigadier, who warned him not to mention it to anybody for fear of being denied permission to leave Pakistan alive. However, Maj. Kalkat's knowledge of the 'Operation Gulmarg' strategy was detected by the Pakistani Army.[16]

As a result, he was placed effectively under house arrest there. The officer, however, made a daring breakout and came to Ambala on 18 October 1947. He boarded a cargo train late at night to travel quickly to Delhi. The following day, he met Sardar Baldev Singh, the Defense Minister, Brig Kalwant Singh, the acting CGS, Col. Thapar, the acting Director of Military Operations (DMO) and others to discuss the Pakistani plan for 'Operation Gulmarg'. However, this did not go over well with them. The hunt for Maj. Kalkat's family, who had travelled to India from Mianwali with the assistance of the regional Deputy Commissioner, began in East Punjab when 'Operation Gulmarg' had already begun on 22 October 1947, just as planned (Prasad & Pal 1987: 17). Now that they had seen the error of their ways, the Indian authorities only discovered Kalkat's whereabouts in Amritsar on 24 October. He was brought before Prime Minister Nehru, who scolded the acting DMO and the defence minister for failing to act quickly enough in the wake of Kalkat's discovery.

The second source was journalist Shri G.K. Reddy. On 21 October 1947, he answered a trunk call and discovered it was from API (Associated Press of India) Lahore to Lt. Col. Alavi, the public relations officer of GHQ, Pakistan Army. Alavi made it obvious that the attack on Ramkot (the J&K Border Post) would start that evening, without realizing he was speaking to anybody other than a Muslim. Every evening, GHQ Rawalpindi would call API Lahore to update them on the progress of the invasion, but they were required to publish the information as a statement from the 'Azad Kashmir Government' with a Palandri date line because Palandri was designated as their headquarters. Reddy shared his account after leaving Pakistan, and it was later printed in *Blitz* weekly of Bombay on 9 June 1948. Apart from the fact that the tightly regulated supply of food and gasoline could not have reached the invaders without government support or connivance, these two independent testimonies, which were based on first-hand information, indicated Pakistan's culpability indisputably in the invasion of J&K (Kalkat 18).

Each Pathan tribe was required to join at least one Lashkar of 1,000 tribesmen as part of the Operation Gulmarg strategy, according to Maj. Kalkat's statement. Separate instructions for the appointment of Political Agents and Deputy Commissioners were given. After recruiting, these Lashkars were to be concentrated at Bannu, Wana, Peshawar, Kohat, Thal, and Nowshera by the first week of September 1947. The Brigade Commanders were instructed to supply them with guns, ammunition, and some essential clothing items at these places while keeping records of these distributions against Pakistani Army soldiers (Kalkat 1983: 18).

Additionally, a Major, a Captain and ten JCOs of the regular Pakistani Army were to be provided to each Tribal Lashkar. The Major was to lead the Lashkar in actual combat and serve as the tribal leaders' 'adviser' of the Malik, the official commander of the squad. While each of the ten JCOs was to be in charge of a company or group of the Lashkar, the Captain was to serve as a staff officer. They were to be Pathans who lived and dressed just like the other Pathans in the Lashkar. Maj Gen. Akbar Khan, known by the code name Tariq, was to be in charge of the entire army. He was to be assisted by Brig. Sher Khan. Their headquarters were situated in the same way as that of the chief of staff of the Pakistan Army, and Gen. Sir Frank Messervy was, of course, aware of the entire scheme.

By 18 October 1947, all units known as Lashkars were to be assembled in Abbottabad. They were to be transported on public buses that had been hijacked, with all trips taking place at night. No civilians or unauthorized individuals were allowed near the designated territory of the Lashkars, located 16 km from Abbottabad. Six Lashkars were to march from Muzaffarabad to Srinagar via Domel, Uri and Baramula in order to capture the airport and then move on to Banihal Pass, as outlined in the general plan of operations. To secure the right flank of the main force as it moved from Muzaffarabad, two Lashkars were to move directly from Haji Pir Pass to Gulmarg. A similar force of two Lashkars was to advance from Tithwal through Nastachhun Pass to capture Sopore, Handwara, and Bandipur.

In order to capture Poonch and Rajauri and subsequently advance to Jammu, another force of 10 Lashkars was to operate in the Poonch, Bhimbar and Rawalkot area. The whole strategy included provisions for the very unrestricted distribution of guides and informants from the so-called Azad Army to all of these tribal

Lashkars. Before departing from Muzaffarabad, each company was required to have a minimum of four guides attached. Gen. Akbar Khan was also tasked with creating the Azad Army, which would be composed mostly of Muslims from the J&K State Forces. By 15 October, weaponry, ammunition, supplies, and clothing dumps were to be set up in the area ahead of Abbottabad. After D-day, these were to be relocated to Muzaffarabad and Domel. Operation Gulmarg's 'D-day' was determined to be 22 October 1947, when the different Lashkars were to enter J&K. By the last light on 21October, the Seventh Infantry Division of the Pakistani Army was to converge in the Murree-Abbottabad region and be prepared to deploy right away into J&K territory to support the tribal Lashkars and strengthen their control over the Valley. At Sialkot, one infantry brigade was also kept in a position to proceed to Jammu (Kalkat 1983: 41).

The main column of the raiders struck Muzaffarabad on 22 October 1947 early in the morning after crossing the border from Garhi Habibullah. The 4 J&K Infantry traitors who were in charge of the outposts in Lohar Gali and Ramkot joined the raiders, provided them with the most accurate information regarding the size and make up of the defending soldiers and assisted them in deploying a sufficient force against each defensive picket. Before the residents of Muzaffarabad could grasp what had transpired, the city was conquered by fire and sword. In particular, the MMG unit of the Dogra pickets, which was stationed on high ground in the school area to the north of the city, fought the enemy with tremendous bravery and inflicted significant fatalities.

However, they were swept away by the onslaught of the invaders as they advanced on the Domel bridge. Lt Col. Narain Singh was at Domel when the unexpected gunfire and yelling in Muzaffarabad shocked him. He soon discovered about the raid from a wounded sepoy who had managed to escape the area. However, the raiders assaulted his own headquarters shortly after this information was released and the Muslim forces at Domel also cooperated with the attackers. Capt. Ram Singh, the adjutant, was murdered while rushing to open the *kot* (armoury) The mortar platoon and the Battalion Headquarters engaged in a daylong, tough battle while taking significant losses. About 15 worn-out and injured soldiers who had survived the day's combat, together with the commanding officer, snuck out of their posts after dusk and headed for the hills. They were never again mentioned (Prasad & Pal 1987: 21).

The stories of other outposts and detachments are similar. They all fought fiercely against overwhelming odds before retreating during the dark hours. The Muzaffarabad detachment under Havildar Bishan Singh managed to withdraw into the hills and reach Srinagar after a gruelling journey. On the night of 26-27 October, the defenders withdrew towards Baramulla, facing several obstacles and fierce fighting along the way. Despite being repeatedly depleted by casualties; the group finally reached a barricade under heavy enemy fire. Here, Brig. Gen. Rajendra Singh and his men made a final stand, sacrificing themselves nearly to the last man. Singh was awarded the Maha Vir Chakra posthumously for his bravery and devotion to duty. He and his men held off thousands of enemy forces for four crucial days, helping to prevent the siege and looting of the entire Kashmir Valley.[17]

Looters rushed into the prosperous town of Baramulla on the evening of 26 October 1947. The place was quickly turned over to looting. Homes in the tribal territory were looted and then burned. A Kashmiri Muslim patriot and an active member of the NC, Maqbool Sherwani was shot dead in public for stalling the raiders (ibid.: 23). As they approached the outskirts of Baramulla town, he rode around on his bike warning them not to move into Srinagar since the Indian Army had already arrived. As per another version, he even misguided them in the wrong direction. His bluff succeeded. For four days, the enemy was stopped in its tracks.[18] His efforts brought more time for Indian Army to advance ahead in the region of Kashmir, An Englishman, Col. Dykes, and several of his assistants who ran the Baramulla Mission Hospital were also shot (ibid.: 23).

In the frenzied excitement of looting and rape, the ultimate goal of their *jihad* or 'holy war' was forgotten. Every man strove to obtain as much wealth or as many girls as he could, and in times of rejection, harassed by the 'Hindu' Maharaja of Srinagar or the 'liberation of the oppressed Muslims' 'in Kashmir. Many raiders returned home with full loot and responded to the officers' reprimands by saying they would be back soon after depositing their treasures in a safe place.[19]

OPERATION DATTA KHEL

On 1 August Maj. Gen. Scott and Lt. Col. Roger Bacon flew out of Gilgit. At that time, fifth J&K Infantry (JAK) was deployed in the G-B area but was scheduled to be relieved soon by 6 JAK Infantry, which had equal ratios of Poonchi Muslims and Sikhs. After the ceremonies got over at Gilgit, Ghansar Singh discovered that all controlled articles like salt, kerosene oil, cloth, sugar, etc., had been unduly consumed or had been intentionally mismanaged and there was nothing left in the stores. It was an obvious attempt on the part of the British to discredit the state administration by creating a shortage of essential commodities in the area. Contrary to what Maj. Brown claimed later in his memoirs, Brig. Ghansar Singh found the public to be happy with the change while being a bit surprised to see the governor arriving without his own team of officials (Raina & Singh 2021: 72).

The battalion was commanded by a Muslim officer, Lt. Col. Abdul Majid Khan. Bunji was located about 35 miles away from Gilgit. However, as per the reports reaching the governor, Muslim troops of the leading company under Capt. Hassan Khan, while on their way to Bunji, had shouted pro-Pakistan slogans not only at Bandipore but also along their route in Gurez as well as Astore. Many civilians sent applications to the governor requesting him not to allow the rest of the battalion into the G-B region. Brig. Ghansar Singh forwarded those applications to Maj Gen. Scott who confirmed the news through a police officer who had been a witness to sloganeering at Warwam near Koorgbal. Maj Gen. Scott then ordered the governor to have an enquiry done and send the culprits back to Srinagar under an escort. A few days later, all officers of 6 JAK Infantry at Bunji, were invited by the governor to participate in the celebrations to mark the birthday of the Maharaja.

There were three Muslim officers, including the CO and as many non-Muslim officers that were unknown to the governor. The Muslim officers used the opportunity to interact with Gilgit Scout officers and JCOs and became part of the plot. Moreover, Maj. Gen. Scott informed the governor that all his attempts to draw the attention of the PM to the issues at Gilgit had failed and the governor would have to fend for himself. The governor then wrote two personal letters to the PM, Maj. Gen. Janak Singh and Dy. PM, Ram Lal Batra, clearly stating that in case the Maharaja went along to India, Gilgit would cede to Pakistan with the help of the Scouts, as well as the Muslim soldiers of 6 JAK Infantry. No reply, as per Brig. Ghansar's memoirs, was ever received (Raina & Singh 78-9). Maj. Brown explained the plan of Operation Datta Khel step by step in his book:

> On D-day, in Gilgit, he was to act as follows:
>
> 1. Put the Governor and his staff under protective custody;
> 2. Put all Hindus and Sikhs in a refugee camp under guard;
> 3. Cut all telephone links;
> 4. Take over the civil wireless station;
> 5. Set up my own administration of the entire Province;
> 6. Signal the Prime Minister of the North-West Frontier Province (NWFP) in Peshawar, to the effect, that there had beena revolt in Gilgit in favour of Pakistan, and with the request that he should inform Pakistan Government;
> 7. Take whatever steps I considered necessary to uphold the new regime. (Brown 2015: 163)

It was the plan hatched by the British, certainly not without the knowledge of the Crown and the government in Britain, to cater to a situation wherein, the Hindu Maharaja of the state decided to go with India. Lord Ismay, the military advisor to the British PM Churchill, had been vocal about the strategic interests of the British in the region and there is enough evidence to prove that he, too, played a major role in the conspiracy. His closeness to Field Marshal (FM) Auchinleck, as well as the Muslim Punjabis leaders was well known. At the middle level, Viceroy Lord Mount-batten, despite his claims to the contrary and Commander-in-

Chief of Pakistan, Gen. Frank Messervy, as well as Governor George Cunningham, played their roles that varied from misleading the Indian leadership to countering any military move that could endanger the very existence of Pakistan into strategizing with Jinnah to marshalling the resources and frenzied men to carry out the undeclared mission of Pakistan. As far as the G-B region, per se, was concerned, the execution plan was devised by none other than Governor Cunningham and Lt. Col. Bacon who then tasked Maj. Brown and Capt. Jock Mathieson to execute the plot mercilessly (Raina & Singh 2021: 95).

It is clear from the accounts of Maj. Brown that he was not sure about the loyalty of Muslim soldiers from the 6th Kashmir Infantry. He was frightened that if they showcased their loyalty towards the Maharaja then their plan would collapse. Maj. Brown planned the operation by keeping this possibility in his plan which he mentions in detail as follows:

> A fighting patrol of three platoons of Scouts would move out from Chilas and move with all haste to the Raikote bridge. From here the patrol would continue on the left hand bank of the Indus and move secretly to Bunji via the Hattu Pir and Ramghat bridge. Their arrival at Bunji would coincide with the start of the operation in Gilgit and Chilas which would be at night. They would then make a lightning surprise attack on the quarter-guard, rifle kotes, and magazine of the 6th Kashmir Infantry. These were all in the same area so the task would not be difficult. They would liquidate the sepoys on duty on the quarter-guard, and secure the rifle kotes and magazine. It had already been ascertained that except for those on quarter-guard duty, all rifles were placed in the kotes at night. The battalion would therefore be hors de combat now, and could easily be made prisoners *in toto*. At the same time as this attack was being carried out, a fighting patrol from Gilgit would liquidate the 6th Kashmir Infantry picquets at Jaglote and Partab Pul Bridge. Scout picquets would then be posted on the bridges at Chamogarh, Partab Pul, Ramghat, and Raikote and our tactical position would be secure for the meantime. If on the other hand, the Muslims of the 6th Kashmir Infantry were prepared to forego their allegiance to the Maharaja and join us, then we would leave the task of crippling the rest of the Battalion to them.
>
> This would be very simple if done with surprise. A patrol from Chilas would merely wipe out the Battalion picquets at Jaglote and Partab Pul Bridge; the Scout patrol would secure the latter to ensure that in the event of the

Muslims in Bunji failing to carry out their task, the Sikhs and Dogras would be unable to cross the river and play havoc in the Sub-division. Prior to D Day I would get rid of Said and Mohammed Khan by some means or other. I would also send the Nagir platoon in Gilgit to Gupis and withdraw the Hunza platoon from Kalamdarchi. The Governor had already agreed to the evacuation of this post. The Mir of Hunza had agreed to garrison it with his own levies. I hoped to have my dispositions on D day as follows: one Nagir platoon, one Punialplatoon, and one Kuh Ghizr platoon in Gilgitheadquarters; one Hunza platoon en route to Gilgit (or actually arrived) from Kalamdarchi; one Nagir platoon and one Hunza platoon in Gupis; one Nagir platoon, one Gilgit platoon, one Hunza platoon, one Yasin platoon, plus about fifty armed levies in Chilas. (Brown 2015: 163-4)

Among the close confidantes of Maj. Brown, were a few JCOs whom he had been able to bring under his absolute control and who, in the days that followed, played a key role in the plot as it was unfolded by Maj. Brown and Capt. Mathieson. The Viceroy Commissioned Officers (VCOs) were mostly from royal families and there was a certain amount of casteism in existence within the ranks and files of Gilgit Scouts. However, given the traditional loyalties, the presence of such royals in Maj. William's coterie meant least friction during the execution. In addition to Sub Maj. Babar Khan (of Nagar), Sub Mohd. Azam Khan (of Koh Ghizr), Jemadar Mohd. Shah Khan (of Hunza), Jemadar Safiullah Beg (of Hunza), Jemadar Fida Ali and Jemadar Sultan Feroze (of Nagar) were the workhorses on whom Maj. Brown had been betting his chances (Raina & Singh 2021: 94).

This well-planned operation was code named Operation Datta Khel which is sometimes mentioned in Maj. William Brown's accounts as a *coup d'état*. One day before the attack, Brown mentioned how he further used the religious sentiments of the Muslim soldiers of Gilgit Scouts to ensure their loyalty and full commitment towards the operation. On the night of 31 October 1947, he said 'Under my personal supervision each man would then swear allegiance to Pakistan on the Holy Quran' (Brown 2015: 202). Even on the day when Operation Datta Khel was executed, the Muslim soldiers of Gilgit Scouts were manipulated once again in the morning. A Holy Quran was placed in front of them on the table, they placed their right hands on the book and swore by

Almighty God that they would be faithful to the cause (Brown 2015: 205).

In order to avoid treachery from any tribe, the three platoons in Gilgit—Nagir, Punial and Kuh Ghizr were reorganized so that each platoon would contain one section of each tribe. This was done to guard the possibility of treachery from one particular tribe. As per Brown's plan, one platoon was to move to the governor's house to place him under arrest and place him in custody. One section was given the task to ensure that no messages were sent out of Gilgit from the post office until the telephone wires had been effectively cut in all directions. Two sections were to be sent to the wireless operator's bungalow to protect Limbuwala and his set. By this time the Sikh and Dogra troops of the 6th Kashmir Infantry were on their way to Gilgit. One heavily armed platoon under Jamadar Safiullah Beg was assigned to proceed for Bhup Singh Parri to wipe off the Sikh and Dogra troops (ibid.: 203).

It is worth noticing, how a British officer, a representative of colonial rule was making relentless efforts to prevent the accession of the Gilgit-Baltistan region to India, trying his best to avoid any scope of treachery or disloyalty, working with every ounce of strength so that Pakistan could get Gilgit-Baltistan. But despite all this planning and plotting Maj. Brown had to face numerous challenges. For starters, there were issues with the repaired radio battery, and to make matters worse, the radio signals from Chilas (It was a sub-division of the Gilgit Agency and was situated in the South on the bank of Indus, Areas of Gor, Kinargarh, Hodar, Buniar, Thak Butgah, Gicha and Thor fell under the subdivision) were weak'. The message for operation Datta Khel could only be delivered by midnight. Albeit, the post office and Gilgit bridges were captured easily and outsiders had collected on the Polo Grounds. After a while, this mob marched towards the governor's residence and raised pro-Pakistan slogans.

Brown mentions that they were turned back by Baber Khan who had considerable influence over them. The kind of influence Baber Khan had over this mob, further supports the claim that most of these men were outsiders and they were to obey the commands given to them by either Maj. Brown or his associates. Till the capture of the post office and Gilgit bridges, everything went more or less as per the plan but the biggest challenge was the unwillingness of governor Ghansar Singh to surrender. He had with him in the house, his orderly, his Sikh servant, the office superintendent and a small Sikh boy. They gathered all the ammunition they had inside and fired substantial rounds to resist the siege from within. Brown said that the Subedar Maj. of Gilgit Scouts obeyed his orders implicitly that the governor was not to be killed. Although a machine gun was fired high over the house, an estimated ten thousand rounds of ammunition were fired uselessly in the hope that this might force the governor to surrender, which was however in vain. Maj. Brown ordered the Scouts to keep the cordon around the house and hoped that the governor would eventually surrender by the morning. The governor surrendered the next morning which was signalled by a green illuminating fire in the sky by the Scouts (Brown 2015: 145).

As per the planning of Operation Datta Khel Maj. Brown was expecting that the 6th Kashmir Infantry en route would consist predominantly of Sikh or Dogra soldiers but to his surprise, one of his trustworthy informants told him that the contingent consisted of about two hundred Muslim Sepoys under Col. Majid and Capt. Mirza Hussain. This was a rather startling news. Evidently, Majid had been clever enough to see the showdown that would result if he brought the Sikhs or Dogras to Gilgit; so, on receipt of the message from the Governor he had set off himself with the Muslims. Majid, however, had far too much control over his battalion. The only way to paralyse the dangerous potentialities of the entire unit was to separate the Colonel completely from his men. So, Maj. Brown said he sent back a message that the Colonel should be placed under arrest immediately and sent to Gilgit. The Muslim troops should remain at Bhup Singh Parri with the Scouts. It was imperative for him that he should see Mirza Hussan immediately so that a plan could be coordinated in the light of this new development. When the governor surrendered, Maj. Brown was at the wireless station. He went there to deliver a message to Khan Abdul Qayum Khan in Peshawar through wireless. This important message has been presented in his memoirs as follows:

To:
KHAN ABDUL QAYUM KHAN PREMIER
N.W.F. PROVINCE
From: MAJOR BROWN 010900

Revolution night 31st to 1st in Gilgit Province entire pro-Pakistan populace has overthrown the Dogra regime—stop—owing imminent chaos and bloodshed Scouts and Muslim State Forces taken over law and order—stop—Scout Officers and Muslim Officers State Forces running administration temporarily—stop—request higher authority be approached immediately and reply through wireless—stop—can carry on meantime Commandant Scouts – stop—messageends. (Brown 2015: 212)

Brown also sent a personal message to Col. Bacon who was now the Political Agent of the Khyber Pass and had his headquarters in Peshawar.

To:
COLONEL BACON
From: BROWN 010900

Coup d'état in favour Pakistan in Gilgit—stop—can carry on meantime but can you help—stop—Brown—stop—message ends. (ibid.: 213)

On the other side of the border, more than 20,000 tribesmen from the NWFP had been gathered and placed at launch pads under the direct supervision of Sardar Abdul Qayyum Khan and Governor Cunningham of NWFP. The Pir of Manki, too, played a crucial role in congregating the Pashtuns. Many volunteers from West Pakistan and soldiers too joined the hordes, in addition to those specifically nominated to lead the Lashkars. As Governor Cunningham boasted later, 'I would only have to hold up my little finger to get a lashkar of 40,000 or 50,000', any attempt by the historians to absolve the British of treachery, would not stand even casual scrutiny. However, no such invading horde had been placed towards Gilgit because as per the British and Pakistan think tanks, Gilgit didn't need outsiders to liberate it.[20]

As for the wishes of the people of Kashmir, an interesting incident is mentioned by Sheikh Abdullah in his memoirs. In May 1944, Jinnah visited Srinagar and during his stay, Ali Mohammad Tariq asked him if the future of Kashmir would be decided by the people living there. Pat came the reply, 'Let the people go to hell'. When people learnt about this, they were quite hurt.[21] Similar was the case with the formation of the government in Pakistan-Occupied Kashmir after these tribal invasions backed by them which they repeatedly preferred to call indigenous uprisings.

PROVISIONAL GOVERNMENT OF PAKISTAN OCCUPIED KASHMIR

As per the official narrative of the Pakistan government, the provisional government of PoK (Pakistan Occupied Kashmir) was declared on 24 October 1947 but as per the memoirs of Col. Akbar Khan, the precise date for the declaration of the provisional government was 27 October 1947.

> On the morning of 27 October 1947, all over Pakistan people who were listening to the news heard of Kashmir's accession and of India's military intervention. . . . Elsewhere the news was spreading fast, whipping up resentment and strengthening the determination to resist. By the evening, the first provisional Government of Azad Kashmir (Free Kashmir) came into existence, with Sardar Ibrahim as President. (Khan 1965: 26-7)

However, Sardar Ibrahim and Justice Saraf presented the date of 24 October in their memoirs for the formation of the provisional government. Interestingly Justice Saraf claimed that even the top leadership of the Muslim Conference was not aware of the declaration of the formation of the provisional government. Not only this, he further stated that even the person who was anointed as the president of Pakistan-Occupied Kashmir had no prior knowledge of these developments which were to take place. To quote his exact words:

> This is not denied by Sardar Mohammad Ibrahim who told this author that on the 23 October, he was awakened almost at the dead of the night by Khwaja Abdur Rahim, then Commissioner, Rawalpindi Division and Nasim Shah Nawaz, then married to General Akbar Khan who told him that it had become necessary to announce the formation of a reconstituted government with himself as the president and that the announcement could not be delayed. It was under these circumstances, he emphasized that his name was announced as President. (*Saraf*, vol. 2, 2015: 547)

Justice Saraf carried on in this regard and wrote:

> The decision to set up a provisional government was no doubt right and timely but cannot approve the fact of its having being taken at such a municipal and limited level, even without the knowledge of the party's top brass (*Saraf*, vol. 2, 2015: 546)

These references further strengthen the argument that not only was the tribal invasion orchestrated by Pakistan, the authorities there played an active and dominant role in directing the formation of the provisional government irrespective of the will of the people and the local leaders.

Now the question arises what the relevance of this date was and why would Pakistan want the world to believe that the provisional government was set up on 24 October 1947 and not on 27 October 1947 as mentioned in the memoirs of Col. Akbar Khan. Well, the plan was to exhibit the formation of the provisional government before the Maharaja signed the letter of accession on 26 October 1947. This way Pakistan intended to challenge the authority of Maharaja and to a broader extent, discard his capacity to sign the letter of accession. It was a matter of disappointment for Sardar Ibrahim Khan that the 'provisional government' was neither recognized by the United Nations, nor by Pakistan. Within two years of taking office, the Muslim Conference leadership and the PoK administration were compelled to sign the Karachi Agreement of 1949 secretly, which gave Pakistan control of more than 80 per cent of the acquired area. Since the arrangement went against the UN resolutions, it was kept confidential. Sardar Ibrahim Khan was fired in 1950, after one year. He denied ever having ratified the Karachi Agreement in subsequent years (Srivastava 2021: 39). The provisional government had no control over its land and armed forces. Its army consisted of tribal raiders who were functioning under the direct command of an officer of the Pakistan Army. Justice Saraf remarked.

> The government had practically nothing to do as the liberated territory was still in a state of disorder and confusion which was quite natural in the circumstances. I have myself seen ministers weighing grain at their Asghar Mall HQ (*Saraf*, vol. 2, 2015: 548)

The United Nations Commission for India and Pakistan (UNCIP) resolutions were passed in the wake of the Indo-Pakistani War of 1947.[22] On the first day of January 1948, India approached the UN with a request for aid, owing to Pakistan's unjust seizure of substantial portions of the state. The Security Council of the UN, in response, passed a resolution on 17 January 1948, exhorting both nations to rectify the situation and to notify the Council promptly of any material alterations. The UN then deemed it fitting to establish UNCIP, which arrived in Karachi on 7 July 1948.[23] In accordance with the recommendations of the UNCIP, the UN passed a resolution on 13 August 1948, mandating a ceasefire to come into effect within four days of its acceptance by both nations. This was to be followed by the withdrawal of Pakistani troops and a portion of Indian forces from Kashmir. The final fate of Kashmir was to be determined in accordance with the will of its people. The ceasefire finally took effect on 1 January 1949.[24] These resolutions aimed to resolve the dispute over the state of J&K, which had acceded to India but was claimed by Pakistan. As per the resolutions, the state of J&K was given the responsibilities of local governance and placed within the jurisdiction of India. This meant that the government of J&K had the authority to make decisions and implement policies concerning the administration and welfare of the local population.

For several years, India awaited Pakistan's compliance with the UN-mandated conditions for a plebiscite, but as that did not occur, the J&K Constituent Assembly ratified the accession of the state to India on 6 February 1954. Later, a new Constitution for J&K was adopted by the Assembly on 17 November 1956 and went into effect on 26 January 1957. The J&K Constitution reaffirmed that 'the state is and shall be an integral part of the Union of India'.

However, in areas under Pakistani control, the UNCIP resolutions stipulated that local authority should be overseen by the UN, instead of being directly governed by Pakistan. This was done to ensure that the rights of the local population were protected and that there was no discrimination on the basis of religion or ethnicity. The government of PoK, on the other hand, had limited autonomy following the signing of the Karachi Agreement in 1949. The primary role of its officials was to promote the region externally, rather than being directly involved in the administration and welfare of the local population. The notion of 'Azad Forces' was used to bolster the illusion of an independent government in PoK, but in reality, these forces were not truly sovereign. They were commanded by Pakistan army officers on temporary leave and their main task was to maintain the security of the region. A notable example of this was Gen. Akbar Khan, who led the tribal raid into J&K in 1947 and later served as the commander of the Azad Forces in PoK (Srivastava 2021: 45).

On 28 April 1949, an agreement was signed in Karachi, solidifying the connection between the regions of Gilgit-Baltistan and Pakistan. This agreement was signed by representatives of 'Azad Kashmir', the influential Muslim Conference and the Government of Pakistan. It declared that the Political Agent in Gilgit would hold ultimate control over the Gilgit and Ladakh areas, thereby bestowing the former with immense powers. Despite the fact that Baltistan was, at the time, still part of the 'Ladakh Wazarat', the agreement referred to this region as Ladakh.[25] It formalized the relationship between the region and Pakistan, with Mushtaq Ahmed Gurmani, minister without portfolio, signing on behalf of the Government of Pakistan, while Sardar Muhammad Ibrahim, the President of 'Azad Jammu and Kashmir' (AJK), and Chaudhary Ghulam Abbas, the President of All Jammu and Kashmir Muslim Conference, signed on behalf of the region. Unfortunately, the agreement was signed under duress, as the local population was not consulted or given a voice in the matter. Since the signing of the agreement, the constitutional status of Gilgit-Baltistan has remained in a state of uncertainty. It is unfortunate that the MC, which had no real presence in the region, was a signatory to the agreement, and even more so as the region was never considered a part of 'Azad' J&K. The legacy of the Karachi Agreement continues to shape the region, and its future remains an important concern for the people who call it home (Warikoo 2014: 172-3).

The Karachi Agreement was a political manoeuvre aimed at using Gilgit-Baltistan as leverage in the ongoing conflict over Kashmir. The government believed that in the event of a plebiscite on J&K, the region would vote in favour of Pakistan. However, the agreement was never truly supported by the people of Gilgit-Baltistan or recognized as legitimate. This is because the signatories of the agreement, including representatives of the government and regional political organizations, did not truly represent the views or interests of the people of Gilgit-Baltistan, nor did they have the authority to speak on behalf of the Maharaja of J&K. The Karachi Agreement remains a contentious issue and its legacy continues to shape the political landscape of Gilgit-Baltistan (Bansal 2018: 79-80).

Sardar Ibrahim Khan, a prominent leader in the Azad Kashmir region, expressed his gratitude towards Gen. Akbar Khan for his contributions in the formation and organization of the Azad Kashmir Army. He recognized the important role that Gen. Tariq, who was actually Col. Akbar Khan using an alias, played in maintaining unity and cohesion among the officers within the organization (Srivastava 2021: 45).

Despite Pakistan's official stance of denying direct control over the Azad Forces, the country has admitted to the UNCIP that it does hold tactical authority over these forces. However, in order to maintain the illusion of autonomy for the Azad Forces and avoid the appearance of interference in the internal affairs of Azad Kashmir, Pakistan has created the illusion that these forces are independent. This allows Pakistan to maintain the appearance of impartiality and non-interference in the region, even as it exerts some level of control over the Azad Forces. This is done in order to maintain the appearance of impartiality and non-interference in the internal affairs of Azad Kashmir and to avoid pulling out its 'Azad Forces' in order to influence the outcome of a potential referendum. The world got to know about the Karachi Agreement through a judgement from the Azad Kashmir High Court (AKHC) in 1993. The judgement claimed that the transfer of territory known as the Northern Areas to Pakistan was a violation of the UNCIP that required the status quo to be maintained for holding a plebiscite (Bansal 2018: 77). The Karachi Agreement helped Pakistan in fulfilling three aspirations. First, to gain control over the day-to-day administration of PoK, second, to take over the territory of Gilgit- Baltistan and third, to take control of the so-called 'Azad Forces'.

After this PM Liaquat Ali Khan made the decision to exclude Gilgit-Baltistan from Pakistan's democratic institutions. This resulted in the region being kept separate from the rest of the country and governed directly by the Ministry of Kashmir Affairs (MKA), located in Karachi. The constitutional separation of Gilgit-Baltistan from Pakistan meant that the region was not given the opportunity to participate in the democratic process, and its residents were effectively ruled from afar. This decision had lasting ramifications for the people of Gilgit-Baltistan.[26] The region of PoK was not governed by the PoK government, rather it was the Spokesperson of the Ministry of Kashmir Affairs and Northern Areas (KANA). Sardar Ibrahim who shed light on its establishment in the region in his memoirs:

> The Azad Kashmir is now ruled by Kashmir Affairs Ministry, a council and one elected assembly. A government is installed there through the assent and blessings of this ministry. (Warikoo 2014: 160)

In 1950, the control of the region was shifted from the Governor of NWFP in Peshawar to the MKA in Karachi and the region was renamed the Northern Areas. To manage this change, a new position was established within the ministry: Political Resident and Chief Adviser to the 'Azad Kashmir' government. The day-to-day administration was handled by the Resident of Gilgit and Baltistan.[27] The Northern Areas were subjected to the Frontier Crimes Regulation (FCR) and the local rulers were brought into the administration through subsidies and the retention of a significant share of the revenues they collected. The hereditary leaders of Hunza and Nagar wielded executive, legislative and judicial authority, all the while operating under the guidance of the Political Agent.[28] As per the provisions of the Karachi Agreement, Pakistan Government-backed MKA was exercising supreme control in that region. In the upcoming years, a new generation of leaders vehemently criticized this structure of power sharing which in reality, only strengthened the dominance of Pakistan over the Gilgit Baltistan region. Justice Saraf further mentioned incidents in his accounts how the President of PoK, named Col. Sher Ahmed was made to sit in a room, waiting just to have a meeting with the Joint Secretary. Over the years the region remained underdeveloped due to a lack of funds and support from the Pakistan government which was unwilling to spend much on that region even when they wanted to keep that territory by any means.[29]

In 1952, the Joint Secretary in the Ministry was appointed as the ex-officio Resident of the Northern Areas, based in Karachi, thousands of miles away from the region. Despite this, he was granted all administrative, judicial, and revenue powers in relation to the Northern Areas. The FCR, which imposed unjust fines and punishments on the tribesmen and treated them as uncivilized, remained in effect.[30] During this period, the Northern Areas were treated as a virtual colony, with political parties and activities prohibited and the local population denied basic rights. There was a lack of investment in developing the infrastructure of the region, particularly in terms of education and health care, and all decisions were made in Islamabad and Karachi, disregarding the will of the local population.

In 1963, Pakistan signed an agreement with China, ceding 2,500 sq miles of territory of the former state of Hunza to China, despite opposition from the Mir of Hunza. The construction of the Karakoram Highway, which passed through the region, also began (Warikoo 2014: 160-1). This agreement altered the alignment between the Xinjiang Province of China and the Gilgit-Baltistan region of J&K, but as there was no representative body in Gilgit-Baltistan, the local population had no say in the matter.

In 1969, Gen. Yahya Khan established the Northern Areas Advisory Council, which was purely an advisory body and functioned under the Residents. The first election for the 16-member body was held in 1970, but it remained a powerless consultative body. The council was initially chaired by the

Resident and later by the Minister for Kashmir Affairs and Northern Areas, who was based in Islamabad (Bansal 2018: 82).

The federal government of Pakistan consistently emphasized the importance of direct communication and interaction between government departments in Pakistan and those in PoK. This is significant as it highlights the government's stance on the status of PoK and the level of autonomy it should have had within Pakistan.

Ghulam Ishaq Khan, who served as cabinet secretary of Pakistan, issued a circular, D.P. No. 8/9/70-Coord.I, on 11 May 1971, directing all Pakistan government departments to communicate directly with those in PoK. This circular further reinforced the government's position that PoK should be treated as an integral part of Pakistan and that all government departments should conduct their business with PoK departments as they would with any other province within Pakistan.[31]

The order also cited an earlier order from the Cabinet Division of the Pakistan government, dated 24 June 1970, which stated that while Azad Kashmir is not technically considered a part of Pakistan, it should be treated as any other province in practical terms. This statement is significant as it shows that the Government of Pakistan recognized that PoK is not legally a part of Pakistan but it should be treated as such in practice. This order emphasized the government's commitment to maintaining close ties with PoK and treating it as an integral part of Pakistan, rather than a separate entity. It also reflected the government's position on the status of PoK, which is a disputed territory between Pakistan and India. Ghulam Ishaq Khan's directive of 11 May 1971 stated:

> The President, in the weekly meeting of 28 April 1971 was pleased to observe once again that the problems of the administration and development of Azad Kashmir should no longer be looked upon as the exclusive concern of Kashmir Affairs Division and every Ministry in the field of its responsibility should look upon and deal with Azad Kashmir as if it were another administrative unit of the country.[32]

Pakistan's internal circulars from 1970 to 1971 reveal that it treated PoK as its own territory, despite claiming to preserve it as a distinct entity awaiting a plebiscite. These circulars, including one issued in 1988, referred to PoK as 'any other province' or 'another administrative unit' of Pakistan, effectively acknowledging that UN resolutions on PoK no longer held any relevance. Interestingly, these circulars did not grant PoK 'provincial status' or representation in the Pakistan National Assembly, further emphasizing the fact that Pakistan had already absorbed PoK in violation of United Nations Security Council (UNSC) resolutions. The PoK government was created and run by Pakistan's KANA, rather than through democratic elections or a constitution. It is worth noting that the first elections based on adult franchise in PoK did not take place until 1970 and the elected legislature and government were soon marginalized by the creation of a council headed by the Pakistan prime minister. These internal circulars provide further evidence that Pakistan had already absorbed PoK and was treating it as a part of its own territory (Srivastava 2021: 55).

In the 1971 Indo-Pak War, Indian army troops under the leadership of Maj. Chewang Rinchen of the Nubra Guards and Ladakh Scouts, were able to secure a total of 804 sq. km of territory in Baltistan, which has since become a part of the Indian state of J&K. During the 23 years of Pakistani rule, the region was neglected and faced numerous challenges, including a lack of funding for development, inadequate infrastructure, and neglected schools, dispensaries, and mosques. The division of families during the war was also a major issue, and despite attempts by the Indian army to reunite them, these efforts were not successful due to a lack of response from the Pakistani side. Following the ceasefire, the Indian government took several steps to improve the living conditions, including posting a Naib Tehsildar and a police inspector to establish law and order, a doctor and medical staff in the local hospital, and setting up fair-price shops and cooperative stores. The Indian army also provided special funds to repair and maintain mosques in the region. In addition to the 804 sq. km of Baltistan territory, Indian troops also recaptured another 110 sq. km in the Kargil sector, which included 36 Pakistani posts which were largely uninhabited. Despite the Simla Agreement, the liberated territory was not returned to Pakistan and remains an integral part of the state of J&K.[33]

Post-war, administrative reforms were carried out in the northern areas by Zulfiqar Ali Bhutto's administration. The region was supposed to be further integrated with Pakistan by the government in Islamabad following the Simla Agreement, which abolished princely states, incorporated Chitral into NWFP, and was administered through temporary ordinances without constitutional or legal backing. The utilization of the term 'northern areas' was meant to disguise Pakistan's illegal occupation and downplay the region's ties to J&K. Historical ethnic identities were also intended to be erased by portraying the region as a result of the 'Two Nation theory'. Ethnic identities and culture have always been viewed as historical connections of the region to India by Pakistan. Despite being ordered by the courts to do so, the Northern Areas have not been returned to 'Azad J&K' by Pakistan, even after the 1949 agreement lapsed with the implementation of the 1970 Act by President Yahya Khan. A resolution was passed in 1972 by the Legislative Assembly of 'Azad J&K' requesting Pakistan to return the Northern Areas, which were temporarily taken over under the Karachi Agreement, but no response has been given by Pakistan (Warikoo 2014: 174).

Pakistan considered it necessary to alter the regional administrative structure in order to eliminate any remnants of the Maharaja's Rule after the UN resolution. To this end, a Presidential Ordinance was passed in August 1972, which abolished the Jagirdari system and, consequently, the institution of Rajas, bringing about significant changes to the administrative structure. The State of Nagar and its hereditary monarchy were dissolved around the same time. The Gilgit and Baltistan Agencies were divided into districts, with their political agents serving as deputy commissioners. The Commissioner for Northern Areas was given the same title as the Resident. In December 1972, the Astor, Chilas, and Darel/Tangir subdivisions were merged to create the Diamer district, which is currently administered by a

Deputy Commissioner. The last princely state of Hunza, which had previously been a vassal of the Maharaja of J&K, was abolished during a visit by Pakistan's Prime Minister, Zulfiqar Ali Bhutto, to the region in September 1974.

In the past, the Ghanche and Ghizer districts were formed, but later, the Khaplu and Kharmong subdivisions of Baltistan's Ghanche district were merged with the Baltistan district and the Gilgit and Ghizer districts were combined as well. While economic reasons were cited as the driving force behind these decisions, Pakistani government officials were also hesitant to serve in remote regions without adequate means of transportation, which played a significant role in the dissolution of the newly established districts.

During this time, the local population had no means of expressing their opinions, as neither the Azad J&K Assembly nor the Pakistani parliament had any representation from the region. The Pakistani government took advantage of this situation to consolidate its hold on the area while avoiding public scrutiny. Political parties were not permitted and traditional administrative systems were abolished, leaving the population governed by the harsh FCR.[34]

The Northern Areas Legal Framework Order, which Bhutto issued in 1974-5, eliminated feudal systems from the area. Bhutto also abolished FCR and subjected the area to the Pakistan Penal Code. Bhutto changed Yahya's Northern Areas Consultative Council (NACC) into the Northern Areas Council in 1974, adding 14 directly elected members, although it was still led by the Commissioner and served largely as an advisory body without any legislative or executive authority.[35]

The creation of the Karakoram Highway (KKH) marked a significant milestone in Pakistan's relationship with China and the region's geostrategic importance. The Pakistani government recognized the need for greater integration and abolished the State Subject Rule, a vestige of the Maharaja's rule, which had prevented non-residents from obtaining citizenship in the state. With the construction of the KKH, outsiders could now easily migrate to the region with the assistance of the Pakistani authorities, further cementing their influence in the area.

The aim was to alter the demographic makeup of the predominantly Shia region. The decision to abolish the State Subject Rule and the construction of the KKH allowed for a significant influx of outsiders, which in turn changed the demographic profile of the region and upset the delicate balance of the local population. This was a deliberate effort by the Pakistan government to alter the cultural, religious, and ethnic composition of the region, and it was perceived as a threat by the indigenous population. There are a lot of Shias in the area, some of them are of tribal ethnicity, and there are also a lot of Ismailis, members of the Aga Khan's Ismaili sect.[36]

> Potential separatist movements are to be found in Pakistan-administered Kashmir and the Northern Areas. Both regions exhibit a strong cultural identity and a sense of alienation from the Pakistan Establishment. 'Azad' Kashmir, on the Pakistani side of the Line of Control, is culturally as close to Pakistan's Punjab as it is to Indian-administered Kashmir. Azad Kashmir is unlikely to opt to leave Pakistan, as is true of the Northern Areas such as Gilgit and Baltistan. Yet grievances do exist.The Northern Areas contain a high percentage of Shi'ia, some tribal in their ethnic origin and many Ismaili—the sect led by the Aga Khan and considered heretics by hard-line Islamists. The Pakistan government has routinely cracked down on 'nationalist' groups in this region, targeting one called the Northern Areas Thinkers' Forum, which advocates the formation of two independent states in the northwest region of the subcontinent.[37]

Since 1974, following the abolition of 'Subject State Rule', opening the way for the settlement of outsiders in the region, with the cooperation of the administration in Islamabad, the region has experienced an influx of non-indigenous population.[38] Pakistani clerics have been propagating the Twelver Shia (Ithna Ashariyyah—the official religion of Iran) and Sunni faith in G-B, leading to the development of a region where sectarian identities often correspond with physical and linguistic borders. Different valleys have distinct dialects and religious traditions, resulting in a diverse mix of beliefs across the region. Today, 60 per cent of the population in Gilgit is Shia, and 40 per cent are Sunni. In Hunza, Punial, Yasin, Ishkoman and Gupis, all are Ismailis. In the Nagar region, everyone is Shia. In Chilas and Darel/Tangir, all persons are Sunnis. In Astor, 90 per cent of the people are Sunnis, and 10 per cent are Shia. Finally, in Baltistan, 96 per cent are Shia, 2 per cent Nurbakhti (or Nurbakhshi—followers of Mohammed Nur Baksh), and 2 per cent are Sunni.[39]

As explained in the first chapter, the people of the region referred to as Dardistan of Turko-Mongoloid ancestry, have a unique ethnic identity and practice Buddhism and Islam in a way that differs from the rest of Pakistan. The majority of the population in Dardistan consists of tribes who speak Indo-Aryan and Iranian-derived Dardic languages, which are vastly different from other languages spoken in Pakistan. Within the region, there are two isolated valleys, Yasin and Hunza-Nagar, where people still speak Burushaski, a distinct language that has no known connection to any other language in the world. Burushaski speakers are a minority in the area but add to the linguistic diversity of the region. In Hunza, there are several areas where Domaaki is spoken. In the higher reaches of the Hunza River and some valleys of Ghizar, Wakhi is also spoken, a language that is also found in Tajikistan, Afghanistan, and China's Xinjiang region. In addition to Burushaski, people in Yasin and Ishkoman also speak Shina, Khowar (the language of Chitral), and Wakhi. Gilgit is a Shina-speaking region, and Burushaski is also spoken in some areas. In contrast, in Chilas and the Indus Valley below Chilas, both Shina and Kohistani are spoken. Shina is also spoken in Diamer and the majority of Ghizar. Baltistan is home to the Baltis, who are of Tibeto-Mongoloid descent and speak Balti. Thus, the region is linguistically diverse, with several languages spoken across different areas.[40]

Gilgit-Baltistan (G-B) has become a hotbed of communal conflict in recent decades due to poor economic conditions and a lack of educational facilities. The dynamics of sectarianism in this region are similar to those in Pakistan, as they share a common historical trajectory and are the result of policies implemented by the same ruling elite. Several factors have contributed to the current sectarian situation, including external involvement from 'brotherly' Islamic countries, a weak judicial system, the proliferation of small arms, and the rise of sectarian madaris (the plural word of a *madrassa* or a school for imparting religious Islamic education). Additionally, religious groups have been used to achieve Pakistan's internal and external policy objectives, further exacerbating the situation. As a result, the people of G-B continue to struggle with communal strife, with the lack of economic development and educational opportunities further complicating the issue. The need for improved governance, better access to education, and efforts to address the root causes of sectarianism remain crucial in promoting peace and stability in the region (Bansal 2018: 104). Unfortunately, poor parents are forced to enrol their kids in *madaris*, the pervasive breeding grounds for Islamic fanaticism. The *ulema* mistakenly and occasionally, actively, incite sectarian hate that frequently results in bloodshed due to a lack of a thorough knowledge of Islamic principles and opposition to contemporary science and technological education (ibid.: 104-5).

Gen. Zia-ul-Haq declared martial law in Pakistan on 5 July 1977. In addition to the four provinces, the Northern Areas were also placed under martial law. It was designated as 'Martial law Zone-E', with four provinces of Pakistan designated as zones A through D. Because of this, the Pakistani military was able to impose its tyranny on the helpless locals who had no say in local government (ibid.: 86-7).

The Karakoram Highway was officially opened by Zia-ul-Haq on 18 June 1978, marking a significant turning point in the history of Gilgit-Baltistan. Prior to its construction, the region was virtually inaccessible to the average Pakistani citizen, thanks in part to the State Subject Rule that had been abolished by Zulfiqar Ali Bhutto. However, the opening of the KKH, coupled with the removal of the State Subject Rule, opened the door for outsiders to enter and settle in the once-pristine territory. This influx of outsiders had a significant impact on the demographic make up of the region, leading to an influx of religious extremists seeking financial gain and promoting their own radical ideologies. Since then, the sectarian tensions in Gilgit-Baltistan have intensified, resulting in frequent conflicts between different groups in the area. The situation is made worse by the lack of economic development and educational opportunities, which exacerbate the underlying issues driving sectarianism in the region (ibid.: 91).

The situation in Gilgit-Baltistan worsened substantially during Gen. Zia-ul-Haq's tenure in the 1980s. To justify his military authority and encourage *jihad* in Afghanistan and the Indian State of J&K, Zia-ul-Haq utilized the slogan of Nizam-e-Mustafa to enforce Sharia law, which was generally interpreted in an anti-Shia manner. Sunni Islamist organizations and Deobandi organizations assisted in this. The Zia era, saw the proliferation of religious extremist outfits such as the anti-Shia, Sipah-e-Sahaba Pakistan (SSP); in response Shia groups such as the Tehreek-e-Nafaz-e-Fiqah-e-Jafaria would come into existence. The SSP established an armed branch called the Lashkar-e-Jhangvi (LeJ) in 1996, while the Shias established their own armed group called the Sipah-e-Mohammedi Pakistan (SMP). The forceful Sunni Islamization campaign led by Gen. Zia had a significantly negative impact on the Shia-dominated Gilgit-Baltistan area. Conflicts between sects were exacerbated by the focus of Islamabad on Sunni *ulema*, Deobandi extremist organizations and the politics of the provincial administrative officials it appointed. Additionally, maintaining sectarian divisions in Gilgit-Baltistan served the interests of the Pakistan Army in maintaining strict control over this crucial strategic region.[41] As mentioned above, the Pakistani government also took part in initiatives to change the demographics of Pakistan occupied Gilgit-Baltistan, making the native population a minority. Large swathes of land were given to non-natives in the Gilgit and Skardu regions. As they were more prosperous than the locals, other strangers bought significant tracts of property. The fast integration of Pushtun and Punjabi foreigners instilled a profound sense of unease among the natives (Swamy 2021: 88). The majority of the commerce in the region is controlled by the outsiders who established themselves there, according to the residents of Kargil who travelled to Gilgit-Baltistan to visit their relatives (ibid. 88). Dr Swamy has pointed out several other reasons behind the increasing militant activities in the region:

> The easy availability of arms in the area, including AK-47 assault rifles and rocket launchers, is another reason for the violence. Despite scores of checkpoints, arms and narcotics flow unabated into the region. The setting up of training camps for the jihadis to fight for the independence of Kashmir has made Gilgit-Baltistan a place where weapons can easily be purchased. Islamabad has turned the whole region into a military depot, which could explode anytime. Many local Sunnis, who had fought. against the erstwhile Soviet Union as

mujahideen (holy warriors) in Afghanistan, returned home after the Soviet withdrawal in the late 1980s, and joined the anti-Shia sectarian groups. In most of the Sunni-dominated areas, there was an increase in the growth of training camps where Sunni militants were given training along with arms and ammunition. The period also witnessed the return of many local Shia graduates of Gilgit-Baltistan from Iran's religious schools. 'With Iranian financial backing and s support,' they formed Shia militant organizations to counter the Sunni extremist groups. Retired Shia officials from the Pakistan Army also started training the Shia youth. (Swamy 2021: 88-9)

The 1999 Kargil War added to the already precarious circumstances in Gilgit-Baltistan. The Pakistani military used the hardline anti-Shia organization Lashkar-e-Taiba (LeT) in addition to regular forces in an effort to take Kargil, escalating an already tense situation. In addition, the existence of extremist groups like Jaish-e-Muhammad (JeM) and Harkat-ul-Mujahideen (HuM) made the area a haven for anti-Shia extremism. It was claimed that Gilgit-Baltistan was home to a sizeable number of training grounds for terrorists, including those at Tangir, Darel, Astore, Darul-Uloom, Juglote, Gilgit, Madrasa Nusratul-Islam, Konodas, Skardu City, and Ghowadi village near Skardu. By fostering the rise of sectarian conflict, these institutions turned the area into a hotbed for terrorism and radicalization (ibid.).

The first significant sectarian conflict in Gilgit-Baltistan began with the anti-Shia riots that erupted in May 1988, triggered by a disagreement over the sighting of the Ramadan moon. Sunnis in Gilgit attacked the Shias who were celebrating Eid-ul-Fitr as they were still fasting, based on their religious leaders' moon sighting. This led to a violent confrontation between the two sects. Local authorities intervened to restore order, but the situation escalated again after a brief lull of four days. The military dictatorship allegedly exploited the opportunity to use the local Sunnis, Afghan and Pakistani Wahhabis—collectively known as the *lashkar*—to 'teach a lesson' to the Shias, resulting in hundreds of deaths over three days. The *lashkars* committed heinous acts of violence and looting, despite the presence of the paramilitary Frontier Police. These events left a lasting impact on the region, with sectarian tensions continuing to simmer and erupt sporadically (ibid.).

The fact that the armed fanatics travelled a great distance to reach Gilgit without being stopped by the security personnel at any stage, reveals the involvement of the state in the attack. Dr Swamy mentions in his book:

> On the fifth day, a huge Lashkar of 80,000 Sunni extremists was sent by Zia-ul-Haq's Government to annihilate the Shias. Villages inhabited by the Shias, Jalalabad, Bonji, Darot, Jaglot, Pari, and Manawar, were completely ruined. Even their animals were slaughtered. The laskhar had travelled a long distance from Mansehra to Gilgit and the Government did not stop it. Instead, it put the blame on RAW (Research and Analysis Wing an Indian intelligence agency) and CIA (Central Intelligence Agency, the US external Intelligence Agency). (Swamy 2021: 90)

On many occasions, organizations have stoked hostility by making use of religious leaders from various religions. One of the strange events involved the release from prison of a Sipah-e-Muhammad cleric from Punjab named Allama Ghulam Raza Naqvi so that he could 'be transported to Gilgit where he would head a seminary to keep the kettle of sectarian strife boiling'. His release served as a barter in exchange for the release of Maulana Muhammad Ludhianvi, the vehemently anti-Shia head of the outlawed Sunni group Sipah-e-Sahaba, and other Lashkar-e-Jhangvi leaders who were detained (Bansal 2018: 107). In order to deny the majority of Sunni population of Gilgit-Baltistan their political rights, the authorities in Islamabad frequently enlisted the help of the Sunni minority of the region. Even Syed Tehseen Anwar, the Inspector General of Police (IGP), the top law enforcement official in Gilgit-Baltistan, acknowledged that police officers were supporting prohibited sectarian organizations in Gilgit-Baltistan and promoting sectarian causes (ibid.). It is estimated that over 1,000 lives have been lost, since the sectarian conflicts surfaced in this region in 1988 (ibid.).

The region was further alienated by President Zia-ul-Haq's attempts to spread 'Sunni-Deobandi' Islam there, as is brought out by Ahmed Khaled in his book, *Pakistan: The State in Crisis:*

> The Deobandi parties, especially Sipah-e-Sahaba spread their influence to the Northern Areas where the Shiites and the Ismailis were made to submit to their puritanical aggression.[42]

The first significant violent demonstration by the Shias in Gilgit occurred in May 1988 as a result of the general assumption that the local government was prejudiced towards Sunni extremists. In reaction, Sunni mobs from outside the area descended and, frequently, with the complicity of the state, destroyed homes and farms while lynching and burning hundreds of people to death (Bansal 2018: 91-2). Sectarian unrest has been widespread since then. The trend revealed that there were disturbances whenever the public demanded their constitutional rights.

Gen. Zia-ul-Haq, the then President of Pakistan, made a significant declaration in 1982, stating that Gilgit, Hunza, and Skardu were not part of the Kashmir issue, but rather integral parts of Pakistan. He reiterated this stance on 9 May 1982, during a press conference in Quetta, stating that the Northern Regions were not recognized as disputed territories. Additionally, he proposed that three individuals from the region serve as observers in Pakistan's National Assembly, known as the Majlis-e-Shura. Gen. Zia was pleased to see representatives from the Northern Regions attend the second session of the Majlis-e-Shura. Zia also organized a dinner for foreign diplomats assigned to Pakistan in Gilgit to demonstrate to the outside world that the area was a part of Pakistan. This declaration by Gen. Zia was an attempt to solidify Pakistan's control over Gilgit-Baltistan and gain the support of the inhabitants of the region. He stated:

> I am not talking of Kashmir; I am talking about the Northern Areas, which make part of Pakistan.[43]

Naturally, there were several severe issues with Zia's position on the status of the region. As this was going on, the 'AJK Legislature' passed a resolution in April 1982 declaring that Gilgit and Baltistan belonged to J&K and should be a part of 'AJK'. By that time, four significant political parties with some sway in the area—the Jammu and Kashmir Muslim Conference (MC), Azad Kashmir People's Party, Jammu and Kashmir Mahaz-e-Raiy Shumari and Azad Muslim Conferencehad joined the Movement for the Restoration of Democracy (MRD), which was leading an anti-Zia movement in Pakistan. On 4 May 1982, the heads of these parties wrote President Zia a letter that they all signed outlining the legal status of the region. They argued that they belonged to the State of J&K and that, like the other members of the state, a decision had not yet been made about their ultimate status. Zia subsequently acknowledged that Gilgit and Baltistan were not a part of Pakistan and were just as contentious as the rest of J&K in an interview with MJ Akbar, the editor of *Sunday* at the time.[44]

In the area, a new battle had started by 1984. An intense conflict between India and Pakistan took place at Siachen Glacier, a completely deserted area of Baltistan that was not clearly delineated as the territory of either country. The two armies fought several battles over this hostile region since 13 April 1984 and they now maintain a continuous military presence at a height of more than 20,000 ft. The conflict in Siachen is a result of the lack of a clear delineation of the region beyond the coordinates NJ9842 (Latitude 35°N Longitude 77°E) in either the Simla Agreement of 1972 or the Karachi Agreement of 1949.[45]

> Even before the armed clash between India and Pakistan in Kargil, their armies were engaged in a bitter and seemingly irrational conflict over control of the Siachin Glacier, located approximately 150 miles northwest of Srinagar, but still part of the state of Kashmir. Siachin has not been resolved, but it has been contained, albeit at a high level of violence and enormous cost. (Chari 2003: 53)

India now has complete control of the 70-km-long Siachen Glacier and all of its tributaries after 15 years of sporadic conflict. Moreover, India is in charge of the three main passes of the Saltoro Ridge, Sia La, Bilafond La, and Gyong La, which are situated west of the Glacier. In contrast, Pakistan is in charge of the glacier valleys to the west of Saltoro Ridge. Pakistan believes that due to its military activities in Siachen, India acquired more than 1,000 sq. miles (3,000 km^2) of land in Baltistan.

On 15 April 1985, Zia reaffirmed that Gilgit-Baltistan would have a representative in the National Assembly and that elections would be held in all three of the region's districts. He said that following a review, the area would have representation in both the National Assembly and the Senate after the Justice Ministry was told to eliminate obstacles to regional participation in the National

Assembly. Nevertheless, no such declaration was ever made, and the region was not represented in any Parliamentary chamber. In order to make decisions on the future of the area, a committee made up of the secretaries of finance, planning, law, establishment, education, interior, and Kashmir and Northern Areas was established in 1984-5. The committee did submit a report, but neither it nor its recommendations were ever made public.[46]

In an effort to attract visitors going from China to Pakistan or the other way round, the Khunjerab Pass was opened to citizens of other countries by May 1986. The ticket was available every year from 1 May to 31 October for international visitors with valid visas and for specific individual travellers up to 30 November, according to a statement released by the Pakistani Embassy in Beijing. The border would be available only for mail and trade services for Chinese and Pakistani authorities at all other times and it would be closed to all other travellers unless special authorization had been obtained. In 1986, five members of the Northern Areas Council—Mir Ghazanfar of Hunza, Mir Shauqat Ali Khan of Nagar, Agha Mohd Ali Shah, Mohd. Jaffar and Ghulam Ali of Baltistan—stated that Kashmir had no connection to the Northern Areas other than the fact that it had been taken over and held there for a short time before being leased to the British (Bansal 2018: 88).

On 28 May 1999, the Supreme Court of Pakistan delivered a decision of considerable historical significance. In this ruling, the Court expressed bewilderment as to the basis upon which the fundamental rights accorded by the Constitution had been withheld from the people of the Northern Areas. The Court proceeded to grant the petitions and directed the federal government to guarantee the enjoyment of basic rights, including the right to select their preferred officials and access to justice, amongst other things. Regrettably, Islamabad displayed no signs of compliance with the verdict of the Supreme Court even as the deadline lapsed six months later (ibid.: 100). This unfortunate development necessitated the diversion of resources to divisive local and sectarian conflicts at the expense of regular political activities (ibid.).

The Sunni Islamization policies of General Zia-ul-Haq were not completely abandoned by the successive Governments. Islamabad's reliance on jihadis for its proxy war in Kashmir and its policy to keep the strategically important region of Gilgit-Baltistan under its absolute control prompted it to fuel the flames of sectarian violence in the region. Chilas and Gilgit have become centres of anti-Shia extremism. Even during the democratic interlude of the 1990s in Pakistan, there was a steady increase in sectarian killings, with seven in 1990, twelve in 1991, and 30 in 1992. Gilgit was in the firm grip of sectarian violence in 1992 following the assassination of Gayyasuddin, a Sunni leader, on May 30, leading to at least 30 killings. The subsequent conciliatory peace talks ended when Latif Hassan, a Shia leader, was shot dead on 4 August 1993, again leading to clashes that claimed more than two dozen lives. In 1993, at least 20 Shias reportedly lost their lives in sectarian riots. (Swamy 2021: 90)

On 17 August 1993, the anniversary of Zia's passing, Gilgit-Baltistan had severe riots during which over 20 people lost their lives before the army was able to restore order. The army said that Shias were gathering weapons from Iran in their mosques. Following this, the Shias were persecuted, and many of them were detained (Warikoo 2014: 295).

Northern Areas Council (NAC) was extended and given the name Northern Areas' Legislative Council (NALC) in 1999. The positions of Speaker and Deputy Speaker were established in 2000 and 2002, respectively. The first NALC, which served from 1999 to 2004, did not pass any legislation. Nevertheless, none of the 18 resolutions it passed suggesting that the Ministry of Kashmir Affairs and 'Northern Areas' (KANA) take action on matters of public interest, were carried out. In May 2005, an appeal court was created, yet, the fact that KANA was in charge of running it, cast doubt on both its independence and its ability to be taken seriously.[47]

GILGIT-BALTISTAN IN THE TWENTY-FIRST CENTURY

These developments make it necessary to analyse the constitutional and legal developments that were being brought about in Gilgit-Baltistan in the twenty-first century. It is evident that the process of directly bringing the region under the control of the Pakistan federal government, began in 1974, with the abolition of the subject state as discussed earlier, in this chapter. However, the tempo to bring about greater federal control would gather steam in the twenty-first century.

Before the changes are assessed, it is first necessary, to look at the legal position of Gilgit-Baltistan with respect to the constitution of Pakistan in the twenty-first century. Gilgit-Baltistan is ruled by the 'order' of the federal Government of Pakistan. In contrast to the situation in Gilgit-Baltistan. PoK is governed by its very own set of laws. Though these two branches are now formally considered to be one in Pakistan, the fact that the elected parliament and the government of the territory, both obtain their power from the executive branch in Islamabad, indicates how precarious their positions are. The Indian position of course, has been that Gilgit-Baltistan is a part of the Indian state of J&K. The Gilgit-Baltistan Order from 2009, specifically its article 9, gives the impression that the territory has already been incorporated into Pakistan (Srivastava 2021: 210). As such the Gilgit-Baltistan Order of 2009 and the subsequent Gilgit-Baltistan Order of 2018, provide important insights into the nature of relationship between Pakistan and Gilgit-Baltistan.

The first major reason for Pakistan to desire for greater control over the region is the strategic nature of the territory. During the Kargil War that was fought in 1999, Pakistan made use of this territory as a staging ground for an invasion that took place over the Line of Control (LoC).[48] It is a strategically important territory that shares borders with China, Afghanistan and India and it is located in the region known as the Pamir Mountains. Both the China-Pakistan Economic Corridor (CPEC) and the Indus River can be found here in their respective courses. Given the region's strategic importance, Pakistan desires to have a greater degree of jurisdiction over it than they would have over PoK. This would allow Pakistan to control the situation there better. People of the region experienced setbacks both in terms of their economic advancement and civil liberties. Inhabitants of the region endured obstacles in both areas. The Human

Development Index (HDI) that Pakistan uses, places the G-B region among the regions that have the lowest score. This is one of the regions that Pakistan possesses. The United Nations Development Programme (UNDP) is the source of this information.

In 2009, the Gilgit-Baltistan Ordinance was published by the Government of President Zardari, who was a member of the Pakistan People's Party (PPP).[49] This was the 18th Constitutional Amendment of Pakistan, and it granted the country's provinces more autonomy than they previously had. Following this, the change was finally approved in the year 2010. Despite the fact that there was some progress in its status, G-B remained subject to stricter regulation than the provinces of Pakistan. This is the case despite the fact that there was some improvement. In defiance of the recommendations issued by UNCIP, it has been successfully assimilated into Pakistan (Srivastava 2021: 210).

The Karachi Accord, which was signed with the Muslim Conference in April 1949, was the agreement that handed over this territory to Pakistan, according to a landmark judgement that was reached by the High Court of the Province of Kashmir in 1993 (ibid.). The agreement was not made public since doing so would have been a breach of both the right of Kashmiris to self-determination as well as the resolutions that were voted by the UNCIP. For this, the agreement was not made public. The court issued an order requiring that the government of PoK assume administrative responsibility for the region, and it asked them to do it in writing. The verdict handed down by the PoK High Court was overturned by the PoK Supreme Court on the grounds that it lacked the legal authority to be rendered in the first place. Since 1994, the region has been managed by the Legal Framework Order that went into effect in order to regulate the area. This order was put into action so that the area could be regulated.

In a landmark ruling that took place in 1999, the Supreme Court of Pakistan ordered the Government of Pakistan to ensure that the people living in the region were granted their basic human rights. This was a very explicit recognition on the part of the highest court in Pakistan as the Pakistan government had, up to this point, denied fundamental rights to the people living in this region (Srivastava 2021: 210). The decision of the court further highlighted the fact that the exercise of these rights ought to be enforced legally. The judgement of the Supreme Court further stated that the Gilgit-Baltistan Council, which was established by the Government of Pakistan in 1994, only possessed the powers of a local government, and that the people of the Northern Areas must be permitted to exercise their right to govern through the representatives that they had chosen for themselves.[50]

The order issued by the Supreme Court effectively extended the court's jurisdiction to the region, which the Pakistani government insisted, on the other hand, did not belong to that country and was currently subject to a vote of popular approval. The Pakistan Government was given a deadline of six months by the court to incorporate any required changes to the constitution, relevant statutes, or orders in order to give effect to the court's verdict. It took Pakistan ten years to accomplish this goal. In comparison to the Legislative Framework Order of 1994, which had been in effect as the governing document of the territory until recently, the Gilgit-Baltistan Order of 2009 did, in fact, broaden the scope of the Council's legislative powers. But even this fell short of the benchmark that was established by the ruling handed down by the Pakistan Supreme Court in 1999.

The decree was issued a decade after the ruling of the Pakistan Supreme Court in 1999 that criticized the absence of representative institutions in the area. Pakistan's answer consisted in a replication of the model of dyarchy, inherent in the PoK Interim Constitution. While establishing an elected Legislative Assembly, all powers were centralized in a Council led by the prime minister of Pakistan. The majority (nine) of the Council's sixteen members represented the federal government. Thus, instead of bridging the democratic, this deficit perpetuated it.

The ruling makes no mention of the UNCIP resolutions cited in the Preamble of the PoK Interim Constitution. Neither is there any mention of a referendum. Contrary to Pakistan's statements in international forums, the exclusion is notable. The contrast conveys a subtle message: in contrast to PoK, G-B is no longer part of the territory susceptible to a referendum. It has been assimilated by Pakistan (Srivastava 2021: 210).

The first section of the order comprises definitions. The Order defines 'Citizen' as follows: 'Unless when otherwise specified in this Order, "citizen" refers to a person with a domicile in Gilgit-Baltistan.' This concept does not differentiate between the original occupants and present-day residents. Maintaining the demographic composition of the territory, a necessary condition for holding a plebiscite to ascertain the will of the people, does not appear to be a priority.

Gilgit-Baltistan has a territorial definition that does not include PoK: 'Gilgit-Baltistan denotes the lands containing the districts of Astore, Diamer, Ghanche, Ghizer, Gilgit, Hunza-Nagar, and Skardu, as well as any other districts that may be constituted from time to time.'[51] The unwillingness to make any reference to the genesis of this region, either in terms of PoK or the state of J&K is noteworthy.

The dilemma over whether the territory should remain a part of the rump territory of J&K under Pakistan control or be made separate from it, has always haunted the legislative and judicial circles in Pakistan. The strategic importance of the region provides a powerful incentive to Pakistan to exercise more direct control over the territory, whereas its political position over the erstwhile Princely State of J&K as a disputed territory, prevents it from doing so, for fear of diluting its international grandstanding on the issue. A further dilemma is provided by its weak legal claim on the territory which also stems from its political position of the region being a part of a disputed territory.

This dilemma is very evident in the famous judgement of 1993 in the case of Malik Muhammad Miskeen & 2 Others vs. Government of Pakistan, wherein the PoK High Court ruled that the area should be returned to PoK.[52] Further, in the 1999 case of Al-Jehad Trust vs. Federation of Pakistan, the Supreme Court of Pakistan criticized, among other things, the lack of fundamental rights that might be enforced by the courts. The Gilgit-Baltistan Order of 2009 attempted to resolve this issue. The order included basic rights in Part II. Article 9 of the Constitution's Freedom of Association Clause contains a unique restriction. No individual or political party in Gilgit-Baltistan is permitted to promote or engage in acts prejudicial or damaging to Pakistan the ideology as stipulated in sub-section (2). Although comparable to the exception stated in Article 4.7(2) of the AJK Interim Constitution Act of 1974, a significant absence exists. It does not state 'the philosophy of the State's admission to Pakistan'. That merely describes Pakistan's ideology. Pakistan says Gilgit-Baltistan has already joined its territory (Srivastava 2021: 211-12).

Regarding the supranational nature of the government of the Gilgit-Baltistan Council, Article 47 of the order on the distribution of legislative functions between the Council led by the prime minister and the assembly is the key to understanding the nature of the government system. Section 47 (2) specifies subject to Clause (3) (ibid.: 212):

(a) The Council shall have exclusive power to make laws regarding any matter in the Council Legislative List set out in the Third Schedule, hereinafter referred to as the Council Legislative List; and
(b) The Assembly shall, and the Council shall not, have power to make laws regarding any matter enumerated in the Fourth Schedule referred to as the Assembly Legislative List.
(c) The Council shall possess the authority to enact any adjustment to the existing laws or any new law in effect in Pakistan.

Article 3, which qualifies the powers of both the Council and the Assembly, states:

(3) The Government of Pakistan shall have the exclusive competence to establish laws regarding any topic not listed in the Council Legislative List or the Assembly Legislative List by order published in the Official Gazette. (ibid.).

The Third Schedule has fifty-five items regarding the legislative powers of the prime minister-led Council, while the Fourth Schedule contains sixty-one articles regarding the legislative powers of the assembly. This gives the impression that the powers of the two bodies were distributed evenly. Nonetheless, the majority of significant issues stayed either with the Council or were not mentioned in either of the two lists, indicating that they were vested in the Pakistani government pursuant to Article 47, paragraph 3 as stated above.

With few exceptions, the Fourth Schedule of the Legislative List of the assembly dealt with municipally-related matters. Yet, even this was an improvement, as the scope of the authority of the assembly was now clearly defined. In fact, this was an improvement over the period when the region was governed by the Frontier Crimes Regulation Act (FCRA) (Srivastava 2021: 213).

The Third Schedule of the Council's legislative agenda featured two crucial subjects that have significant implications for Pakistan's international relations and economic growth. Important to the development of the CPEC, roadways were included in item 19. The subject of point 34 was electricity and bulk storage which has the potential to generate huge hydroelectric revenue for the territory (ibid.).

However, the conditions attached in the case of motorways and the provision of the Pakistani Constitution (Article 161) in the case of electricity prevented G-B from invoking them to its advantage. Then, why were they included? The inclusion of these issues on the legislative agenda of the Council removed them from the jurisdiction of the G-B Assembly and precluded the Assembly from introducing legislation in the future to utilize these resources for the benefit of the G-B people. According to Article 47 (2) (a), the Council led by the prime minister of Pakistan had exclusive jurisdiction over these things.

Gilgit-Baltistan can generate substantial earnings due to its strategic location and the CPEC's traversal of the territory. However, the item was included on the legislative list of the Council, headed by the prime minister, rather than the legislative list of the assembly—Item 19 on the Third Schedule of the

Legislative list of the council says: 'Highways, continuing beyond the region of Gilgit-Baltistan, excluding routes recognised to be of vital importance by the Government of Pakistan'.[53]

The Council had sole control over the subject matter of the Third Schedule. The addition of roadways to the Council list had the consequence of removing a significant revenue stream from the jurisdiction of the local government. In reality, the 2009 Gilgit-Baltistan Empowerment and Self-Governance Order disempowered the territory. Even the Council was prohibited from having control over roads identified by the Government of Pakistan to be of strategic importance, as the text of the document reveals.[54] Article 47(3) stipulates that things excluded from both the Council and assembly lists fall under the jurisdiction of Pakistan. Consequently, the critical roadways comprising the CPEC will fall totally under Pakistan's control. The same consideration is given to energy and water, two more possible sources of income. It is part of Item 34, titled 'Electricity and Bulk Water Storage'.

The exclusive competence granted to the Council by Article 47 (2) (a) over items on its list has barred the assembly from considering any legislation on the issue. Yet, this is a tricky subject. There is a notion that this requires a constitutional amendment in Pakistan. According to Article 161, Gilgit-Baltistan, which is not a province, is ineligible to collect 'Net Hydel Profit' (NHP) or royalty on hydroelectric power which it generates.

Article 47 (3), which was cited a few paragraphs before, is an ideal match to the plan for disempowering Gilgit-Baltistan. It gives the Government of Pakistan authority over any topic not included in the Council list or the legislative list of the parliament. It is easier to empower Pakistan at the expense of the region and its people through silence or omission (Srivastava 2021: 214).

Comparing Article 47 (3) of the Gilgit-Baltistan Order of 2009 to a similar clause in the Azad J&K Interim Constitution Act of 1947 demonstrates that G-B has been treated more harshly than PoK. Article 31 (3) on the 'Legislative Authority of AJK' excludes four specific subjects from the Council or the competence of the assembly, reserving them for the Pakistan government. These are Pakistan's UNCIP resolution responsibilities: defence, currency, and external affairs. The exclusion mentioned in Article 47 (3) of the Gilgit-Baltistan Order did not specify prohibited items, making it more expansive. It gave the Pakistan government authority over any matter not listed on the legislative agendas of the Council or the parliament.

According to the Pakistan narrative, Gilgit-Baltistan no longer belongs to PoK. In that case, the Constitution of Pakistan would serve as a better comparative point than the PoK Constitution in terms of residual powers. The relevant section of Article 142 of the Pakistan Constitution is as follows:

142: Subject matter covered by Federal and provincial statutes:

(a) The Majlis-e-Shoora (Parliament) has the only authority to enact legislation pertaining to any matter on the Federal Legislative List.
(b) Majlis-e-Shoora (Parliament) and a Provincial Assembly have the authority to enact legislation pertaining to criminal law, criminal procedure, and evidence.
(c) Subject to subparagraph (b), a Provincial Assembly, and not the Majlis-e-Shoora (Parliament), shall have the authority to legislate on any subject not included in the Federal Legislative List.
(d) Majlis-e-Shoora (Parliament) shall have exclusive legislative authority over all matters pertaining to territories of the Federation not under the jurisdiction of a province.[55]

Point (c) in the preceding article makes it apparent that Pakistan's Constitution vests residual powers in the 'Provinces'. G-B falls under Point (d), which pertains to 'those territories of the Federation that are not part of a Province'. In their case, the Pakistan Parliament holds residual authority. This is a divergence from the model applied to the provinces of Pakistan. Gilgit-Baltistan is considered differently and on a lower level than the provinces of Pakistan. The land was separated from PoK but was not granted provincial status. It received the most restrictive treatment of the two. G-B is thus subject to twofold peril (Srivastava 2021: 216).

Article 142 (d), which says that 'such areas in the federation as are not involved in any Province' is intriguing. If G-B and PoK are awaiting a referendum and are not a part of Pakistan, they should not be included in the Constitution of Pakistan. In UN phraseology, they are referred to as non-self-governing territories or colonies if they are not members of the federation but are under its supervision (ibid.: 216).The argument that G-B is not a part of Pakistan and hence is not entitled to the economic benefits provided to the 'provinces' of Pakistan is illogical. The unique status of G-B in Pakistan could have allowed for a more generous treatment, or at least an equal treatment, without changing the distribution of provincial authorities.

Further, there is much to be said about the legislative powers of the Gilgit-Baltistan Assembly. Sixty-one topics were included in the Fourth Schedule as the legislative competence of the Gilgit-Baltistan Assembly. In contrast to the 'AJK Interim Constitution Act, 1974', which did not define the powers of the assembly, this bill broke new ground by defining their scope (ibid.). If this was in response to the 1999 order of the Pakistan Supreme Court, it was only a partial remedy. The Supreme Court had made a caustic statement that the Northern Areas Council, created in the wake of the 1993 PoK High Court verdict, was entrusted with the functions of a municipal government.[56] The court had ordered the Pakistani government to take administrative or legislative action within six months to ensure that the people of G-B enjoy 'their above fundamental rights, namely to be governed by their elected representatives'. An assembly has replaced the Council. The majority of the powers delegated to the elected 'assembly' by the Gilgit-Baltistan Order, 2009, pertain to municipal functions such as libraries, botanical surveys, theatres and cinemas, markets and fairs, inns and innkeepers, orphanages and poorhouses (ibid.).

The Gilgit-Baltistan Order of 2009 was a welcome experiment in the devolution of power, given the territory's banal history of administration under the British-era Frontiers Crime

Regulations (FCR). However, this experiment was short-lived, and the Government of Gilgit-Baltistan Order of 2018 eliminated the separate list for an elected legislature.

Further, the executive authority of the Gilgit-Baltistan assembly is quite limited. Article 31 of the Gilgit-Baltistan Order of 2009 defines the executive authority of the government as follows: '(1) Subject to this Order, the executive authority of the Government shall extend to the matters with respect to which the Assembly has power to make laws'.[57]

As the Council was granted the majority of legislative authority, the executive authority of the government was similarly constrained. Complex government organization and procedure was irrelevant. It was simply intended to create the impression that adequate powers had been delegated to the local administration in the absence of actual powers. Without delegating meaningful powers, a top-heavy administration brought off the loyalty of significant portions of the local elite through the provision of sinecures.

Gilgit-Baltistan also suffered from having to pay taxes to Pakistan without having any representation in the Pakistani legislature. No taxation without representation is one of the fundamental tenets of democratic government. The Gilgit-Baltistan Order of 2009 attempted to sidestep the issue by referencing statutes. The pertinent Article 48 is as follows:

> 48. Tax to be levied by laws only. No tax shall be levied for the purposes of the territories of Gilgit-Baltistan except by or under the authority of an Act of the Council or the Assembly and all taxes and levies competently imposed under an Act of the Assembly or the Council or under any law made by the Government of Pakistan shall remain in force.[58]

Customs charges, excise duties, non-agricultural income tax, corporate tax, sales tax, and capital gains tax on immovable property were included on the legislative agenda of the Council. The assembly legislative list included land revenue, toll tax, taxes on automobiles, taxes on luxury, entertainment tax, etc. Under Article 56, the budget of G-B must be submitted before the assembly.[59] Yet, the budget-making job was largely symbolic due to the Council's control over the primary sources of taxation. Under the Gilgit-Baltistan Order of 2009, the assembly and the government primarily had tasks without authority.

Further, it was the objective of these legal provisions to emphasize the Islamic character of the people at the cost of their Kashmiri identity. The Gilgit-Baltistan Order of 2009 was mute on the Kashmiri ethnicity of its inhabitants, but stressed their Islamic identity. Article 49 of the Islamic Provisions section of Part VIII specified that no law should contradict the teachings and requirements of Islam. Article 50 addressed legislative reference to the Council of Islamic Ideology by the legislature or the Council (Srivastava 2021: 218).

Part XI (Articles 60 to 79) of the Gilgit-Baltistan Order of 2009 established a complex organization, comprising the Gilgit-Baltistan Supreme Appellate Court, the Supreme Judicial Council, and the main court. On the advice of the governor, the prime minister of Pakistan was to nominate all levels of judges as head of the Council. The process did not involve the elected chief executive. This also precluded the collegium of judges from participating in appointments to the superior judiciary. This left no room for the Pakistan Supreme Court to make appointments in the judiciary (ibid.: 218-19).

A judiciary so reliant on the nation's prime minister is unlikely to render decisions that are detrimental to Islamabad. From the Gilgit-Baltistan Order of 2009, it appears that the G-B Supreme Appellate Court would be the highest court of appeal. In 2018, however, the Supreme Appellate Court's challenges to Islamabad's power were swiftly overturned wherever they arose. The Supreme Court of Pakistan reinstated the 2018 Government of Gilgit-Baltistan Order, which the Supreme Appellate Court had declared null and void. The latter affirmed its jurisdiction over the territory in the ruling it rendered on the Government of Gilgit-Baltistan Order, 2018. The decision of the Supreme Court suggested a slightly amended order, renamed the 'Gilgit-Baltistan Government Reform, 2019'.

People protested against the old Gilgit-Baltistan Order of 2018, which was promulgated on 15 May 2020. This section demonstrates that in addition to merging administrative and legislative responsibilities, the Council led by the prime minister of Pakistan would also oversee judicial nominations.

Under conditions of an emergency, Article 87 authorized the prime minister of Pakistan, as chairman of the Gilgit-Baltistan Council, to issue an emergency declaration. The justifications for such a proclamation were 'war, external aggression, or internal unrest'. The chairman could act on receipt of a report from the governor of G-B or otherwise. Likewise with judicial appointments, the chief minister played no role in this procedure; he remained a figurehead.[60]

In the event that the chairman of the Council declared a foreign or domestic emergency, it was possible that all executive powers of the G-B government would be undertaken by the chairman of the Council of the governor on his behalf. A proclamation of emergency could be followed by an order suspending fundamental rights, as per Article 88.[61] Under Article 89 (2), neither the declaration of emergency nor the suspension of fundamental rights was subject to judicial review: 'The validity of any Proclamation issued or order made under Article 87 or Article 88 shall not be questioned in any Court'.[62]

The Gilgit-Baltistan Order of 2009 was a step forward, despite its many limits, in that it granted the assembly limited but defined legislative authority. The experiment was replaced in 2018 by the Government of Gilgit-Baltistan Order, which is a throwback to a time when Islamabad exercised greater centralized control. The loss of the 2009 order was lamented by the local populace. There is speculation that the Shia-dominated region received concessions under the tenure of Asif Zardari, who was sympathetic to their objectives. Since the CPEC became increasingly important in the scheme of things, a more secular reading may be that the military sought to consolidate its control on the territory (Srivastava 2021: 220).

The Gilgit-Baltistan Governance Reform Order of 2019 was to be proclaimed by the Pakistan Government within fifteen days following the ruling of the Supreme Court of Pakistan in January 2019 (Srivastava 2021: 238). The Pakistan Government continued to implement the previous order of 2018 with an addendum extending the Election Act of 2017 to the region for more than fourteen months. The Supreme Court approved the modification, despite the fact that it amounted to an executive defiance of the highest court.

According to the presidential decree, the version on which the Supreme Court ruled in January 2019 remains the 'proposed Gilgit-Baltistan Government Reforms 2019'. The area lacks a written constitution. These directives are executive decrees issued by Islamabad that provide the legal framework within which G-B must operate. If they are subject to such frequent change, ambiguity is inevitable.

The Gilgit-Baltistan Order of 2009 was enacted under the administration of Asif Zardari. It gave some respite to the inhabitants of the region by broadening the scope of the legislative powers of the assembly, while the Council led by the prime minister of Pakistan remained responsible for the majority of crucial subjects.[63] The 2018 Government of Gilgit-Baltistan Order downgraded the Council to an advisory capacity.[64] Yet, the authority of the Council was not passed to the elected parliament. Instead, they were assumed by the prime minister of Pakistan. The latter would wield authority directly, rather than via the Council, where the local community was re-presented. In addition, the distinct listing of the powers of the elected assembly was eliminated, leaving it with ambiguous, undefined authority. There is nothing equivalent in Pakistan's provinces to the structure of the Order in which the prime minister of Pakistan wields supreme legislative and executive authority in the nation.

The 2009 G-B Order came into effect before the 2010 18th Amendment to the Constitution of Pakistan, which delegated additional authority to provinces. The Government of Gilgit-Baltistan Order of 2018 was enacted eight years later and resulted in a more centralized rule over the region. Different trajectories followed by G-B and the provinces of Pakistan demonstrate the prejudice against the G-B population. They are viewed as inferior individuals.

The narrowing political space for the people of G-B must be attributed to the alteration of the internal and foreign situation of Pakistan in the meantime. By 2018, the political landscape of Pakistan had shifted. The PML-N government succeeded the Zardari administration in 2013. This was then followed in 2018 by Imran Khan's PTI. The military had made a return. Qadri's public protests against Nawaz Sharif's government were supported by 'invisible forces', or 'Khalai Maqhlooq', as the embattled prime minister referred to the intelligence agencies (Srivastava 2021: 240).

The Government of Gilgit-Baltistan Order of 2018 has two notable provisions. It unites the region in everything but name with Pakistan, and the prime minister of Pakistan takes direct responsibility for the most essential legislative tasks. They go beyond the three issues often cited by Pakistan, including defence, foreign policy, and currency. Under the Third Schedule of this order, there are sixty-eight issues designated for the exclusive competence of the prime minister. Among them are immigration, citizenship, critical roads and highways, energy, and bulk water storage, in addition to the vast majority of the essential taxes.[65] The Pakistan Citizenship Act of 1951 is particularly included in the definition of citizenship. Accession is seen as a fait accompli.[66]

The allocation of powers between the Council and the elected assembly demonstrates that the true 'authority' does not rest with the 'local authority', which Pakistan says is the foundation for its control over the area. Earlier, it was vested in the Council led by the prime minister of Pakistan. It currently resides solely with the prime minister. Part IX of the Gilgit-Baltistan Government Reform, 2019 now includes a chapter on Islamic Provisions. The second factor is the disenfranchisement of the inhabitants of the territory. A list of sixty-one subjects that the elected assembly could formerly legislate on has been entirely eliminated. This foreshadows future events should the area become a 'province' of Pakistan. In a democracy, the clause giving immunity to the military forces is contrary to the norm.

According to the Gilgit-Baltistan Order of 2018, a citizen was defined as 'a person who has a domicile or residence of Gilgit-Baltistan and who is a citizen under the Pakistan Citizenship Act, 1951 (II of 1951)'.[67] This equates to applying the Pakistani law directly to Gilgit-Baltistan. Obviously, this is nothing new. From its creation, the territory has been governed by Pakistani law. This definition makes demographic change possible by enabling any Pakistani to claim Gilgit-Baltistan citizenship on the basis of residency; it is also an explicit acknowledgement that the region has been incorporated with Pakistan. That is a divergence from Pakistan's view on the application of UNSC resolutions to Kashmir on both points. The concept of citizenship is based on 'domicile' or 'residence'; there is no mention of the 'State Subject Rule', which restricts citizenship to the original occupants prior to 1947 and their descendants. This opened the door for an inflow of Pakistani people entering the country.

The phrasing of the clause on joining Pakistan is slightly different in the Interim Constitution of PoK and the Government of Gilgit-Baltistan Order, 2018. The Interim Constitution of PoK suggests that it supports and stands for accession to Pakistan, which implies that accession is incomplete and yet to happen.[68] However, in the Government of Gilgit-Baltistan Order, the wording implies that the territory has already joined Pakistan. Article 17(2) of the 2018 Order states that 'No person or political party in the area comprising Gilgit-Baltistan shall propagate against, or take part in activities prejudicial or detrimental to the ideology of Pakistan'.[69]

Part VII of the Constitution of Pakistan specifies the distribution of legislative powers between the federal and state governments. Article 60 outlines the legislative powers of the prime minister and the elected assembly. In Gilgit-Baltistan, a region of Pakistan, there are no high-ranking officials such as a prime minister or president. Instead, the region has a chief minister and governor.[70]

Although this appears to follow the power distribution framework of the constitution, the prime minister holds supra-constitutional authority in Gilgit-Baltistan because the region is not considered a province. Consequently, the prime minister is not accountable to the elected assembly. Additionally, the executive authority of the government is restricted to areas where the elected legislature has jurisdiction, but the list of such areas no longer exists, essentially rendering the chief minister powerless.

The 2018 Government of Gilgit-Baltistan Order further strengthens the prime minister's power by transferring all the powers of the Council to them. Previously, the Council had a prime minister and members elected by the Gilgit-Baltistan Assembly. However, the Council now has only an advisory role, and the prime minister has assumed all its powers. This contradicts Prime Minister Shahid Khaqan Abbasi's promise to transfer the powers of the Council to the elected assembly.

The prime minister in Pakistan is the head of the executive branch of government; however, his jurisdiction in Gilgit-Baltistan includes both executive and legislative powers. This grants him a degree of absolute authority over the people of Gilgit-Baltistan, which he cannot exercise over Pakistani citizens under Pakistani law. The prime minister's powers in Gilgit Baltistan is therefore similar to those of the Viceroy in British India.

There are different variations of the Government of Gilgit-Baltistan Order from 2018. One version of this order specifies that there are 68 items in the Third Schedule that outline the power of the prime minister of Pakistan (Srivastava 2021: 246). However, the version under consideration here divides the prime minister's powers into two parts. Part I comprises 62 items on which the prime minister does not require consultation with either the elected assembly or the government of Gilgit-Baltistan. These include items such as national highways and strategic roads that extend beyond Gilgit-Baltistan (item 30)[71] and electricity and bulk water storage (item 44).[72]

This division of power means that the elected assembly and government of Gilgit-Baltistan will have no control over CPEC or the mega dams to be constructed with Chinese assistance. This situation is problematic because it limits the ability of the elected representatives of Gilgit-Baltistan to manage their own affairs significantly, even with regard to issues that affect their immediate environment and resources.

The lack of control over such issues could lead to the exploitation of the resources of the territory by external actors and might not benefit the local population. This concentration of power in the hands of the prime minister raises concerns about the democratic process and could lead to the marginalization of the elected representatives of Gilgit-Baltistan. Additionally, it raises concerns about the possibility of the prime minister using his powers to further his own interests at the expense of the people of Gilgit-Baltistan.

The Government of G-B Order, 2018, Part II of the Third Schedule lists five types of taxes. These are income tax, corporation tax, sales tax, tax on the capital value of assets, capital gains tax or property tax, and tax on production. The prime minister has the power to pass laws and put these taxes into effect, but there is a rule that says he or she must talk to the governor and chief minister first. Also, the chief minister can bring these laws to the assembly so that they can be talked about (Srivastava 2021: 246).

Even though this provision lets elected officials and the assembly talk with G-B officials and discuss the issue, it does not mean that the elected officials or the assembly agree or give their approval. This provision is just a token to make up with the people of the territory, who were upset about having to pay taxes without being able to vote on them. In the end, the prime minister is in charge of all tax laws and how they are carried out. G-B officials and the assembly don't have much of a say in the process.[73] This shows how power is shared unequally in the territory, where the prime minister is in charge of everything.

The intervention of the Pakistan Supreme Court in Gilgit-Baltistan has had significant implications for the region. Gilgit-Baltistan has been a disputed territory since 1947, with both Pakistan and India claiming sovereignty over the region. The region is strategically important, as it borders China and is home to significant natural resources, including minerals and water.

One of the primary outcomes of the intervention of the court was the equating of Pakistan's de facto control over Gilgit-Baltistan with sovereignty (Srivastava 2021: 195). This meant that Pakistan was considered the ultimate lawgiver for the region and it could act through executive fiat or legislative enactment without challenge from the Supreme Appellate Court. However, this interpretation of sovereignty suggested that Pakistan's *de jure* claim over the territory was weak, and the wishes of the people of Gilgit-Baltistan were irrelevant if they conflicted with the laws of Pakistan.

The jurisdiction of the Supreme Court was based on Article 184 (3) of Pakistan's constitution, which allows for the enforcement of fundamental rights.[74] However, the judgement of the court did not address the fundamental rights of the people of Gilgit-Baltistan. Instead, it was limited to quashing the judgement of the Supreme Appellate Court and promulgating the G-B Order, 2019. This was a departure from the Court's earlier 1999 judgement, which had instructed the granting of judicially enforced fundamental rights and participation in representative government.[75]

The caution shown by Pakistan in granting fundamental rights to the people of Gilgit-Baltistan reflects a concern that it may prejudice its claim over Kashmir. However, this caution is not reflected in the court's assertion of federal authority, which disregards UN resolutions. A 2019 judgement by the Pakistan Supreme Court ruled that the Gilgit Baltistan Supreme Appellate Court cannot give rulings as a 'constitutional court' on matters pertaining to the federal government. This positions the Supreme Appellate Court within a legal administrative framework of Pakistan's federal framework despite the region not being a part of Pakistan's territory under the Pakistan Constitution.

Overall, the judgement of the Court did not address the issues that led to protests in Gilgit-Baltistan, specifically the lack of control over the region's destiny and the complete rollback of the legislative powers of the elected assembly. This has led to a sense of frustration among the local population, who feel that their voices are not being heard and that their future is being decided without their input. The court's intervention has further complicated the already complex issue of the status of Gilgit-Baltistan and has left many questions unanswered.

THE CHINESE INTERESTS IN GILGIT-BALTISTAN

The second major reason for Pakistan to desire direct control over the territory, is its close association and increasing dependence on China. While the first reason was the strategic importance because of its location as a frontier territory, providing access into Central Asia and China, the second reason is a direct consequence of the increasing economic linkages and trade linkages between China and Pakistan. This would not be possible without Pakistan's direct control over Gilgit-Baltistan. It is not a coincidence that with Pakistan's greater economic and strategic dependence on China in the twenty-first century, one sees a simultaneous number of regulations being passed by Pakistan to bring about a more direct control over the territory which has acquired an even greater importance for the country.

Gilgit-Baltistan has always been adjacent to Tibet and as such has traditionally provided access through passes from the latter into the subcontinent. However, with the rise of China in the twentieth century the nature of Chinese interests and roles in the region have undergone a metamorphosis. One modern example of the Chinese interests in the region is the China Pakistan Economic Corridor or CPEC which in turn is a part of the Chinese Belt and Road initiative.

The CPEC was introduced in 2013, but the relationship between China and Pakistan goes back much further. In fact, the first formal trade agreement between the two countries was signed in 1963,[76] which coincided with the signing of the Sino-Pakistan Treaty, in which Pakistan gave China 5,180 sq. km of land in PoK.[77] These events followed the India-China War in the previous year. While Pakistan's trade and economic ties with China are a component of its political relationship, China's interests are mainly geopolitical. China seeks to build-up Pakistan as a counterbalance to India and to address its Malacca Strait predicament. The CPEC provides China with access to ports on the Arabian Sea, with the Karakoram Highway and Gwadar being two endpoints that precede the initiative. While the Chinese presence in Gwadar has garnered more media attention, there will actually be more Chinese investment in PoK and Gilgit-Baltistan. This investment is expected to boost the region's development, and will also help tighten Pakistan's grip on the territory, limiting political space for its inhabitants.

The China-Pakistan Free Trade Agreement (CFTA) was signed on 24 November 2006, and it came into force in July 2007. This applies solely to commerce in products thirty-five per cent of these items fell into the category of zero-rated items. The pact increased bilateral trade from US$ 2.2 billion in Fiscal Year (FY) 2005 to US$ 13.8 billion in FY 16 (Srivastava 2021: 304-5).

It was unsurprising that Pakistan's trade deficit increased after signing the Free Trade Agreement with China since China possesses a stronger and more diverse manufacturing base than Pakistan. This reality also has implications for the CPEC. While almost the entire amount of US$50 billion under CPEC is designated for power and infrastructure, they have a substantial local cost component, which will improve Pakistan's foreign exchange position during the initial period of project execution.[78] However, neither of these sectors generates export revenue, primarily because of endemic problems of Pakistan's economy and power distribution system.[79] As a result, profit repatriation and loan repayment will necessitate foreign exchange earnings from other sectors. The CPEC is thus, only expected to further exacerbate Pakistan's persistent trade deficit with China.

Pakistan's motive for joining CPEC is not to correct its trade imbalance with China but to seek investment in the power and infrastructure sectors. Nonetheless, it cannot ignore the negative effects of the CPEC on its trade and current account deficits. Although China is not Pakistan's primary export market, the country is undertaking various projects in Gilgit-Baltistan under the CPEC initiative. These projects comprise two hydropower stations, road construction, and optical fibre projects, including the Phandar and Gilgit KIU hydropower stations with 80 and 100 MW capacities, respectively, with no further details provided.[80] The road construction and optical fibre projects will be financed under concessional loans from the Chinese government and the total cost of infrastructure projects in Gilgit-Baltistan under CPEC will amount to around US $2,130 billion (Srivastava 2021: 313). The Pakistan government is expected to take on the debt obligation in addition to the Chinese investment in the hydropower projects that will be carried out under the Independent Power Producer mode.

As per a media report, an agreement has been signed by Pakistan and China to construct five dams, collectively known as the Indus River Cascade, which will have a total capacity of 22.5 GW (ibid.: 314). The Memorandum of Understanding (MoU) encompasses the construction of the Daimer Bhasha project with a capacity of 4,500 MW, valued at US $14[81] billion and is expected to be completed in nine years, the Patan Dam with a capacity of 2,400 MW, the Thakot Dam with a capacity of 4,000 MW, the Bunji Dam with a capacity of 7,100 MW, and the Dasu Dam with a capacity of 4,320 MW.[82] It is uncertain whether an investment decision has been made for all the dams, except for the Daimer Bhasha Dam.

The acting chief secretary of PoK stated that the Sixth Pakistan-China Joint Cooperation Committee has decided to incorporate the 1,124 MW Kohala and 720 MW Karrot hydroelectric plants, located in PoK, under the CPEC. The Mansehra-Muzaffabad-Mirpur-Mangla Expressway and the Mirpur Special Economic Zone are other projects that will be included in CPEC (ibid.).

Chinese companies investing in hydropower projects in PoK and Gilgit-Baltistan are guaranteed a tariff of US cents 7.1 per KWh per unit and a thirty year concession, even though the region continues to be paid one-seventh the rate paid to Khyber-Pakhtunkhwa and Punjab. These projects are separate from the three large dams built in the 1960s and 1970s, namely Tarbela and Chashma on the Indus and Mangla on the Jhelum, which were primarily designed to supply water for irrigation and have a total live storage capacity of 19.4 billion cubic m. China has become the largest lender in the world.

Considering the relatively smaller size of the economies of PoK and Gilgit-Baltistan, Chinese investment under CPEC will have a considerably greater impact here than in Pakistan. The residents of Gilgit-Baltistan may not gain until Pakistan fulfils its promise of last year to pay water usage fees on line with Khyber-Pakhtunkhwa and Punjab. Payment of Net Hydel Profit (NHP), which is a larger amount, would necessitate amending Article 161 of Pakistan's constitution, which states that such payments are to be provided to either Pakistan's provinces or specifically to the province in which the power station is located.[83] Until the current constitution is altered, PoK and Gilgit-Baltistan would be excluded from any advantages and will experience flooding and population relocation.

Road development and the installation of optical fibre lines[84] will bring in Chinese and Pakistani labourers from outside the country. This could upset the delicate racial and religious balance in this area. The Pakistani military will lay the optical fibre connection. The development of road and optical fibre networks in Gilgit-Baltistan is driven entirely by shared strategic requirements of China and Pakistan. In a similar manner, Punjab and other provinces of Pakistan will be the primary beneficiaries of power projects, as they will be the regions from which electricity is evacuated. Pakistan would also absorb the foreign exchange gain of monies provided by China via CPEC.

Geopolitical interests of China will dictate the speed and direction of CPEC. Pakistan is a junior partner. Its market size is insufficient for China and if there is a revision of the Belt and Road Initiative (BRI) in the Chinese calculus, whether as a result of a shift in strategic goals or a slowdown in the Chinese economy, it will have immediate repercussions on CPEC. Former PM Imran Khan promised Gilgit-Baltistan 'provisional provincial status'. The region of Gilgit-Baltistan is at a serious risk of land loss and population displacement. The resources of PoK and the Northern Regions are exploitable, however they do not qualify for hydro-electricity royalty payments. In the case of the Mangla Dam, which is located entirely in Pakistan-occupied Kashmir, the royalty payment began thirty-six years after the completion of the dam, and the amount paid is still a fraction of what is owed.[85] In the case of Gilgit-Baltistan, the negotiating position of the local people is considerably weaker. If Gilgit-Baltistan is included in Pakistani territory, this will be another violation of Pakistan's UNCIP resolution and will undermine Pakistan's claim to Kashmir further.

It is therefore clear, that while the basis of Pakistan's legal claim on the region is tenuous at best, and the local people may not be the beneficiaries of the financial proceeds from the local resources as a result of a series of rules and regulations, yet the federal government in Pakistan continues to pass an increasing series of laws which undermine the local sovereignty of the people. This, however, is nothing new in the frontier where the larger adjoining states have always interfered in the local politics to leverage their own interests. It was certainly true in the nineteenth century when the Russians and the British were engaged in the Great Game and it is certainly true now when the Chinese recognize the importance of the region for the success of their Belt and Road Initiative and have developed interests there.

From the strategic point of view, it has been repeated several times over in earlier chapters, that the region has always been the gateway to the Indian subcontinent. There is however, one very fundamental difference in the nineteenth-century Anglo-Russian rivalry in the region and the twenty-first century Sino-Pakistani interests there.

While, in the nineteenth century the idea of increasing influence in Gilgit-Baltistan was for the British to defend its Indian Empire and in doing so, to acquire control over the strategic heights and the passes leading into India. To this effect, expeditions were launched to map the region and explore new routes and their feasibility for trade. The Russians, on the other hand, wanted to colonize and Russify land lying to their east and develop their own overland trading infrastructure. Thus, one can say, that the thrust of geopolitical power was towards Central Asia, with the British moving for consolidation of their north-western frontiers while Russians moving south-west with Central Asia emerging as the point of convergence of their power.

The twenty-first-century rise of China and its emergence as a pre-eminent power has disturbed this traditional equilibrium. Further, the de facto control over this strategic frontier was left with Pakistan, which is the smaller of the two states which emerged from British India. The insignificant relative gross national power of Pakistan, vis-à-vis China has made it effectively economically and politically dependent on the latter, which is dominant in this bilateral relationship and desires access to the Pakistani market and its Indian Ocean ports. Therefore, unlike the nineteenth century, the direction of geopolitical power projection, is not towards Central Asia but into the Indian subcontinent because of an unfavourable balance of power. The subcontinent provides a market for Chinese goods and access into the Arabian Sea, both of which are crucial to Chinese economy and security. Nevertheless, this only goes on to prove the continuing geostrategic importance of the Gilgit-Baltistan frontier in the twenty-first century as a gateway to the Indian subcontinent.

NOTES

1. '1947 Indian Independence Act.' UK Parliament, https://www.parliament.uk/about/living-heritage/evolutionofparliament/legislativescrutiny/parliament-and-empire/collections1/collections2/1947-indian-independence-act/
2. Vappala P. Menon, *The Story of the Integration of the Indian States*, Orient Longmans, India, 1961, p. 271.
3. Ajay K. Raina, and Rajendra Singh, *Treachery & Gallantry*, Sabre & Quill Publishers, New Delhi, 2021, p. 77.
4. William A. Brown, *The Gilgit Rebellion, 1947*, Pen & Sword Books Ltd., South Yorkshire, 2014, p. 156.
5. Kulwant R. Gupta, *India-Pakistan Relations with Special Reference to Kashmir*, Atlantic Publishers & Distributors Limited, India 2006, p. 170.
6. V.P. Menon, *The Story of the Integration of the Indian States*, Orient Longmans, India, 1961, p. 272.
7. M. Mahajan, *Accession of Kashmir to India*, Sulakhani Devi Mahajan Trust, New Delhi, 1969, p. 10.
8. Akbar Khan, *Raiders in Kashmir*, Rebus Publishing House, Srinagar, 1970, p. 2.
9. Dinkar P. Srivastava, *Forgotten Kashmir*, Harper Collins Publishers India, Noida, 2021, p. 21.
10. S. Ibrahim Khan, *The Kashmir Saga*, Verinag Publishers, Mirpur, 1965, p. 65.

11. Muhammad Y. Saraf, *Kashmiris Fight for Freedom, Volume I (1819 -1946)*, Ferozsons Ltd., Lahore, 1977, p. 634.
12. Note on the Gilgit Agency by F.P. Mainprice, late Assistant Political Agent, Gilgit dated, 10 October 1947, Gilgit Agency, Government of India, 1947, File No. 45/GG/47.
13. Ibid.
14. Ibid.
15. S.N. Prasad, & Dharm Pal, *History of Operations in Jammu & Kashmir-1947-8*, Thomson Press (India) Ltd, New Delhi, 1987, p. 17.
16. Onkar S. Kalkat, *The Far-Flung Frontiers*, Allied Publishers, New Delhi, 1983, pp 40-2.
17. The Tribune.com, 'The valiant Dogra who saved the "paradise on earth"' by S.S. Chib dated 8 December 2001, accessed on 5 February 2023. https://www.tribuneindia.com/2001/20011208/windows/main4.htm
18. Times of India.com, 'Who changed the face of '47 war?' by Rahul Singh dated 14 August 2005, accessed on 6 February, 2023.https://timesofindia.indiatimes.com/india/Who-changed-the-face-of-47-war/articleshow/1200682.cms
19. Ibid.
20. Muhammad Y. Saraf, *Kashmiris Fight for Freedom, Volume 2 (1947- 78)*, National Institute of Kashmir Studies, Mirpur, 2015, p. 94.
21. Sheikh Abdullah, *Flames of the Chinar*, Penguin Books India, New Delhi, 1993, p. 60.
22. Peacekeeping.un.org, 'United Nations India-Pakistan Observation Mission (UNIPOM)', accessed on 7 April 2023.https://peacekeeping.un.org/mission/past/unipombackgr.html
23. B.G. Verghese, *A Jammu and Kashmir Primer: From Myth to Reality*, India Research Press, New Delhi, 2007, p. 8.
24. Alok Bansal, *Gilgit—Baltistan and Its Saga of Unending Human Rights Violations*, Pentagon Press, New Delhi, 2018, p. 77.
25. Kulbhushan Warikoo, (ed.), *The Other Kashmir: Society, Culture and Politics in the Karakoram Himalayas*, Pentagon Press, New Delhi, 2014, p. 160.
26. Owens Bennett-Jones, *Pakistan Eye of the Storm*, Penguin Books India Private Limited, New Delhi, 2002, p. 70.
27. Ahmad H. Dani, *History of the Northern Areas of Pakistan*, National Institute of Historical and Cultural Research, Islamabad, 1991, p. 414.
28. Crisisgroup.org 'Discord in Pakistan's Northern Areas' dated 2 April 2007, accessed on 3 March 2023.https://www.crisisgroup.org/asia/south-asia/pakistan/discord-pakistan-s-northern-areas

29. Qudratullah Shahab, *Shahabnama*, Sang-e-meel Publications, Lahore, 1999, p. 424.
30. Jasjit Singh (ed.), *Pakistan Occupied Kashmir: Under The Jackboot*, Siddhi Books, New Delhi, 1995, pp. 131-2.
31. Syed Manzoor H. Gilani, *The Constitution of Azad Jammu and Kashmir*, National Book Foundation, Islamabad, 2008, p. 834.
32. Ibid., p. 836.
33. Virendra Verma, *A Legend in His Own Time, Chewang Rinchen*, Young India Publications, Dehradun, 1998, pp. 115-18.
34. Alok Bansal, 'In Pursuit of Forced Assimilation: Sectarian and Ethnic Marginalisation in Gilgit-Baltistan', *India Quarterly*, vol. 63, No. 2, April-June 2007, pp. 56-80.
35. Ibid.
36. Stephen Philip Cohen, *The Idea of Pakistan*, New Delhi, Oxford University Press, 2005, p. 222.
37. Ibid.
38. European Foundation for South Asian Studies.org, 'An introduction to the disputed territory of Gilgit Baltistan: The Himalayan flashpoint', accessed on 22 March 2023.https://www.efsas.org/publications/study-papers/an-introduction-to-the-disputed-territory-of-gilgit-baltistan-the-himalayan-flashpoint/
39. 'Story of Gilgit Deaths Foretold', Editorial, *Daily Times*, 10 January 2005.
40. Tariq Rahman, *Language and Politics in Pakistan*, Oxford University Press, Karachi, 1988, p. 220.
41. A.N. Swamy, *Talibanization of Gilgit-Baltistan and Sectarian Killings*, Surendra Publications, New Delhi, 2021, p. 87.
42. Khaled Ahmed, *Pakistan: The State in Crisis*, Vanguard Books Pvt. Ltd., Lahore, 2002, p. 38.
43. Institute of Policy Studies.com, 'Northern Areas of Pakistan: Facts, Problems and Recommendations', date 17 April 2004, accessed on 8 February 2023. https://www.ips.org.pk/northern-areas-of-pakistan-facts-problems-and-recommendations/
44. Ibid.
45. P.R. Chari, *Politics and Security in South Asia: The Compound Crisis of 1990*, Routledge, London, 2003, p. 53.
46. Institute of Policy Studies.com, 'Northern Areas of Pakistan: Facts, Problems and Recommendations', date 17 April, 2004, accessed on 8 February, 2023.https://www.ips.org.pk/northern-areas-of-pakistan-facts-problems-and-recommendations/

47. Waheguru P.S. Sidhu, et al. (ed.), *Kashmir: New Voices, New Approaches*, Lynne Rienner Publishers, Colorado, 2006, p. 43.
48. Sumantra Bose, *Kashmir at the Crossroads: Inside a 21st-Century Conflict*, Yale University Press, London, 2021, p. 108.
49. Satish Kumar, *India's National Security: Annual Review 2010*, Taylor & Francis, India, 2013, p. 300.
50. Nirmal C. Vij, *The Kashmir Conundrum: The Quest for Peace in a Troubled Land*, HarperCollins, India, 2021, p. 31.
51. Nosheen Ali, *Delusional States: Feeling Rule and Development in Pakistan's Northern Frontier*, Cambridge University Press, United Kingdom, 2019, p. 12.
52. Pakistan Annual Law Digest 1993, Pakistan Annual Law Digest Office, Pakistan, 1993, p. 6.
53. Gilgit-Baltistan.gov.pk, 'An Order, Government of Pakistan, Ministry of Kashmir Affairs and Northern Areas', Islamabad, dated 9 September, 2009, p. 56, accessed on 24 February 2023.
54. Ibid.
55. National Assembly of Pakistan.pk, 'The Constitution of the Islamic Republic of Pakistan', as modified up to 18 February 2012, p. 74, accessed on 9 February 2023. https://na.gov.pk/en/index.php.
56. Henry S. Rowen and Rafiq Dossani, *Prospects for Peace in South Asia*, Stanford University Press, United States, 2005, p. 120.
57. Gilgit-Baltistan.gov.pk, 'An Order, Government of Pakistan, Ministry of Kashmir Affairs and Northern Areas', Islamabad, dated 9 September 2009, p. 12, accessed on 24 February, 2023. See also Dinkar P. Srivastava, *Forgotten Kashmir*, Harper Collins, India, 2021, p. 217.
58. Ibid., pp. 22-3.
59. Ibid., p. 27.
60. Gilgit-Baltistan.gov.pk, 'An Order, Government of Pakistan, Ministry of Kashmir Affairs and Northern Areas', Islamabad, dated 9 September 2009, p. 45, accessed on 24 February 2023. See also Dinkar P. Srivastava, *Forgotten Kashmir*, Harper Collins, India, 2021, p. 219.
61. Ibid., p. 46.
62. Ibid.
63. Gilgit-Baltistan.gov.pk, 'An Order, Government of Pakistan, Ministry of Kashmir Affairs and Northern Areas', Islamabad, dated 9 September 2009, p. 22, accessed on 24 February 2023.
64. Gilgit-Baltistan.gov.pk, 'An Order to provide for political empowerment and good governance in Gilgit-Baltistan', Islamabad, dated 21 May 2018, p. 32, accessed on 3 March 2023.

65. Gilgit-Baltistan.gov.pk, 'An Order to provide for political empowerment and good governance in Gilgit-Baltistan', Islamabad, dated 21 May 2018, p. 78, accessed on 3 March 2023.
66. Ibid., p. 1.
67. Ibid.
68. Azad Jammu and Kashmir Assembly.gok.pk, 'The Azad Jammu and Kashmir Interim Constitution Act', Muzaffarabad, dated 31 August 1974, p. 5, accessed on 5 March 2023.https://ajkassembly.gok.pk.
69. Gilgit-Baltistan.gov.pk, 'An Order to provide for political empowerment and good governance in Gilgit-Baltistan', Islamabad, dated 21 May 2018, p. 8, accessed on 7 March 2023.
70. National Assembly of Pakistan.pk, 'The Constitution of the Islamic Republic of Pakistan', as modified up to 18 February 2012, p. 93, accessed on 9 February 2023. https://na.gov.pk/en/index.php
71. Gilgit-Baltistan.gov.pk, 'An Order to provide for political empowerment and good governance in Gilgit-Baltistan', Islamabad, dated 21 May 2018, p. 80, accessed on 3 March 2023.
72. Ibid., p. 81.
73. Siegfried O. Wolf, *The China-Pakistan Economic Corridor of the Belt and Road Initiative: Concept, Context and Assessment*, Springer International Publishing, Germany, 2019, p. 95.
74. National Assembly of Pakistan.pk, 'The Constitution of the Islamic Republic of Pakistan', as modified up to 18 February 2012, p. 99, accessed on 9 February 2023. https://na.gov.pk/en/index.php.
75. Priyanka Singh, *Gilgit Baltistan: Between Hope and Despair*, Institute for Defence Studies and Analyses, India, 2013, p. 22.
76. Jyoti Bhusan Das Gupta, *Jammu and Kashmir*, Springer, Netherlands, 2012, p. 300.
77. Fozia Nazir Lone, *Historical Title, Self-Determination and the Kashmir Question*, Brill, Netherlands, 2018, p. 19.
78. Tom Miller, *China's Asian Dream: Empire Building Along the New Silk Road*, Bloomsbury Publishing, United Kingdom, 2019, p. xvii.
79. Sarwar A. Kashmeri, *China's Grand Strategy: Weaving a New Silk Road to Global Primacy*, ABC-CLIO, United States, 2019, p. 47.
80. Sanika Sulochani Ramanayake and Reena Marwah, *China's Economic Footprint In South And Southeast Asia: A Futuristic Perspective: Case Studies of Pakistan, Sri Lanka, Myanmar And Thailand*, World Scientific Publishing Company, Singapore, 2021, p. 101.

81. Julien Chaisse, *China's International Investment Strategy: Bilateral, Regional, and Global Law and Policy*, Oxford University Press, United Kingdom, 2019, p. 393.
82. Amit Ranjan, *Water Issues in Himalayan South Asia: Internal Challenges, Disputes and Transboundary Tensions*, Springer Nature Singapore, Germany, 2019, p. 179.
83. National Assembly of Pakistan.pk, 'The Constitution of the Islamic Republic of Pakistan', as modified up to 18 February 2012, p. 86, accessed on 9 February 2023. https://na.gov.pk/en/index.php
84. Siegfried O. Wolf, *The China-Pakistan Economic Corridor of the Belt and Road Initiative: Concept, Context and Assessment*, Springer International Publishing, Germany, 2019, p. 237.
85. Business Recorder.com, 'AJK to get Rs. 750 million as Mangla royalty annually', dated 15 January 2004, accessed on 15 March 2023.https://fp.brecorder.com/2004/01/20040115191208/

REFERENCES

Bansal, Alok, *Gilgit-Baltistan and its Saga of Unending Human Rights Violations*, Pentagon Press, New Delhi, 2018.

Brown, William A., *The Gilgit Rebellion, 1947*, Pen & Sword Books Ltd., South Yorkshire, 2014.

Chari, P.R., *Politics and Security in South Asia: The Compound Crisis of 1990*, Routledge, London, 2003.

Dani, Ahmad H., *History of the Northern Areas of Pakistan*, National Institute of Historical and Cultural Research, Islamabad, 1991.

Kalkat, Onkar S., *The Far-Flung Frontiers*, Allied Publishers, New Delhi, 1983.

Khan, Akbar, *Raiders in Kashmir*, Rebus Publishing House, Srinagar, 1970.

Khan, S. Ibrahim, *The Kashmir Saga*, Verinag Publishers, Mirpur, 1965.

Menon, Vappala P., *The Story of the Integration of the Indian States*, Orient Longmans, India, 1961.

Prasad, S.N., & Dharm Pal, *History of Operations in Jammu & Kashmir 1947-8*, Thomson Press (India) Ltd., New Delhi, 1987.

Raina, Ajay K. and Rajendra Singh, *Treachery & Gallantry*, Sabre & Quill Publishers, New Delhi, 2021.

Saraf, Muhammad Y., *Kashmiris Fight for Freedom*, Volume 2: *(1947-78)*, National Institute of Kashmir Studies, Mirpur, 2015.

Srivastava, Dinkar P., *Forgotten Kashmir*, Harper Collins, India, 2021.

Swamy, A.N., *Talibanization of Gilgit-Baltistan and Sectarian Killings*, Surendra Publications, New Delhi, 2021.

Warikoo, Kulbhushan (ed.), *The Other Kashmir: Society, Culture and Politics in the Karakoram Himalayas*, Pentagon Press, New Delhi, 2014.

CHAPTER 5

Conclusion

It is clear that the region of Gilgit and the Khyber Pass has been historically significant as a natural frontier of the Indian subcontinent and has been the subject of much political manoeuvring and conflict over the centuries. From the Delhi Sultanates to the Mughals, to the Sikh Empire and the British, various powers have sought to control these strategic areas in order to defend themselves from external threats and expand their influence. The region of Gilgit, in particular, has seen a complex interplay of local power struggles, with rulers of Yasin and Chitral attempting to exert their control over the area, and eventually succumbing to the influence of the Dogras under Gulab Singh. Despite initial resistance and uprisings, the region eventually came under the control of the Dogras, with the support of the British. The history of the region serves as a testament to the enduring importance of natural frontiers and the strategic value of controlling them. The geopolitical struggle between the British and Russian empires for dominance over Central Asia and control over the passages to India, known as the Great Game, shaped British policy in Gilgit-Baltistan and influenced major conflicts with India's northern and western frontiers. The fear of Russian access to the Black Sea and subsequently cutting off British access to its Indian colony was a primary driving factor behind the British involvement in the Crimean War. While some British explorers suggested leaving Gilgit-Baltistan as a neutral buffer zone between British and Russian zones of influence, the British desire to extend their position as a paramount power in the region led to the rule of Gulab Singh, who served the British well in projecting power into the region. The Great Game reflected British strategic thinking throughout the nineteenth century and highlights the enduring impact of geopolitical struggles on international relations.

The nineteenth-century British concern over Russian expansion in Central Asia played a crucial role in shaping their policies towards the northern Indian frontier region of Gilgit-Baltistan. The recognition of Gulab Singh as the ruler of Jammu & Kashmir and the extension of British control over minor states in the region, provided an official political representation for the British in the strategically important region. The British would continue to extend their grip on the larger frontier region from Ladakh to the Durand Line in Afghanistan, with all reports from the Gilgit-Baltistan region and Chitral categorized under 'Frontier' in British indices. The Great Game as it came to be known between the British and Russian empires in Central Asia, would determine all British policies in the region, with the threat of Russian access to the Black Sea and consequently cutting off of British access to India being the primary driving factor behind British involvement in the Crimean War. As the Russians consolidated their position in Central Asia, the British adopted a more cautious and methodical approach towards securing their northern frontiers. The British policies towards Gulab Singh and the region of Gilgit-Baltistan too, would be shaped by their concerns over Russian inroads into Central Asia and their desire to pre-empt any possible Russian moves in the region.

The events surrounding the Witkiewicz Mission and the subsequent Russian expeditions in Afghanistan also had significant implications for British policies towards the North-West Frontier. The Russian expansion into Khiva and their moves in Central Asia only added to the British concerns over their northern borders. The strategic importance of the Gilgit-Baltistan region was realized by the British and this would lead to a series of missions and reports that recommended the need for greater control over the region to counter the perceived Russian threat. The two possible alternatives, direct annexation or the use of princely states like J&K to exert control, were both considered but ultimately the latter was chosen. These events would play a crucial role in shaping

British policies towards the North-West Frontier in the nineteenth century and beyond.

The meetings between Viceroy Lord Lytton and Maharaja Ranbir Singh in November 1876 resulted in the decision that small principalities such as Yasin and Chitral, lying beyond the then northern borders of J&K State, should come under the control of J&K rather than under the influence of some foreign power. The British were concerned about maintaining their political stability and winning over the local population and therefore preferred a negotiated settlement between J&K and the frontier states with their support. The appointment of Major Biddulph as the first British Political Officer to Gilgit was crucial in this regard, as he was expected to develop relationships with the local tribes in the frontier region and control the access of people into the frontier regions on political grounds. This focus on frontier issues was not a coincidence considering the several contemporary Russian territorial acquisitions in Central Asia which had occurred in quick succession. The decision to bring the frontier regions under the control of J&K was an important step towards securing the northern borders of India and maintaining British influence in the region.

The Gilgit Agency was established by the British as an instrument of control over the region and to maintain friendly relations with the local tribes of the remote frontier of the Indian subcontinent. However, it soon became clear that the policy followed by the British had been unsuccessful in pacifying the frontier and establishing friendly relations with the local tribes. The Dogras, who were acting essentially as British agents to expand their power, were seen as the pre-eminent threat by Chitral and Hunza who used every opportunity to resist the Dogra rule. This role and position of the agency in itself, would turn out to be major factors in its failure. The British expected that after the withdrawal of their agent from Gilgit, the role of providing up-to-date information on the affairs of the frontier would be fulfilled by the J&K State. However, the British were disappointed as often, the Maharaja did not provide the same quality of information that was expected.

The Panjdeh incident resulted in the significant deterioration of relations between Russia and Great Britain, triggering major British military preparations for the defence of the frontier. In the end, Foreign Secretary, Sir Mortimer Durand, proposed that the Gilgit Agency should be re-established under one more English officer supported by Dogras from the local Muslim kingdoms.

The uprising of Hunza and Nagar in 1888 against the Kashmir Darbar highlighted the need for British intervention in the region. Captain Algernon Marion Durand's tour of Gilgit, Chitral, and other places, as well as subsequent appointment as the British Agent of the reconstituted Gilgit Agency in 1889, marked a significant turning point in the British presence in the region. With the shared expenses of the agency between Kashmir and British India, Durand was able to make overtures to Hunza and Nagar, countering Russian influence in the area. The unique position of the Gilgit Agency under Durand's leadership allowed him to carry out foreign relations with nearby states, despite the complicated system of authority within the region. Under Durand's administration, significant measures were undertaken to improve the supply situation for the Kashmir troops, including refurbishing forts and establishing new mule tracks. Overall, the establishment of the Gilgit Agency under Durand's leadership helped to bring stability to the region and establish British influence in the area. The events of 27 May 1891 and the subsequent Chitral crisis of 1895 were significant in shaping the British policy towards the frontier and the region. The capture of the strategically located fortress of Nilt by Durand's composite force marked a significant achievement for the British. However, the Chitral crisis brought about a change in the British attitude towards the frontier and the actions of Sher Afzul and Umra Khan were seen as an act of war. The British government took decisive action to relieve the garrison at Chitral and to further give no quarter to Umra Khan. The Chitral crisis also brought about the recognition of Shuja-ul-Mulk as the provisional Mehtar by Robertson pending approval from the Government of India. The events that unfolded during the crisis highlighted the complex political dynamics of the region and the involvement of various factions in the conflict. The Chitral crisis of 1895 would mark a turning point in the history of the region and its impact was felt for years to come. The Chitral Campaign of 1895 in response to this crisis was a significant event that had far-reaching consequences for the region and the policies of the British government's in the area.

By April 1895, the Chitral Crisis was showing signs of ending when the British troops, led by Major General Sir Robert Low, began to withdraw from the place, which marked the end of the campaign. The decision of Dr Robertson to send Lieutenant Gurdon to Chitral was seen as an act of aggression, and the fact that Chitral was a tributary state of Jammu & Kashmir, added to the complexity of the situation. The campaign resulted in direct instability in the adjoining states and a collapse of the British frontier policy, which had been built-up over several years under the Gilgit Agency. Eminent Englishmen such as Lord Roberts and George Curzon were concerned that a British withdrawal would imply Russian involvement in the region. Overall, the Chitral Campaign was a watershed event that had significant implications for the future of the region.

The Great Game between Britain and Russia, meanwhile was cooling down towards the end of the nineteenth century. The Chitral crisis and the subsequent British response to it, essentially delimitated the frontier between the British and Russian empires. On 11 March 1895, negotiations were ongoing between the Russians and the British to demarcate the spheres of influence of the two great powers. The signing of the Pamir Boundary Commission on 10 September 1895 was understood to have officially ended the Great Game of the nineteenth century between Russia and Britain. The report of this boundary commission pointed clearly to the fact that the region to the east of Badakhshan had relatively few entry routes into India and almost none of them was suitable for military force to cross over. The boundary report went into extensive details about the routes taken by major invasions of the Indian subcontinent and came to the conclusion that it was the mountain passes to the west of the Indus River as it flows southwards. It concluded that the Gilgit Agency as it remained after 1896 after the separation of Chitral, did not sit adjacent to the primary invasion routes into India. It pointed out that while the routes to the north of Gilgit were occasionally used by trade caravans, it had never been a primary invasion route. The Gilgit Agency was divided between the North-West Frontier facing Afghanistan and by extension, the Russian Empire under the Chitral Agent, and the northern frontier facing Qing China under the oversight of the Gilgit Agent.

This was due to the anticipation of a Russian movement across the Pamirs and the danger of antagonistic views between the regional rulers. Additionally, the larger state of Chitral further to the west, was a source of concern for the British due to its historical status as an Afghan tributary and it would be this geopolitical environment and the military experiences of the 1895 campaign in Chitral, that convinced the British to carry out regional military reforms.

All this while, the costs of maintaining a military force in the Gilgit Agency were becoming very high, so the Government of India decided to streamline the logistics by concentrating the troops in fewer locations and reorganizing the Kashmir Imperial service troops. This would reduce the expenditure on the defence of the Agency by approximately eighty-four thousand rupees and to British revenues by a further forty-one thousand rupees along with a reduction in the number of troops under the Agency. This reduction of officers together with the withdrawal of the separate complement of the bodyguard of the agent contributed to a further reduction of military expenditure. However, this was in no way indicative of a change in British policy towards the people of the region or towards the state of Kashmir.

Over the next few years, there was a debate about increasing the use of Imperial colonial troops from various princely states in the defence of the North-Western Frontier. This was accompanied by a restructuring of the military units and its organization. Additionally, regulations were introduced in 1901 under which Imperial troops could be commanded under law by British officers while they were on duty as part of a British military effort within or outside India. This reliance on levies would continue until 1913, when the Government of India created the Gilgit Scouts to replace the local levies in the Agency. The cost of raising this new military force was to be borne equally by the Kashmir State and the British government. The Political Agent's military assistant was made the commandant and the Political Agent was the final authority in all the matters relating to the Scouts including those related to appointments and promotions. The Gilgit Scouts would have important implications for events that were to transpire later in the century.

It was painfully clear by this time that the Kashmir State troops were inadequate to meet the emerging challenges of the frontier and had limited offensive capability, while the tribes across the Indian frontier were becoming better armed with modern weapons. Additionally, all other measures to reduce the cost of the Gilgit Agency had already been expended and the role being fulfilled by the levies was essential to the safety of the frontier. Therefore, the best option was to rationalize the security solution by replacing the levies with a more efficient military force. Finally, an over dependence on the Kashmir troops gave the impression of an occupying military force to the fiercely independent tribals, making the region vulnerable to external political activity by hostile powers such as Afghanistan or Russia. To change this perception, the most appropriate way forward was the creation of an indigenous military unit like the Gilgit Scouts.

The internal and external geopolitical situation significantly changed by the beginning of the twentieth century. The Great Game had withered away after the delimitation of the boundary between the Russian and British empires at the end of the nineteenth century and the de-facto status of Afghanistan as a neutral buffer state between the two empires. The defeat of Russia in the Russo-Japanese War in 1904-5 contributed to a political realignment between Britain and Russia with the realization in Britain that Germany was a far more significant military and strategic threat with imperial ambitions. In 1903, it was considered doubtful if the British would be able to reach Kabul before the Russians in the event of a war. The defence of the Indian frontier rested on three important factors: the loyalty of the Amir and the frontier tribes, development and maintenance of transportation infrastructure, and a promise of military reinforcements. Under

Lord Kitchener, a series of military reforms were undertaken with the main emphasis on making the British Indian Army capable of missions relating to war.

The Dane Mission was sent to Afghanistan in 1904 to ensure the allegiance of the Amir of Afghanistan. The mission was intended to give British officials privileges and allow British subjects safe entry into Afghanistan for purposes of trade. The Amir of Afghanistan became increasingly eager for an official treaty with the British, but the Indian government under Curzon believed that this was undesirable. After a number of discussions and negotiations, the treaty between Britain and Afghanistan was signed on 21 March 1905, which effectively gave Afghanistan British military support in the event of war, but at the cost of the Amir dictating terms to the British. The overall assessment of the treaty by Curzon was that it had not improved the security situation on the Indian frontier tribes materially. The Russo-Japanese War was raging in the far east, and the Japanese victory in the war had two important security implications for the British.

The second decade of the twentieth century saw a shift from a Russia focused threat to a threat based around pan-Islamism emanating from Central Asia. This changed the nature of the threat and the security requirements on the frontier, as the Afghans and the tribals on the frontier were convinced that there was an alliance between the British and the Russians to bring about the downfall of the Ottoman empire and the Caliphate. This led to the conclusion that there would be no British troops being deployed to Manchuria or Japanese troops to the North-West Frontier of India with the common agreement of both the new Viceroy Lord Minto and Lord Kitchener. The British policies in the implementation of British policies in Gilgit-Baltistan in the aftermath of the 1907 Anglo-Russian Entente focused on the Kashgar region in western Tibet. The shift in military requirements in the frontier led to the move towards abandoning the system of levies in favour of the Gilgit Scouts.

The Frontier Constabulary was established to cater to the changed strategic situation, and the Gilgit Agency was relieved of its charge over Chitral and the north-western passes. Boundary demarcations and military rationalization of the frontier were being carried out but the Great War had broken out in Europe, diverting the entire focus there. The Ottoman Empire was aligned with the Central Powers, against the Entente, and the frontier and Afghanistan had enormous latent sympathy for the Ottomans, further heightened by conspiracy theories of a Christian plot against the Caliph. The Amir's control over Afghanistan was weakening, partly due to his pro-British position. After the outbreak of the War, the Amir remained neutral towards the British despite large sections of the population and powerful factions at his court desiring otherwise.

Eventually in February 1915, the Great War arrived in the region when Ottoman agents and seditionists were sent into Afghanistan through Persia to stir up 'pan-Islamic anti-British sentiment'. This was not unique to the Ottomans, as the British had sent agents such as Major Lawrence to Arabia to rouse the Arab tribes into revolt. The Germans attempted to make overtures to the Afghans, using groups like the Niedermayer-Hentig Mission, which arrived in Kabul on 28 September 1915. The mission was isolated from everyone to prevent the pro-Ottoman factions in court from getting access to the mission, and promised the Amir of German military aid if he agreed to wage war against the British. However, the Amir explained his intention of remaining neutral in the war and not breaking off diplomatic relations with the British on his own initiative. Nasrullah, his younger brother, publicly declared that he would not abide by the British treaties if he came to power, and appealed to the anti-British factions in the country as well in the Afghan army.

The Third Anglo-Afghan War of 1919 saw the dismissal of the Niedermayer mission from Afghanistan on 22 May 1916 and the assassination of Amir Habibullah in February 1919. This set the stage for the Treaty of Rawalpindi of 1919, which recognized the independence of Afghanistan and stopped British subsidies to Afghanistan. This conflict and the resulting treaty led to a renewal of the Great Game with Afghanistan no longer a British bulwark on the frontier against Russia. Local princes and rulers began to pledge the services of their state troops to the British in the defence of the frontier regions, including the state troops of Jammu & Kashmir. However, the boundary demarcation of the Gilgit Agency was still not clearly understood, and the 1917 Russian Revolution had triggered the Russian Civil War and British troops were part of it.

By the end of Second World War, the British had come to the conclusion that they could no longer hold India in thraldom, and on the Viceroy Lord Mountbatten's recommendation, they announced a plan for the Partition of India. The Indian Independence Act, passed on 18 July 1947, stated that the British would relinquish their rule over India on 15 August 1947, at which point India would become an independent nation. East and West Pakistan were to be established as autonomous, sovereign states in a portion of its borders that had a predominance of Muslims. The Maharaja of J&K was willing to maintain the status of the princely state as independent, but he soon realized that after a certain point, it was not going to be possible. He presented a 'Standstill Agreement' to both the dominions of India and Pakistan, but India did not exhibit any haste in doing so and wanted to examine its implications. The communal riots before Indian Independence further acted as a catalyst for the Maharaja's anxiety, and he dismissed the Pakistan-inclined PM Ram Chandra Kak on 11 August 1947 and appointed a former officer of Jammu and Kashmir State Forces, Major General Janak Singh as temporary PM of the state.

Brigadier Ghansar Singh, the Dogra cousin of the Maharaja, was appointed governor of Gilgit in 1947, but his appointment was fraught with complications due to his lack of support from Ram Chandra Kak, the then-prime minister of Jammu & Kashmir. Following the collapse of British paramountcy on 1 August 1947, the area was given back to the Jammu & Kashmir Princely State and Brig. Singh was appointed as the first governor of Gilgit Agency and Gilgit Wazarat by Hari Singh. General Janak Singh was also succeeded by Mehr Chand Mahajan soon as prime minister on 15 October 1947, but Pakistan was still pressurizing Hari Singh and violating the terms of the agreement to compel J&K for accession to Pakistan. The object of the Standstill Agreement, drafted by the British Indian government (Political Department) on 3 June 1947, was to provide for the continuance of economic and administrative relations between the two neighbours on the same basis as had existed before the creation of the new dominions.

There is enough extant evidence available today to indicate that the intervention in Kashmir was planned and supported by Pakistan, with the raiders attacking the princely state on 22 October 1947 thereby setting in motion a series of events that would largely determine the relations of the South Asian neighbours until the twenty-first century. At the end of this conflict which would morph in 1948, into the first Indo-Pak War, with the State of Jammu & Kashmir acceding to India and Pakistan being left in control of the strategic region of Gilgit-Baltistan.

The United Nations Commission for India and Pakistan (UNCIP) resolutions were passed in the wake of the Indo-Pakistani War of 1947 to resolve the dispute over the state of Jammu & Kashmir. India approached the United Nations with a request for aid and the Security Council of the United Nations passed a resolution on 17 January 1948, exhorting both nations to rectify the situation and to promptly notify the Council of any material alterations. The UNCIP then recommended a ceasefire to come into effect within four days of its acceptance by both nations, followed by the withdrawal of Pakistani troops and a portion of Indian forces from Kashmir. The ceasefire finally took effect on 1 January 1949.

The 1971 Indo-Pak War saw Indian army troops secure 804 sq. km of territory in Baltistan, which has since become a part of the Indian state of Jammu & Kashmir. During the 23 years of Pakistani rule, the region was neglected and faced numerous challenges, including a lack of funding for development, inadequate infrastructure, and neglected schools, dispensaries, and mosques. The division of families during the war was also a major issue, and despite attempts by the Indian army to reunite them, these efforts were not successful due to a lack of response from the Pakistani side.

Post-war, administrative reforms were carried out in the Northern Areas by Zulfiqar Ali Bhutto's administration to consolidate Pakistan's control over the region, but the region was not returned to Pakistan. Ethnic identities and culture have always been viewed as historical connections of the region to India by Pakistan, after the 1949 agreement lapsed with the implementation of the 1970 Act by President Yahya Khan. The Legislative Assembly of 'Azad Jammu and Kashmir' passed a resolution in 1972 requesting Pakistan to return the Northern Areas which were temporarily taken over under the Karachi Agreement. This resolution made it necessary to alter the regional administrative structure in order to get rid of any leftover signs of the Maharaja's Rule. In August 1972, the State of Nagar and its system of a hereditary monarch were dissolved, and districts were established for the Gilgit and Baltistan Agencies.

In December 1972, the Astor, Chilas, and Darel-Tangir Sub-Divisions were merged to establish the Diamer district and the last princely state of Hunza was abolished in September 1974 during a visit by prime minister of Pakistan, Zulfiqar Ali Bhutto. The formation of the Ghanche and Ghizer districts and the merger of the Khaplu and Kharmong subdivisions of Baltistan's Ghanche district were later combined with the Baltistan district. Pakistan used this opportunity to strengthen its grip on the area while avoiding public scrutiny. The Northern Areas Legal Framework Order, which Bhutto issued in 1974-5, eliminated feudal systems from the area and subjected it to the Pakistan Penal Code.

The construction of the KKH was a significant development that solidified Pakistan's relationship with China. The decision to abolish the State Subject Rule and the construction of the KKH allowed for a significant influx of outsiders, which in turn changed the demographic profile of the region, upset the delicate balance of the local population, and was a further step in the establishment of direct federal control over the region. This was a deliberate effort by the Pakistani government to alter the cultural, religious, and ethnic composition of the region, something that was perceived as a threat by the indigenous population.

In April 1982, the AJK Legislature passed a resolution declaring that Gilgit and Baltistan belonged to Jammu & Kashmir and should be a part of 'Azad Jammu & Kashmir'. Four significant political parties with some sway in the area joined the MRD and signed a letter outlining the legal status of the region. The 1984, would witness a local contest between India and Pakistan over control of the Siachen Glacier, a completely deserted area of Baltistan that was not clearly delineated as either country's territory, but had strategic significance and would give a tactical advantage to whoever would hold it. The two armies have fought several battles over this hostile region since 13 April 1984 and both sides have maintained a continuous military presence at a height of more than 20,000 ft. India now has complete control of the 70 km-long Siachen glacier and all of its tributaries after 15 years of sporadic conflict, and the three main passes of the Saltoro Ridge, Sia La, Bilafond La, and Gyong La. Pakistan controls the western glacial valleys of the Saltoro Ridge and believes that due to its military activities in Siachen, India acquired more than 1,000 sq. miles (3,000 km^2) of land in Baltistan.

On 15 April 1985, Zia reaffirmed that Gilgit-Baltistan would have a representative in the National Assembly and that elections would be held in all three districts of the region. However, no such declaration was ever made and the region was not represented in any Parliamentary chamber. In order to take decisions on the future of the area, a committee made up of the secretaries of finance, planning, law, establishment, education, interior and Kashmir and Northern Areas was established in 1984-5, but neither it nor its recommendations were ever made public. In 1986, five members of the Northern Areas Council stated that Kashmir had no connection to the Northern Areas other than the fact that it had been taken over and held there for a short time before being leased to the British. The Khunjerab Pass which was temporarily opened for foreigners in May 1986, but subsequently closed again, was a reflection of Pakistan's insecurities stemming from the legality of its claim over the region.

Moreover, a number of recent judicial rulings have attempted to exert greater central control over the region at the cost of local autonomy. In 1999, the Supreme Court of Pakistan issued a historic ruling on 28 May 1999, stating that the people in the Northern Areas may be denied the fundamental rights granted under the Constitution. However, Islamabad showed no sign of intending to abide by the ruling of the Supreme Court. A series of orders were passed by the Ministry of Kashmir Affairs and Northern Areas by the Government of Pakistan, beginning with the 2009 Gilgit-Baltistan Order, which reserved certain subjects under the Federal Government of Pakistan. This included strategic highways and roads which were traversing the strategically important frontier territory. Policies such as these would have a deleterious effect on the local populace which would not benefit from the potentially lucrative proceeds of the CPEC.

Attempts to have a direct control on the frontier would undermine the local demands for federal autonomy and also divert locally earned earnings away from the indigenous population. Further orders such as the 2018 Gilgit-Baltistan Order would further strengthen central control over the region. The 2018 Government of Gilgit-Baltistan Order further strengthens the Pakistan prime minister's power by transferring to him, all the legislative powers of the Gilgit Baltistan Council. This contradicts Prime Minister Shahid Khaqan Abbasi's promise to transfer the Council's powers to the elected assembly. The Pakistan prime minister's executive and legislative powers over Gilgit-Baltistan, both de-jure and de-facto are more absolute and complete than they are over the citizens of Pakistan. This situation is problematic because it significantly limits the ability of the elected representatives to manage their own affairs, even with regard to issues that affect their immediate environment and resources.

Despite these attempts at direct control, the underlying theme of Pakistan's legal terminology has been to identify the region as distinct from Kashmir which it has always considered a disputed territory. Nevertheless, as Gilgit-Baltistan was a part of the princely state of Jammu & Kashmir at independence, Pakistan finds it difficult to accommodate this inherent dichotomy in its position, of Jammu & Kashmir as a disputed territory with its intentions of greater control over the Gilgit-Baltistan frontier.

Further, the more recent trend of intervention by the Pakistan Supreme Court has had significant implications for this strategically important frontier region, with its significant natural resources. Consequent to its inherent confusion about the nature of Pakistan's relationship with the region, the Supreme Court's interpretation of sovereignty suggested that the former's *de jure* claim over the territory was weak, and the wishes of the people of the territory were irrelevant if they conflicted with Pakistan's laws. This has naturally led to a sense of frustration among the local population, who feel that their voices are not being heard and that their future is being decided without their input.

An important factor driving this desire for greater control over Gilgit-Baltistan, is Pakistan's close and increasing association with China. The strategic territory with its long history of providing access into Central Asia and China, is now acquiring a new significance for Pakistan with its ever-greater economic dependence on the former. Pakistan's greater economic and strategic dependence on China in the twenty-first century has seen a simultaneous number of regulations being passed by Pakistan to bring about a more direct control over the region.

While the CPEC was introduced in 2013, this relationship between China and Pakistan has a much older background. The CPEC is expected to further exacerbate Pakistan's persistent trade deficit with China. Pakistan's motive for joining CPEC is to seek investment in the power and infrastructure sectors, but it cannot ignore the negative effects of the CPEC on its trade and current account deficits. China has become the largest lender in the world, and Chinese investment under CPEC will have a considerably greater impact here than in Pakistan. Road development and the installation of optical fibre lines will bring in Chinese and Pakistani labourers from outside the country, upsetting the delicate racial and religious balance in this area. The development of road and optical fibre networks in Gilgit-Baltistan is driven by China and Pakistan's shared strategic requirements, but it will be Punjab and other provinces of Pakistan which will benefit primarily from such projects, as they will be the regions, which consume the electricity produced in the Gilgit Frontier.

China's geopolitical interests will dictate the speed and direction of CPEC, and Pakistan is a junior partner. The region of Gilgit-Baltistan is at a serious risk of land loss and population displacement due to the lack of hydroelectricity royalty payments. Pakistan's legal claim on the region is tenuous at best, and the local people may not be the beneficiaries of the financial proceeds from the local resources. However, the Federal government in Pakistan continues to pass an increasing series of laws which undermine the local sovereignty of the people. This is nothing new in the frontier where the larger adjoining states have always interfered in the local politics to leverage their own interests.

Thus, the significance of Gilgit-Baltistan, for Pakistan, has a acquired a degree of criticality which it probably never had for the British in the nineteenth century or at any time in the history of the Indian subcontinent. The British, the astute students of history, that they were, realized the significance of this frontier and made efforts to control and secure it against any prospective incursions and threats. Judiciously they sent expeditions and retained the most important passes and routes under their control for the security of their Indian Empire. For Pakistan on the other hand, it is through Gilgit frontier that it has its proverbial umbilical cord with China, and the only land connection which makes this close and increasingly one-sided collaboration possible.

Therefore, the nineteenth-century Anglo-Russian rivalry in the region and the twenty-first-century Sino-Pakistani interests there differ in that the British interests in the frontier were essentially defensive in nature while the Russians went about their enterprise of Russification in Eurasia. The traditional thrust of geopolitical power was towards Central Asia, with the British consolidating their north-western frontiers and the Russians moving south-west. As such the frontier during British rule was controlled by the political centre in India, and this naturally helped the British in consolidating their British Indian Empire. With Pakistan's control over the frontier after 1947, this traditional geopolitical stability was disturbed. With the twenty-first-century rise of China and the increasing dependence of Pakistan on China, the direction of geopolitical power projection has now moved in the opposite direction towards the Indian subcontinent, with the risk that a power outside the subcontinent may achieve de facto control over this strategic northern frontier of the Indian subcontinent.

Bibliography

PRIMARY SOURCES

National Archive Documents

A.C. Lyall to F. Henvey, No. 2085 E.P., 8 August, 1879, Government of India, Foreign, Secret, October 1879, Nos. 267-310.

Abortive attempt made upon Hunza by Wazir Muhammad Shah and Raja Alif Khan, Government of India, Foreign, Political-A, October 1881, Nos. 268-73.

Action taken by Government for securing political control on the frontier territories of Chitral and Yassin, Government of India, Foreign, Secret, July 1877, Nos. 34-60B.

Address by Maharaja of a Kharita to Lord Ripon on assumption of the Viceroyalty of India, Government of India, Foreign, A. Political-E, September 1882, Nos. 266-72.

Administration of Kashmir by Golab Singh, Government of India, Foreign, India despatch to secret committee, January 1848, No. 10.

Aman-ul-Mulk to Maharaja, Government of India, Foreign, Secret, July 1877, Nos. 34-60B.

Aman-ul-Mulk to the Viceroy, No. 20, 1889, Government of India, Foreign, Secret-F, February 1890, Nos. 85-113.

Amir's refusal to assist the people of Hunza to attack the English, Government of India, Proceedings, Foreign, Secret-F, October 1894, Nos. 358-73.

Application of Aman-ul-Mulk, Ruler of Chitral to be admitted into direct political relations with the British Government, Government of India, Foreign, Secret, July 1881, Nos. 314-99.

Arrangements for administration of Kashmir on transfer to Golab Singh, Government of India, Foreign, Governor-General's despatch to Secret Committee, 1846, No. 57.

Attempt of Mir Ghazan Khan, Chief of Hunza, to incite Yassin, Darel and Chilas to unite in some hostile movement against Kashmir, Government of India, Foreign, Secret, July 1878, Nos. 53-94.

Biddulph to Henvey, 25 July 1879, No. 149, Government of India, Foreign, Secret, October 1879, Nos. 402-5.

Biddulph's (Major) letter said to have caused vexation to Aman-ool-Moolk, Government of India, Foreign, May 1879, Nos. 128-30.

Boundaries between Lahore and Kashmir, Government of India, Foreign, Governor-General's despatch to Secret Committee, 1848, No. 8.

British Agent to Resident Kashmir, 29 December 1889, Government of India, Foreign, Secret-F, May 1890, Nos. 37-43.

British Consulate General, Kashgar to Sir A.H. Grant, dated 19 February, 1918, Corruption of Cypher telegram to Kashgar, Government of India, Foreign and Political Department, 1919, Nos. 45.

Bunji Fort fixed as the limit of travel in the Gilgit direction for visitors, Government of India, Foreign, A. Political-E, April 1884, Nos. 75-6.

Chitral Affairs. Threatening attitude of the Kohistanis and other tribesman in regard to the opening up of the Khagan-Chilas Road, Government of India, Foreign, Secret-F, September 1893, Nos. 443-99.

Chitral-Afghan boundary dispute. Raids by Afghans on Chitral territory. Decision not to remind the Amir unless there are further complaints, Government of India, Proceedings, Foreign and Political, Secret-F, December 1914, Nos. 1-8.

Claims of the Mir of Hunza to lands in Yasin; action of the Chinese and Russian authorities, Government of India, Foreign, Secret-F, August 1899, Nos. 168-201.

Closing of the Gilgit Agency, Services and Pay of Colonel Tanner and Dr J. Duke, Government of India, Foreign, Secret, November 1881, Nos. 4-11.

Closing of the route to India through Hunza and Nagar against European and American travellers, Government of India, Foreign, Secret-F, January 1894, Nos. 153-8.

Col. Prideaux to Secretary, Government of India, Foreign, No. 59-515, 15 February 1892 (Confidential), Government of India, Foreign, Secret-F, March 1892, Nos. 185-94.

Colonel R.C.F. Schomberg's complaint about maladministration in Gilgit Agency, and consequent misery and hardship among the people of Gilgit, Government of India, Office of the P.S.V., General Branch, 1945, File No. 1195-G/43.

Confidential memo by T.C. Plowden on the new policy for the protection of the north-western frontier of Kashmir, Government of India, Foreign, Sec-F, July 1888, Nos. 63-86.

Confidential Report Yarkand Mission by Sri Douglas Forsythe, Government of India, Foreign, Secret, August 1875, Nos. 68-81.

Copy of a letter from the Political Agent, Gilgit, No. 36-S/16-X, dated 30 April 1928, to the Resident in Kashmir, India's concern with Sinkiang, Government of India, Foreign and Political Department, File No. 37-X, Secret, 1928, Nos. 1-12.

Decision that Gilgit is an administered area in an Indian State and therefore cannot be described as a 'Centrally Administered Area' Government of India, External Affairs Department, External, File No. 130-X, 1937, No. 19.

Defence Scheme regarding a report of the committee convened to revise that portion of the Chitral-Gilgit defence scheme which affects Kashmir and Gilgit, Government of India, Foreign, Secret-F, April 1910, Nos. 1-2, Part A.

Diary of political events at Kashmir, Government of India, Foreign, S.C., October 1847, Nos. 145-6.

Dr G.S. Robertson's Mission to Chitral, Government of India, Foreign, Secret-F, July 1893, Nos. 571-741.

Dy. No. 4733-X/28, Visit to Chinese Turkestan in 1929, Government of India, Foreign and Political Department, File No. 115 (3)-X, External, 1928, Nos. 1-52.

Enquiry about non-Muslims in Gilgit, Government of India, Ministry of States, Kashmir Branch, 1948, File No. 7(4)-K/48.

Expedition against Darel and Tangir by Kashmir and Chitral for harbouring Pahalwan Bahadur, Government of India, Foreign, Secret, May 1880, Nos. 50-2.

F. Henvey to A.C. Lyall, 11 January 1879, Government of India, Foreign, Secret, October 1879, Nos. 267-310.

F.E. Younghusband to R. Parry Nisbet, 24 October 1889, Government of India, Foreign, Secret-F, February 1890, Nos. 59-84.

Forsyth's (Sir Douglas) proposal for establishing an Agency at Gilgit, Government of India, Foreign, Secret, August 1875, Nos. 68-81.

Ghazan Khan of Hunza suggests that Chaprote, be completely occupied by Kashmir Government, Government of India, Foreign, Secret, January 1879, Nos. 311-13.

Gilgit Agency, Government of India, 1947, File No. 45/GG/47.

Gilgit Diary No. 107 of 27 April, 1880, Government of India, Foreign, Secret, December 1880, Nos. 117-66.

Government of India to H.H. Fowler, No. 66, 17 April 1895, Government of India, Foreign, Secret-F, July 1895, Nos. 1-433.

Government of India to Secretary of State for India, 103, 15 July 1881, Government of India, Foreign, Secret-E, August 1884, Nos. 4-19.

Government of India to Secretary of State for India, No. 142, 11 July 1893, Government of India, Foreign, Secret-F, August 1893, Nos. 6-34.

Government of India to Secretary of State for India, No. 192, 19 October 1892, Government of India, Foreign, Secret-F, December 1892, Nos. 430-41.

Government of India to Secretary of State for India, No. 4, Frontier, 6 January, 1892, Government of India, Foreign, Frontier-A, January 1892, Nos. 15-130.

Government of India, Foreign and Political Department, File No. 248-X, Secret, 1928, Nos. 1-217.

Government of India, Foreign and Political, External, No. 612-X, Secret, 1927, Nos. 1-2.

Government of India, Foreign and Political, Secret, File No. 401-X of 1933, Nos. 1-57.

Government of India, Foreign Department Proceedings, Secret, July 1877, No. 39.

Government of India, Foreign Department Proceedings, Secret, July 1881, Nos. 314-97.

Government of India, Foreign, Political A, May 1868, Nos. 121-2.

Government of India, Foreign, Secret, June 1882, Nos. 53-5.

Government of India, Foreign, Secret-F, July 1874, Nos. 129-30.

Government of India, Foreign, Secret-F, March 1892, Nos. 185-94.

Government of India, Foreign, Secret-F, September 1889, Nos. 231-52.

Governor of Yasin against the alleged proposal to transfer the Mastuj District to the Mehtar of Chitral, Government of India, Foreign, Secret-F, October 1907, Nos. 9-12.

Inclusion of Rs. 2,25,590 in the military budget estimates for 1900-1901 on account of the Gilgit Agency, Government of India, Military Department, Accounts Budget-A, Proceedings, April 1900, No. 3036.

Intelligence of Political events in Kashmir, Government of India, Proceedings, Foreign, Secret, December 1846.

Intention of Kashmir Durbar regarding Chaprote, Government of India, Foreign, Secret, January 1879, Nos. 341-3.

Lapse of paramountcy-Handing over of cash balance, etc. of Gilgit Treasury to the Kashmir Government, Government of India, Kashmir Residency Office, 1947, No. 24.

Letter from Sardar Nizam-ul-Mulk to the British Agent at Gilgit, 19 December, 1892, Dr G.S. Robertson's Mission to Chitral, Foreign, Secret-F, July 1893, Nos 571-741.

Major Biddulph's correspondence with Maharaja of Kashmir, Government of India, Foreign, Secret, October 1879, Nos. 154/59.

Major Biddulph's proposed visit to Chitral, Government of India, Foreign, Secret, October 1879, Nos. 252/54.

Major Biddulph's proposed visit to Darel, Government of India, Foreign, Secret, October 1879, Nos. 232-51.

Major Biddulph's visit to Chitral, Government of India, Foreign, Secret, October 1879, Nos. 255/66.

Major Biddulph's visit to Yassin and Chitral, Government of India, Foreign, Secret, October 1879, Nos. 267-310.

Map of Gilgit and surrounding country, Government of India, Foreign, General-B, January 1881, Nos. 125-32.

Marlow, B.W., Estimate of the Kashmir Durbar share of expenditure during 1914-15, Government of India, Foreign Department, Establishment-B, January 1914, Nos. 176-7.

Measures for the Effective Control and Discipline of the Imperial Service Troops Under All Conditions of Service, Government of India, Military Department, Special and Miscellaneous, Political-B, August 1901, Nos. 256-64.

Meer's Correspondence with Abdul Rahman and looks to Russia for aid, Government of India, Foreign, Political-A, July 1874, Nos. 129-30.

Memorandum by Sir John Ardagh, KCB advocating the incorporation within the British frontier of country admittedly Chinese for the purpose of frustrating a Russian advance on India via the Kilik, Mintaka, Shimshal, Khunjerab, Mustagh and Karakoram Passes, Government of India, Foreign, Secret-F, January 1898, Nos. 160-9.

Memorandum from the Resident at Kashmir, No. F. 317/27, dated the 30 March 1928, Increase in the 'Darbar Presents' grant of the Gilgit Agency, Government of India, Foreign and Political Department, Accounts, 1928, No. 88-A.

Memorandum No. 369 from J.B. Wood, Resident Kashmir to the Political Secretary to the Government of India, dated 28 January, 1926, Additional Grant in the Gilgit Agency, Government of India, Foreign Department, Accounts, No. 55-A, 1926, No. 18.

Memorandum on Gilgit and Chitral by Pundit Munphool, Government of India, Foreign, Political-A, May 1868, No. 8/11.

Military operations in and around Chilas, Government of India, Proceedings, Foreign, Secret-F, July 1893, Nos. 190-330.

Mr Harvey's opinion that the Ruler of Kashmir should be brought under the control of the paramount power, Government of India, Foreign, Secret-E, March 1883, No. 86.

News furnished by the Maharaja of Kashmir regarding Chitral and Gilgit, Government of India, Foreign, S.M., 1871, Nos. 1-2.

Note from O.K. Caroe dated 27 January 1941, Status of Hunza and Nagir and Political Districts of Chilas, Koh Ghizar, Ishkoman and Yasin vis à vis the Kashmir State, Government of India, Political Department, Secret, 1941, File No. 112-P, Nos. 1-5.

Note on Chinese Turkistan by Colonel Schomberg, Government of India, Foreign and Political, External, No. 583-X, Secret, 1927.

Notice to visitors in consequence of unsettled state of the Gilgit Border, Government of India, Foreign, Political-B, April 1881, Nos. 159-60.

Objection to banished Chitralis settling in Gilgit, Government of India, Proceedings, Foreign, Secret-F, November 1893, Nos. 70-86.

Officer on Special Duty in Shignan and Wakhan requested to obtain information regarding affairs from the Darbar, Government of India, Foreign, Secret-E, September 1883, Nos. 1-6.

Pahalwan Bahadur's occupation of the fort of Roshan, Government of India, Foreign, Secret-E, June 1884, Nos. 342-8.

Periodical occupation of Roshan by Mulk Aman—His retreat of the hearing of approach of Kashmir Troops, Government of India, Foreign, Secret-F, July 1886, Nos. 450-1.

Peshawar Confidential Diary No. 17 of 14 September, 1887, Government of India, Foreign, Secret-F, January 1888, Nos. 246-69.

Policy to be pursued towards Maharaja Golab Singh for his conduct during the war of 1848-9, Government of India, Foreign, S.C., December 1850, Nos. 114-61.

Political Agent to Resident Kashmir, No. 402-T, Government of India, Foreign, Secret-F, May 1913, Nos. 95-102.

Political separation of Chitral from Gilgit, Government of India, Foreign, Secret-F, April 1897, Nos. 12-21.

Position of Gilgit & Chitral, Dhir etc vis à vis J&K in connection with the Indo-Pakistan Canal Dispute, Government of India, Ministry of States, Kashmir Section, Group B, 1953, F1(2)-K/53.

Position of Hunza, Nagir, Chilas, Koh Ghizar, Ishkuman and Yasin in the event of Kashmir acceding to the Federation, Government of India, External Affairs Department, External Branch, Secret, 1937, File No. 676-X/37, Nos. 1-9.

Position of Russia in Central Asia, Government of India, Foreign, Secret-I, 1869, Nos. 63-5.

Proposal to sever the Mir of Hunza's connection with China and to grant him money and suitable jagirs in Kashmir as compensation, Government of India, Proceedings, Foreign, Secret-F, September 1900, Nos. 16-27.

Proposed formation of a North-West Frontier Agency, Minute by his Excellency the Viceroy, Government of India, Proceedings, Foreign, Secret-F, September 1900, No. 37.

Proposition of Aman-ul-Mulk of Chitral to subdue Hunza not accepted by Kashmir Darbar, Government of India, Foreign, Secret-E, April 1883, Nos. 211-26.

Relations between the Maharaja of Kashmir and the tributary states of Kashmir, Government of India, Foreign, Secret, December 1880, No. 36.

Relations of Shignan and Wakhan with Kashmir, Government of India, Foreign, Secret, July 1881, No. 48.

Report on Gilgit under Pakistan occupation, Ministry of States, Kashmir Branch, New Delhi, 1951, File No. 8(18)-K/51.

Report on the Frontier, 1885-86, by Colonels Lockhart and Woodthorpe, Government of India, Foreign, Secret-F, September 1889, Nos. 282-5.

Report on the Pamirs by The Earl of Dunmore, External, Confidential, 1892.

Reports regarding Nagar and Shignan and Wakhan, Government of India, Foreign, Secret-F, December 1884, Nos. 7-12.

Restoration of Mastuj and Laspur, to the Mehtar of Chitral, Government of India, Proceedings, Foreign and Political, Secret-F, August 1914, Nos. 1-15, Part-B.

Rising in Gilgit. Withdrawal of Gilgit Agency. Policy to be adopted towards Ruler of Chitral, Government of India, Foreign, Secret, July 1881, Nos. 314/99.

Rumoured military preparation at Kashmir in view of attacking Hunza, Government of India, Foreign, Secret-E, September 1882, Nos. 586-628.

Russian designs on Tagharma in consequence of the cession by China of the valley to Russia, Government of India, Foreign, Secret-F, May 1899, Nos. 84-7.

S.E. Pears to A.H. Grant, Proposed boundary between the North-West Frontier Province and the Gilgit Agency, 1914, Government of India, Foreign and Political Department, Frontier-A, August 1914, Nos. 1-2.

Schedule of Proposals Involving Considerable Military Expenditure for 1902-3, September 1901, Government of India, Military Department, Accounts Budget-A, Proceedings, November 1901, Nos. 42-3.

Secretary of State for India to Government of India, No. 35, Secret, 3 September, 1880, Government of India, Foreign, Secret, December 1880, No. 361.

Secretary to the Government of India to Col. Lockhart, No. 1043-F, 6 June, 1885, Government of India, Foreign, Secret-F, August 1885, Nos. 12-81.

Selected articles on Kashmir question, Government of India, Ministry of External Affairs, Kashmir (NGO) Unit, 1957, File No. 145-KU/57.

Sino-Soviet Pact on Sinkiang. Certain developments in Sinkiang, Government of India, Ministry of External Affairs, Central Asian Branch, 1949, File No. 303 CAK/49.

Sir-i-Kol, Chilas and the North-eastern boundary of Afghanistan, Government of India, Foreign, Secret, March 1879, Nos. 35-7.

State of Affairs in Gilgit (Gilgit Diaries), Government of India, Foreign, Secret-F, November 1893, Nos. 636-55.

State of Affairs in Gilgit (Gilgit Diaries), Government of India, Foreign, Secret-F, July 1893, Nos. 742-61.

Succession to the throne of Kashmir—Serious illness of the Maharaja, Government of India, Foreign, Secret-E, January 1883, Nos. 427-30.

Telegram from Private Secretary to the Viceroy to Secretary to the Government of India, 1 February, 1915, General War Diary, Army Headquarters, India, (F.S.R., Part II, Section 140; and Staff Manual, War, Section 20), Confidential, Foreign and Political Department, 1915, vol. 14.

Telegram from the Resident of Kashmir, No. 2053, 26 May 1919, Offers of services, gifts and assistance made by Ruling Princes and Chiefs and private individuals in connection with the war with Afghanistan, Government of India, Foreign and Political Department, Internal-A, Proceedings January 1920, Nos. 1-230.

Tender of allegiance made by the Chief of Shignanto the Maharaja of Kashmir, Government of India, Foreign, Secret, July 1877, Nos. 73/81.

Termination of Gilgit Lease, Government of India, Foreign, Secret-F, October 1907, Nos. 9-12.

Termination of the Gilgit Lease, Government of India, Kashmir Residence Office, 1947, F.9-C/35.

Translation of a letter from the Amir to Sher Afzul, 29 November 1892, Dr G.S. Robertson's Mission to Chitral, Foreign, Secret-F, July 1893, Nos. 571-741.

Srinagar State Archive Documents

Assessment Report Skardu Tehsil of Baltistan, Government of Jammu and Kashmir, Revenue, Samvat 1958 (1901), No. 2184.

Government of Jammu and Kashmir Administration Report 1892-3, No. 1711.

Government of Jammu and Kashmir administration Report 1904-5, No. 1719.

Government of Jammu and Kashmir, Addenda and Corrigenda at the revised list of Ruling Princes, Chiefs and leading personages of the Jammu and Kashmir State and the Gilgit Agency, Miscellaneous, No. 23, Samvat 1997 (1941), No. 1543.

Government of Jammu and Kashmir, Assessment Report of the Gilgit District, Samvat 1973 (1916), No. 2165.

Government of Jammu and Kashmir, Ex-Governor, Register 1, Serial No. 1523, Remittance of Rs. 70,000 to Gilgit, Samvat 1962 (1905), No. 289.

Issue of grains to the military detachment at Skardu, Government of Jammu and Kashmir, Revenue Secretariat, Samvat 1948 (1891), No. 317.

Raids of the Hilly Tribes, Government of Jammu and Kashmir, Jammu and Kashmir State Council, Police Branch, Samvat 1979 (1922), No. 1895.

Reoccupation of Giligt Ilaqa, Government of Jammu and Kashmir, Revenue Secretariat, Samvat 2004 (1947), A/817/47, No. 75.

Report by R.T. Clarke on Baltistan and Ladakh, 1904, No. 2046.

Official Reports

Crisisgroup.org, 'Discord in Pakistan's Northern Areas' dated 2 April 2007, accessed on 3 March 2023. https://www.crisisgroup.org/asia/south-asia/pakistan/discord-pakistan-s-northern-areas

Pakistan Annual Law Digest 1993, Pakistan Annual Law Digest Office, Pakistan, 1993.

United States Institute of Peace.org, 'Conflict Dynamics in Gilgit-Baltistan', by Izhar Hunzai dated 22 January 2013, accessed on 12 December 2022. https://www.usip.org/publications/2013/01/conflict-dynamics-gilgit-baltistan

University of Nebraska Digital Commons.edu, 'Report on the proceedings of the Pamir Boundary Commission' by M.G. Gerard 1896, p. 12, accessed on 9 December 2022. https://digitalcommons.unomaha.edu/afghandocsreports/8/

Laws and Treaties

Azad Jammu and Kashmir Assembly.gok.pk, 'The Azad Jammu and Kashmir Interim Constitution Act', Muzaffarabad, dated 31 August 1974, accessed on 5 March 2023.https://ajkassembly.gok.pk

Euro Docs Brigham Young University.edu, Anglo-Afghan Treaty of 1919, accessed on 25 December 2022.https://eudocs.lib.byu.edu/index.php/Anglo-Afghan_Treaties#Anglo-Afghan_Treaty_of_1919

Gilgit-Baltistan.gov.pk, 'An Order to provide for political empowerment and good governance in Gilgit-Baltistan', Islamabad, dated 21 May 2018, accessed on 3 March 2023.https://gilgitbaltistan.gov.pk

Gilgit-Baltistan.gov.pk, 'An Order, Government of Pakistan, Ministry of Kashmir Affairs and Northern Areas', Islamabad, dated 9 September 2009, accessed on 24 February 2023.https://gilgitbaltistan.gov.pk

Legislation.gov.uk, Government of India Act 1935, accessed on 14 January 2023.https://www.legislation.gov.uk/ukpga/Geo5and1Edw8/26/2/contents/enacted

National Assembly of Pakistan.pk, 'The Constitution of the Islamic Republic of Pakistan', as modified up to 18 February 2012, accessed on 9 February, 2023. https://na.gov.pk/en/index.php

Parliament.uk, '1947 Indian Independence Act', accessed on 4 January 2023. https://www.parliament.uk/about/living-heritage/evolutionofparliament/legislativescrutiny/parliament-and-empire/collections1/collections2/1947-indian-independence-act/

First Hand Accounts

Abdullah, Sheikh, *Flames of the Chinar*, New Delhi: Penguin Books India, 1993.

Beynon, William G.L., *With Kelly to Chitral*, London: Edward Arnold, 1896.

Biddulph, John, *Tribes of the Hindoo Koosh*, Calcutta: Superintendent of Government Printing Press, 1880.

Brown, William A., *The Gilgit Rebellion, 1947*, South Yorkshire: Pen & Sword Books Ltd., 2014.

Burnaby, Fred, *A Ride to Khiva*, London: Cassel and Company, 1895.

Charak, Sukhdev S. and Anita Billawaria, *Gulabnama of Diwan Kirpa Ram* (*Translated from Persian*), Light & Life Publishers, 1977.

Drew, Fredrick, *The Jummoo and Kashmir Territories*, London: Edward Stanford, 1875.

Drew, Fredrick, *The Northern Barrier of India. A Popular Account of the Jummoo and Kashmir Territories*, London: Edward Stanford, 1877.

Durand, Algernon, *The Making of a Frontier*, London: John Murray, 1900.

Keay, John, *The Gilgit Game: The Explorers of the Western Himalayas 1865-95*, Frome and London: Butler and Tanner Ltd., 1979.

Khan, Akbar, *Raiders in Kashmir*, Srinagar: Rebus Publishing House, 1970.

Khan, S. Ibrahim, *The Kashmir Saga*, Mirpur: Verinag Publishers, 1965.

Knight, Edward F., *Where Three Empires Meet*, London: Longmans Green and Co., 1905.

Leitner, Wilhelm G., *Dardistan in 1866, 1886 and 1893*, New Delhi: Asian Educational Services, 1996.

Murray, Charles A., *The Pamirs*, Volume I, London: John Murray, 1893.

Murray, Charles A., *The Pamirs*, Volume II, London: John Murray, 1893.

Nevill, Hugh L., *Campaigns on the North-West Frontier*, London: John Murray, 1912.

Robertson, George S., *Chitral the Story of a Minor Siege*, London: Methuen & Co., 1899.

Schomberg, Reginald C.F., *Between the Oxus and the Indus*, London: Martin Hopkinson Ltd., 1935.

Schomberg, Reginald C.F., *Peaks and Plains of Central Asia*, London: Martin Hopkinson Ltd., 1933.

Shahab, Qudratullah, *Shahabnama*, Lahore: Sang-e-meel Publications, 1999.

Thomson, Harry C., *The Chitral Campaign*, London: William Heinemann, 1895.

Younghusband, George J. and Younghusband, Francis, *The Relief of Chitral*, London, Macmillan and Co., 1910.

Younghusband, Sir Francis, *The Light of Experience*, Houghton, Boston and New York: Mifflin Company, 1927.

Newspaper Articles

'Kashmir', *Madras Mail*, 4 November 1889.

'Russia and Kashmir', *Madras Mail*, 30 August 1889.

'Story of Gilgit Deaths Foretold', Editorial, *Daily Times*, 10 January 2005.

'The New Administration in Kashmir', *Madras Mail*, 29 October 1889.

Business Recorder.com, 'AJK to get Rs. 750 million as Mangla royalty annually', dated 15 January, 2004, accessed on 15 March, 2023.https://fp.brecorder.com/2004/01/20040115191208/

Khan, Ismail, M., 'Avoiding the Highway of Death', *The International News*, Internet Edition, 5 May 2005.

Mahmud, Ershad, 'Challenges before the New Government in NAs', *The News*, Internet Edition, 11 December 2004.

SECONDARY SOURCES

Books

Adamec, Ludwig W., *Afghanistan, 1900-1923 A Diplomatic History*, Berkeley: University of California Press, 1967.

Ahmed, Khaled, *Pakistan: The State in Crisis*, Lahore: Vanguard Books Pvt. Ltd., 2002.

Alder, Garry J., *British India's Northern Frontier 1865-1895 A Study in Imperial Policy*, London: Longmans Green and Co. Ltd., 1963.

Ali, Nosheen, *Delusional States: Feeling Rule and Development in Pakistan's Northern Frontier*, United Kingdom: Cambridge University Press, 2019.

Allworth, Edward (ed.), *Central Asia: A Century of Russian Rule*, New York: Columbia University Press, 1967.

Andreeva, Elena, *Russia and Iran in the Great Game*, New York: Routledge, 2007.

Bamzai, Prithvi N.K., *Culture and Political History of Kashmir*, Volume 1: *Ancient Kashmir*, New Delhi: MD Publication Pvt. Ltd., 1994.

——, *Culture and Political History of Kashmir*, Volume 2: *Medieval Kashmir*, New Delhi: MD Publication Pvt. Ltd., 1994.

——, *Culture and Political History of Kashmir*, Volume 3: *Modern Kashmir*, New Delhi: MD Publication Pvt. Ltd., 1994.

Bansal, Alok, *Gilgit-Baltistan and Its Saga of Unending Human Rights Violations*, New Delhi: Pentagon Press, 2018.

Barthorp, Michael, *Afghan Wars and the North-West Frontier 1839-1947*, London: Cassell, 2002.

Bazaz, Prem N., *The Struggle for Freedom in Kashmir*, New Delhi: Kashmir Publishing Company, 1954.

Beatson, Stuart, *A History of the Imperial Service Troops of Native States*, Calcutta: Office of the Superintendent of Government Printing, India, 1903.

Bennett-Jones, Owens, *Pakistan Eye of the Storm*, New Delhi: Penguin Books India Private Limited, 2002.

Bhatt, A., *Inside PoK The Gilgit Grumble*, New Delhi: Surendra Publications, 2020.

Bose, Sumantra, *Kashmir at the Crossroads: Inside a 21st-Century Conflict*, London: Yale University Press, 2021.

Bryant, Edwin and Patton, Laurie (ed.), *The Indo-Aryan Controversy Evidence and Inference in Indian History*, Routledge, 2005.

Chaisse, Julien, *China's International Investment Strategy: Bilateral, Regional, and Global Law and Policy*, United Kingdom: Oxford University Press, 2019.

Charak, Sukhdev S., *A Short History of Jammu Raj*, Pathankot: Ajaya Prakashan, 1985.

——, *Life and Times of Maharaja Ranbir Singh (1830-1885)*, Jammu Tawi: Jay Kay Book House, 1985.

Chari, P.R., *Politics and Security in South Asia: The Compound Crisis of 1990*, London: Routledge, 2003.

Chohan, Amar S., *The Gilgit Agency*, New Delhi: Atlantic Publishers and Distributors, 1997.

Chowdhary, Rekha, *Jammu and Kashmir Politics of identity and separatism*, New York: Routledge, 2016.

Cloughley, Brian, *A History of the Pakistan Army*, New York: Skyhorse Publishing, 2016.

Cohen, Stephen Philip, *The Idea of Pakistan*, New Delhi: Oxford University Press, 2005.

Colquhoun, Archibald R., *Russia against India The struggle for Asia*, New York and London: Harper and Brothers, 1900.

Crooke, W., *The Tribes and Castes of the North-Western Provinces and Oudh*, Volume I, Calcutta: Office of the Superintendent of Government Printing, India, 1896.

——, *The Tribes and Castes of the North-Western Provinces and Oudh*, Volume II, Calcutta: Office of the Superintendent of Government Printing, India, 1896.

——, *The Tribes and Castes of the North-Western Provinces and Oudh*, Volume III, Calcutta: Office of the Superintendent of Government Printing, India, 1896.

——, *The Tribes and Castes of the North-Western Provinces and Oudh*, Volume IV, Calcutta: Office of the Superintendent of Government Printing, India, 1896.

Dani, Ahmad H., *History of Pakistan*, Lahore: Sang-e-Meel Publications, 2008.

——, *History of the Northern Areas of Pakistan*, Islamabad: National Institute of Historical and Cultural Research, 1991.

Datta, C.L., *Ladakh and Western Himalayan Politics: 1819-48*, New Delhi: Mushiram Manoharlal Publishers Pvt Ltd., 1973.

Davies, Collins C., *The Problem of the North-West Frontier 1890-1908*, London: Cambridge University Press, 1932.

d'Encausse, Hélène C. (ed), *Central Asia: A Century of Russian Rule*, New York: Columbia University Press, 1967.

Dodwell, Henry, *The Cambridge History of the British Empire*, Volume 4: United Kingdom: Macmillan, 1929.

Dutt, Nalinaksha and Shivnath Sharma (ed.), *Gilgit Manuscripts*, Volume I, Delhi, 1984.

Ewans, Martin, *Securing the Indian Frontier in Central Asia*, New York: Routledge, 2010.

Fisher, Margaret W., Leo E. Rose, and Robert A. Huttenback, *Himalayan Battleground Sino-Indian Rivalry in Ladakh*, New York: Frederick A. Praeger, 1963.

Fuller, William C., *Strategy and Power in Russia 1600-1914*, New York: The Free Press (Macmillan), 1992.

Gadru, S.N. (ed.), *Kashmir Papers, British Intervention in Kashmir*, Srinagar: Freethought Literature Company, 1973.

Gilani, Syed Manzoor H., *The Constitution of Azad Jammu and Kashmir*, Islamabad: National Book Foundation, 2008.

Gupta, Jyoti Bhusan Das, *Jammu and Kashmir*, Springer, Netherlands, 2012.

Gupta, Kulwant R., *India-Pakistan Relations with Special Reference to Kashmir*, India: Atlantic Publishers & Distributors Limited, 2006.

Gupta, Virendra (eds.) and Alok Bansal (ed.), *Pakistan Occupied Kashmir*, New Delhi: Manas Publications, 2016.

Gupte, Pranay, *India the Challenge of Change*, United Kingdom: Mandarin, 1989.

Hall, Kira (ed.), *Studies in Inequality and Social Justice Essays in honor of Ved Prakash Vatuk*, Meerut: Archana Publications, 2009.

Hopkirk, Peter, *The Great Game On Secret Service in High Asia*, Great Britain: John Murray, 2006.

Hussain, Serena (ed.), *Society and Politics of Jammu and Kashmir*, London: Palgrave Macmillan, 2021.

Kalkat, Onkar S., *The Far-Flung Frontiers*, Allied Publishers, New Delhi, 1983.

Kashmeri, Sarwar A., *China's Grand Strategy: Weaving a New Silk Road to Global Primacy*, United States: ABC-CLIO, 2019.

Kaul, Jawaharlal, *Jammu and Kashmir: The Wounded Paradise*, New Delhi: Khama Publishers, 2021.

Kaul, Maharaj, *Essays in Inequality and Social Justice (Essays in honor of Ved Prakash Vatuk)*, Edited by Kira Hall, Meerut: Archana Publications, India, 2009.

Kendall, Elisabeth and Ewan Stein (eds.), *Twenty-First Century Jihad Law Society and Military Action*, London: I.B.Tauris, 2015.

Khan, Amanullah, *Gilgit Baltistan: A Disputed Territory or a 'Fossil of Intrigues'?*, Gilgit: Javed Printers (Pvt.) Ltd., 1999.

Khan, I.K., *Geopolitics of Gilgit-Baltistan*, New Delhi: Sumit Enterprises, 2018.

Kumar, N., George van Driem, and P. Stobdan (ed.), *Himalayan Bridge*, New Delhi: Knowledge World (Routledge), 2021.

Kumar, Satish, *India's National Security: Annual Review 2010*, India: Taylor & Francis, 2013.

Lamb, Alastair, *Kashmir: A Disputed Legacy 1846-1990*, Hertingfordshire: Roxford Books, 1991.

Lone, Fozia Nazir, *Historical Title, Self-Determination and the Kashmir Question*, Netherlands: Brill, 2018.

Mahajan, Meher, C., *Accession of Kashmir to India*, New Delhi: Sulakhani Devi Mahajan Trust, 1969.

Margolis, Eric S., *War at the Top of the World: The Struggle for Afghanistan, Kashmir and Tibet*, New York: Routledge, 2001.

Menon, Vappala P., *The Story of the Integration of the Indian States*, Orient Longmans, India, 1961.

Miller, Tom, *China's Asian Dream: Empire Building Along the New Silk Road*, United Kingdom: Bloomsbury Publishing, 2019.

Minassian, Taline T., *Most Secret Agent of Empire*, New York: Oxford University Press, 2014.

Moulton, Edward, *Lord Northbrook's Indian Administration, 1872-76*, New York: Asia Publishing House, 1968.

Murphy, Dervla, *Where the Indus is young*, London: Clio Press (John Murray), 1988.

Nish, Ian H., *The Anglo-Japanese Alliance*, University of London: The Athlone Press, 1966.

Omrani, Bijan (ed.), *Great Potential, Many Pitfalls*, New York: Routledge, 2018.

Prasad, S.N., & Dharm Pal, *History of Operations in Jammu & Kashmir-1947-48*, New Delhi: Thomson Press (India) Ltd., 1987.

Prescott, John R.V., *The Geography of Frontiers and Boundaries*, New York: Routledge, 2015.

Radloff, Carla F. and Shakil Ahmad S., *Folktales in the Shina of Gilgit*, Islamabad: National Institute of Pakistan Studies, 1998.

Rahman, Tariq, *Language and Politics in Pakistan*, Karachi: Oxford University Press, 1988.

Raina, Ajay K. and Rajendra Singh, *Treachery & Gallantry*, New Delhi: Sabre & Quill Publishers, 2021.

Raina, Niranjan N., *Kashmir Politics and Imperialist Manoeuvres: 1846-1980*, New Delhi: Patriot Publishers, 1988.

Ramanayake, Sanika Sulochani, and Reena Marwah, *China's Economic Footprint In South And Southeast Asia: A Futuristic Perspective—Case Studies of Pakistan, Sri Lanka, Myanmar And Thailand*, Singapore: World Scientific Publishing Company, 2021.

Ramusack, Barbara N., *The New Cambridge History of India*, Volume 3, Part 6: *The Indian Princes and Their States*, United Kingdom: Cambridge University Press, 2008.

Ranjan, Amit, *Water Issues in Himalayan South Asia: Internal Challenges, Disputes and Transboundary Tensions*, Germany: Springer Nature Singapore, 2019.

Richard, D.S., *The Savage Frontier: A History of the Anglo-Afghan Wars*, London: Macmillan, 2003.

Robinson, Cabeiri D., *Body of Victim, Body of Warrior Refugee families and the making of the Kashmiri Jihadists*, Berkeley: University of California Press, 2013.

Rowen, Henry S. and Dossani, Rafiq, *Prospects for Peace in South Asia*, United States: Stanford University Press, 2005.

Saraf, Muhammad Y., *Kashmiris Fight for Freedom*, Volume 1: *1819-1946*, Lahore: Ferozsons Ltd., 1977.

Saraf, Muhammad Y., *Kashmiris Fight for Freedom*, Volume 2: *1947-1978*, Mirpur: National Institute of Kashmir Studies, 2015.

Saxena, Hori L., *The Tragedy of Kashmir*, New Delhi: Nationalist Publishers, 1975.

Schofield, Victoria, *Kashmir in Conflict: India, Pakistan and the Unending War*, London: I.B. Taurus, 2003.

Sehgal, Narender, *A State in Turbulence Jammu & Kashmir*, New Delhi: Ocean Books, 2013.

Sidhu, Waheguru P.S. et al (eds.), *Kashmir: New Voices, New Approaches*, Colorado: Lynne Rienner Publishers, 2006.

Singh, Harbans, *A Modern History of Jammu and Kashmir*, vol. 1, New Delhi: Speaking Tiger Books, 2023.

——, *Maharaja Hari Singh: The Troubled Years*, New Delhi: Brihaspati Publication, 2011.

Singh, Jasjit (ed.), *Pakistan Occupied Kashmir: Under The Jackboot*, New Delhi: Siddhi Books, 1995.

Singh, Priyanka, *Gilgit Baltistan: Between Hope and Despair*, New Delhi: Institute for Defence Studies and Analyses, 2013.

Snedden, Christopher, *Understanding Kashmir and Kashmiris*, London: Hurst, 2015.

Srivastava, Dinkar P., *Forgotten Kashmir*, India: Harper Collins, 2021.

Stellrecht, Irmtraud, *Perspectives on History and Change in the Karakorum, Hindukush, and Himalaya*, University of Michigan: Rüdiger Köppe, 1997.

Stobdan, Phunchok and Suba Chandran (ed.), *The Last Colony Muzaffarabad-Gilgit-Baltistan*, New Delhi: India Research Press, 2008.

——, *The Great Game in the Buddhist Himalayas*, India: Vintage Books, 2019.

Swamy, A.N., *Balochistan, PoK and Gilgit Baltistan Fact File*, New Delhi: Surendra Publications, 2017.

Swamy, A.N., *Talibanization of Gilgit-Baltistan and Sectarian Killings*, New Delhi: Surendra Publications, 2021.

Swinson, Arthur, *North-West Frontier*, London: Transworld Publishers Ltd., 1969.

Teng, Mohan K., Ram K.K. Bhatt and Santosh Kaul, *Kashmir Constitutional History and Documents*,Volume I, *Constitutional History*, Jammu: Jay Kay Book House, 1999.

Teng, Mohan Krishen et al., *Kashmir: Constitutional History and Documents*, New Delhi: Light & Life Publishers, 1977.

Toynbee, Arnold, *The New Europe: Some Essays in Reconstruction*, New York: J.M. Dent & Sons Limited, 1916.

Verghese, B.G., *A Jammu and Kashmir Primer: From Myth to Reality*, New Delhi: India Research Press, 2007.

Verma, Virendra, *A Legend in His Own Time, Chewang Rinchen*, Dehradun: Young India Publications, 1998.

Vij, Nirmal C., *The Kashmir Conundrum: The Quest for Peace in a Troubled Land*, India: HarperCollins, 2021.

Warikoo, Kulbhushan (ed.), *The Other Kashmir: Society, Culture and Politics in the Karakoram Himalayas*, New Delhi: Pentagon Press, 2014.

Waugh, Daniel C., *Etherton at Kashgar: Rhetoric and Reality in the History of the Great Game*, Seattle: Bactrian Press, 2007.

Wolf, Siegfried O., *The China-Pakistan Economic Corridor of the Belt and Road Initiative: Concept, Context and Assessment*, Germany: Springer International Publishing, 2019.

Wolpert, Stanley, *Jinnah of Pakistan*, London: Oxford University Press, 1984.

Wolpert, Stanley, *Shameful Flight: The Last Years of the British Empire in India*, New York: Oxford University Press, 1984.

Wyatt, Christopher M., *Afghanistan and the Defence of Empire*, London: I.B.Taurus, 2011.

Journal Articles

Bansal, Alok, 'In Pursuit of Forced Assimilation: Sectarian and Ethnic Marginalisation in Gilgit-Baltistan', *India Quarterly*, vol. 63, No. 2, April-June 2007, pp. 56-80.

Copland, Ian, 'Islam and Political Mobilization in Kashmir, 1931-34', *Pacific Affairs*, vol. 54, No. 2, Summer 1981, pp. 228-59.

Dad, Aziz A., 'Boundaries and Identities: The Case of Gilgit-Baltistan', *Crossroads Asia Working Paper Series*, No. 34, 2016, pp. 1-32.

Joshi, Prateek, 'Supreme Court Ruling on Gilgit Baltistan: A Legacy of Unfulfilled Promises', *National Security*, vol. II, Issue I, pp. 27-34.

Khan, Ehsan M., 'Constitutional Status of Gilgit-Baltistan: An Issue of Human Security', vol. XXI, Issue 1, December 2021, pp. 85-103.

Kreutzmann, Hermann, 'Boundaries and Space in Gilgit-Baltistan', *Contemporary South Asia*, vol. 23, No. 3, 2015, pp. 276-91.

Lambah, Satinder, K., 'The Tragic History of Gilgit-Baltistan since 1947', *Indian Foreign Affairs Journal*, vol. 11, No. 3, July-September, 2016, pp. 227-37.

Mackinder, H.J., 'The Geographical Pivot of History', *The Geographical Journal*, vol. 23, No. 4, April 1904, pp. 421-37.

Mishra, Vivek K., 'Sectarian Violence in Gilgit-Baltistan', *Jadavpur Journal of International Relations*, vol. 23, Issue 1, 2018, pp. 1-23.

Muhammad, Ghulam, 'Festivals and Folklore of Gilgit', *Memoirs of the Asiatic Society of Bengal*, vol. I, No. 7, 1905, pp. 93-127.

Roy, Kaushik, 'Feeding the Leviathan: Supplying the British-Indian Army, 1859-1913', *Journal of the Society for Army Historical Research*, vol. 80, Summer 2002, pp 144-61.

Stöber, Georg, 'The Gilgit Textbook Controversy' and its Conflictual Context', *Internationale Schulbuchforschung*, vol. 29, No. 4, 2007, pp. 389-411.

WEBSITES

'Recent Developments in Gilgit-Baltistan' by Ashish Shukla dated 19 March, 2019, accessed on 18 March, 2023.https://icwa.in/show_content. php?lang=1&level=1&ls_id=2727&lid=2023

Brill and The Hague Academy of International Law, Northern Areas (Pakistan) reference map for Gilgit District showing Yasin, Hunza, and Nagar valleys, accessed on 30 August 2022.https://commons.wikimedia.org/wiki/File:Gilgit-Baltistan_map_with_tehsils_labelled.png

Dailyexcelsior.com, 'Maharaja Hari Singh and his era of social reform in J&K' dated 23 September 2015, accessed on 16 December 2022.https://www.dailyexcelsior.com/maharaja-hari-singh-and-his-era-of-social-reform-in-jk/

European Foundation for South Asian Studies.org, 'An introduction to the disputed territory of Gilgit Baltistan: The Himalayan flashpoint', accessed on 22 March, 2023.https://www.efsas.org/publications/study-papers/an-introduction-to-the-disputed-territory-of-gilgit-baltistan-the-himalayan-flashpoint/

Gutenberg.org, Map from 'Dardistan in 1866, 1886 and 1893' by G.W. Leitner, accessed on 31 August 2022.https://www.gutenberg.org/files/60590/60590-h/images/illus1.jpg

Indian Council of World Affairs.in, 'Gilgit Baltistan, China and Pakistan' by Dhrubajyoti Bhattacharjee, dated 3 June 2015, accessed on 16 March 2023.https://www.icwa.in/show_content.php?lang=1&level=3&ls_id=5108&lid=830

Peacekeeping.un.org, 'United Nations India-Pakistan Observation Mission (UNIPOM)', accessed on 7 April 2023. https://peacekeeping.un.org/mission/past/unipombackgr.html

Picryl.com, 'Relief map of Gilgit-Baltistan and adjoining regions', accessed on 30 August 2022.https://picryl.com/media/map-from-the-making-of-a-frontier-five-years-experiences-and-adventures-in-d283a4

The Tribune.com, 'The valiant Dogra who saved the "paradise on earth"' by S.S. Chib dated 8 December 2001, accessed on 5 February 2023.https://www.tribuneindia.com/2001/20011208/windows/main4.htm

Times of India.com, 'Who changed the face of 47 war? by Rahul Singh' dated 14 August 2005, accessed on 6 February 2023.https://timesofindia.indiatimes.com/india/Who-changed-the-face-of-47-war/articleshow/1200682.cms

Index